Praise for *Customized Parenting*

"As parents we always wonder, are we doing a good job? But 'parenting is not static, and neither is your Parenting Plan' is the supportive, encouraging, and hopeful message that author Bailey Gaddis shares with her readers. As a mom of three kids, I wish I had this book at the beginning of my parenting journey, one that began over a decade ago. This informative and accessible book is filled with ideas and suggestions that all new parents (and perhaps even some seasoned ones) should use to help guide meaningful decisions that will impact your daily life. It provides innovative strategies for creating respectful and important boundaries with children, navigating social challenges like building relationships and bullying, and encourages readers to be confident, adaptable, and intuitive on their parenting journey."

—**Rekha Rajan**, author of *The Read Aloud Factor*

"If you're hoping to discover your unique parenting style, *Customized Parenting* is your answer. Gaddis is the judgment-free, funny-but-real friend you want with you on the parenting journey, helping you create a practical parenting plan that is just right for your family."

—**Meghan Rudd, PhD**, licensed clinical psychologist

"Bailey is an extraordinary teacher and mother. While many offer theories on parenting, Bailey lives it—the proof is in her children, who are present, kind, curious, and deeply compassionate. Her approach is grounded in lived experience and humor, rooted in the belief that each parent must find their own authentic way while raising children with empathy and a sense of responsibility. Her teachings are remarkably accessible—and they work."

—**Rachel Kolar McCord**, integrative therapist, educator, and founder of The Veil and Mother Medicine

"Clears away all the mental clutter of parenting and offers a clear path parents can follow to create more intuitive, fulfilling, and effective parenting strategies. Gaddis has distilled an incredible collection of top child development and family research into easily digestible forms, making it easy for parents to become well-informed, without the overwhelm. This is the go-to guide for choosing your own adventure when raising humans, and having fun along the way."

—**Katy Snow, PhD**, research program in child development, University of Amsterdam

CUSTOMIZED PARENTING

CREATING EASY, INTUITIVE PARENTING PLANS FOR EVOLVING FAMILIES

BAILEY GADDIS

CHICAGO

Published by Parenting Press
An imprint of Chicago Review Press Incorporated
814 North Franklin Street
Chicago, Illinois 60610
ISBN 978-1-64160-972-2

Library of Congress Control Number: 2025935299

Cover design: Jonathan Hahn
Typesetting: Nord Compo

Printed in the United States of America

To Hudson and Grace,
for making motherhood the greatest adventure

And Eric and Mom,
for being my constant companions on the journey

CONTENTS

Introduction

THE SEED OF YOUR PLAN

I FELT LIKE A DECENT MOM until my son Hudson started walking. During his first year of life we were in a cocoon, largely protected from the prying eyes and intrusive opinions of society. My intuition blossomed in this environment, as did my relationship with Hudson. This all went to hell when he became a toddler and craved interaction with a wider variety of humans. As we began spending more time with family and attending play groups, I began questioning everything.

You might be surprised to hear that all the self-proclaimed parenting experts at various gatherings had opinions about how Hudson should be parented and regularly spit up said opinions on my husband and me. "He's just manipulating you with his crying"; "You should make him clear his plate"; "Do you really let him go out in public in his pajamas?" Um yes, yes, I do. This opinion vomit would inflame my anxiety, cause me to retreat, and confuse me, but inexplicably caused my husband to nod in agreement. The result: I felt resentful and defeated, and my husband decided that all the parenting stuff we were doing was wrong. This led to serious discord, which I'll get into later.

In the play groups I met amazing women, many of whom are still in my life almost ten years later. But initially I hated these groups as I witnessed the other moms parenting with finesse and success. They never judged me, but I did. When Hudson and I were stuck to the confines of home, I had no one to compare my parenting to. But now, I was shown all the other ways you could handle feeding, safety, keeping the poop in the diaper, and so on. I felt lost and lacking. But something kept pulling me back to these groups. Each time I'd connect with these women we'd go a little deeper, and then eventually there was the *aha* moment: I realized all these other mamas also felt lost and lacking. Huzzah!

My new mom crew and I began sharing how unprepared we felt for parenting and how all the bestselling parenting books made us feel like subpar parents. Many seemed to be written with a tone that was a cross between our mother-in-law's voice (need I say more?) and an expert who wanted you to know how much better equipped they were at handling all of this. And they all failed to transport us to their magical land of children who prefer veggies over buttered pasta, use sign language instead of tantrums, and decide, "Hey, my parents work so hard, I think I'll just potty train myself." Where was the book that wasn't trying to teach the one right way to parent? Where was the book that guided us back to our instincts? Where was the book that helped us craft a customized parenting philosophy for our unique families? I became determined to find it—or write it.

As I began outlining what this book would entail, I decided to explore my ideas with clients in my hypnotherapy practice who were also struggling with parenting. Throughout the years that followed, I worked with my clients and fellow mamas to fine-tune the parenting process that became this book. We discovered our unique, authentic parenting values. We used tools for guiding ourselves back to our inner wisdom. We customized strategies for adjusting to our evolving children and roles as parents. We created bespoke Parenting Plans that enhanced our authenticity—not only as parents, but also as people. These plans put into words how we wanted to be as parents, partners, and individuals.

A crucial component of crafting my Parenting Plan was exploring my values and discovering what was actually important to me. I asked myself, *Do I care more about a tidy house or my family feeling free to eat popcorn while having a dance party inside a pillow fort? Do I want my son to always agree with me or to feel safe expressing his opinions? Is it more important for me to answer all my e-mails or say yes when Hudson, and now my two-year-old Grace, ask me to show them how to work a whoopee cushion?* By asking these questions, and many more, I began shifting and clarifying my parenting choices. But to create a complete Parenting Plan, I needed more—I needed a framework to fill in.

As I explored my parenting experiences and beliefs, and listened to my clients and fellow parents, I saw that there are nine essential aspects of parenting we need to address, with each aspect infused by our own insights and guided by our own values.

The Nine Essential Elements of Parenting

Here's an overview of the parenting elements we'll explore in the book.

1. **Communication.** Children have so much to say but so few tools to help them say it, which is why they sometimes use wailing, fists, and feet. We'll consider an array of kid-friendly communication tools you can both use to feel more heard, especially when resolving a conflict. We'll also discuss elements of communication like active listening, tone of voice, body language, eye contact, facial expressions, posture, and touch that can enhance the parent-child bond.

   As you contemplate this part of your Parenting Plan, I'll help you create a customized vocabulary and blended style of communication you can use with your child and your family unit, so you can be more effective communicators in every area of your lives.
2. **Navigating emotions.** Children feel stuff, lots of stuff, and express this stuff in big ways. Parents also have big feelings, especially if we feel judged, inadequate, stressed, or painfully tired. In this chapter we'll talk about creating space and coping strategies for both you and your child to process the full range of emotions. There is reciprocity in learning how to honor and express feelings, so as we model for our children how to be fully aware of and handle emotions in a healthy way, they will likely begin to show enhanced emotional intelligence. And because our child's emotions can be super triggering, we'll explore how you can meet those emotions with empathetic objectivity instead of with your own breakdown.

I'll also offer options such as movement, play, and other tools that can support children in understanding their emotions and effectively moving through them. You'll then customize these tools for your child, so when big emotions hit, you have a plan to help your child face them with empathy, acceptance, and even a sense of humor.

3. **Building boundaries.** If you find yourself unable to use the bathroom without your offspring sitting on the floor in front of you, you are a candidate for boundaries. Children can be terrible at boundaries, which is normal. They need a lot of support in learning to develop and maintain healthy boundaries for themselves and honor the boundaries of others. The primary benefit of creating boundaries is a fostering of respect, balance, and autonomy for both child and parent.

   This chapter examines the benefits of emotional and physical boundaries, includes a review of current research on setting boundaries for children, and offers simple questions and brainstorming prompts you can use to both define your personal and family boundaries and assist your child in establishing their own boundaries.

4. **Disciplining.** Children are not currently accepting memos outlining the aforementioned boundaries their parents feel are needed to keep them physically and emotionally safe. So parents have to use discipline. Together we'll dive into effective disciplining strategies, such as being consistent in parental reactions when boundaries are pushed, following through with consequences that have been clearly and calmly explained to the child, and resisting the urge to be too wordy when disciplining.

   We'll also explore how to validate a child's feelings while staying firm, anticipate the breaking of boundaries and take steps to prevent it, keep cool when the kiddo resists disciplining efforts, and create a safe and cozy space for the child to process the frustration of being disciplined. You'll have a clear and custom plan for using discipline to shift your family boundaries from fantasy to reality.

5. **Instilling values.** While it's natural for children to be raving egomaniacs, it's never too early to plant the seeds that help them bloom into good citizens of the world. Every time we help our littles engage with others in ways that promote empathy, altruism, and social justice, we're not only supporting their development but also adding value to society. We're all in this together, so exposing our kids to activities such as recycling, volunteering, or just good old-fashioned helping out teaches them that we are all vulnerable and valuable. Children are great companions for activities such as walking the dog, making a card for a sick relative, or visiting a nursing home to offer companionship to those without a family.

   In this chapter, you'll explore the values you want to instill in your child and then create a plan for structuring your time with your offspring to infuse them with these values. You'll ask questions such as *What activities could we engage in that will promote a sense of purpose, belonging, security, trust, responsibility, self-discipline and control, empowerment to make decisions, or acceptance of mistakes?* We'll also consider how play, art, and stories can be tools for promoting positive values.

6. **Navigating the social scene.** As you might have noticed, children gravitate to other children, which can lead to peals of laughter or tussles and tears. The social dynamics of the child community can be challenging, and doubly so when parents get involved.

   This chapter will support you in creating an ideal formula of social interaction for your child—for example, a mix of playdates, park play, and kid tai chi classes (it's a thing)—and then help you brainstorm about the timing, level of freedom, dispute resolution, big emotion management, and boundaries you want to use during these social interactions. We'll also discuss how you can move through the making (and occasional breaking) of parent-child friendships with confidence, authenticity, and minimal anxiety, even if you, like myself, have social insecurities. By the end of the chapter, you will have a plan for exploring this new social landscape so these interactions can be enjoyable for both you and your kiddo.

7. **Creating a family schedule and routines.** "Winging it" with a child can be akin to sailing into a storm without a navigation system. That's why it's so important to develop a clear plan for managing your personal and family schedule, in addition to routines for chores and quality (or at least good enough) hygiene and potty learning. The resulting consistency can help your family, children especially, experience more peace, clarity, and emotional stability. When an organized schedule and set of routines are established and honored, blocks of free time often appear because you and your people are no longer wasting time trying to figure out what you need to do next.

   To create your customized family schedule and routines, which honor the natural rhythm and needs of your child's and family's life, we'll look at your core parenting values, your daily obligations (including work), your child's eat-sleep-play cycle, and current research.
8. **Promoting healthy food, sleep, and safety choices.** Guiding your kids toward healthy choices such as eating nutritious food, getting quality sleep, and utilizing safe practices can be one of the hardest elements of parenting because most kids want their food fried or sugared, their sleep only when all fun things in the world stop for the night, and their safety protocols, well, never, no fun in that. We have our work cut out for us. To get more than French fries and grilled cheese into your child, this chapter offers an array of strategies to help you align the food choices you make for your child with your own so you can explore healthy eating together. To support this exploration, you'll look at the nutritional landscape of your child's diet as it relates to your unique family eating values and goals, consider current research on the dietary needs of children, then establish a family food philosophy that will become a cornerstone of your Parenting Plan.

   I'll also share the most relevant evidence-based information on slumber and help you determine the sleep strategies that will best suit your kids. And yes, trial and error will be part of the process. In addition to crafting a customized sleep plan, we'll also examine how to deal with the judgment you might receive for your plan and how to stand tall in your choices. Finally, we'll figure out the safety plans you want to implement in each area of your child's life.

9. **Parenting with your people.** For better or (sometimes) worse, we aren't in this parenting thing alone. Many of us are navigating relationships with caregivers that range from extended family members to babysitters to teachers, not to mention our coparent if we're partnered in this adventure. So how do you have a conversation with your partner about screen time without fighting the urge to hop in the car and head for Mexico? How do you communicate expectations for discipline with the babysitter in a way that will make the sitter more receptive than defensive? Because navigating these dynamics can be tricky, this chapter examines strategies for effectively communicating, resolving conflicts, creating a united front, scheduling, and forming routines with the adults who play a significant role in your child's life. The tools you choose to utilize can support your child in developing strong, healthy emotional and social bonds with other adults—even those who may have different beliefs or values than yours.

   We'll also home in on the type of child care you feel would best suit your child by creating a tiered list of criteria and then using it to select the options that meet your needs. We'll then explore how to move through the decision-making process in an organized and objective manner.

As you contemplate these aspects of parenting and discover what they mean for you and your family through the writing prompts in each chapter, you'll be creating a solid draft of your Parenting Plan. To support this exploration and stimulate your creativity, you'll also find simple relaxation exercises, links to guided meditations, and more tools throughout the book.

For me, the act of writing down what I believed, what I hoped for my family, and what we needed to get there transformed my parenting experience. As a result, my family is blossoming in exciting, unexpected ways after years of struggle. Because I'm no longer groping in the dark for answers outside myself, I can relax: my kids sense this and seem freer to be their wild, sweet, complex selves. What's so fantastic about this Parenting Plan is that it's a living document that loves being revisited and revised, flexing and growing as you and your children do, while also releasing anxiety and judgment around your role as parent.

To help you craft your Parenting Plan, I also provide research-based parenting strategies and ideas that have worked for me and my clients. This isn't to tell you how you should parent. This is to provide you with options. You can use these options, craft some hybrids, or throw them all out and do your own thing.

So let's take a deep dive into your values and dreams for your parenting journey and mix a special sauce of quality information with your instincts so you can create a style of parenting that's all your own. No two Parenting Plans will be the same, but they'll all achieve the same goal: enhanced equilibrium, competence, and empowerment, supporting you in approaching your role of parent with an open mind and heart, and renewed sense of adventure.

Onward!

Meditations, Writing Prompts, and Parenting Plan Outline

You're busy. So busy you might think it's a miracle that you've gotten this far in the book. And the idea that I'm going to ask you to do more than just read this book might be annoying. But here's the thing: committing to answering the prompts is the key to transforming your parenting experience and crafting your customized Parenting Plan. The good news: there is no deadline. While I encourage you to regularly interact with this book, the meditations, and the writing prompts, don't feel like you have to get it all done in a week, or even six months. Just keep coming back and gradually making your way through every chapter and every question.

If you're wondering why I'm so cruel as to give you homework, here's why. The guided meditation for each chapter supports you in synthesizing and exploring the chapter's ideas. The writing prompts then allow you to explore what the ideas in the chapter mean to you and your unique family. By answering these prompts, you will have a complete Parenting Plan by the time you finish the book. You can record your answers in whatever medium you prefer: writing them in a notebook (or the book itself if you own the print edition); typing them into your phone, tablet, or computer; or speaking voice memos into a speech-to-text program. You can insert your answers directly into the Parenting Plan template found at the following link: https://www.baileygaddis.com/parenting-plan.

Writing everything down is so important because it means you'll actually use it—at least most of the time. A study done by the department of psychology at Dominican University of California found that those who write down their goals accomplish significantly more than those who don't write them out. The study also found that the chance of success was increased when people shared their goals with someone else.

Speaking of sharing your goals, if you're parenting with a partner, you can answer these prompts together, you can individually answer them and then compare and discuss your answers as you go, or you can answer on your own and then discuss the complete Parenting Plan when you've reached the end of the book. Getting on the same page with this plan helps ensure you and your partner present a united front, your children receive fairly consistent messages, and you and your partner hold one another accountable to your parenting goals.

My hope is that by the time you reach the last page, you will have life-changing insights about your relationship with your children and self, and how you can journey forward with passion, purpose, and clarity.

Parenting Older Children

If you're reading this book after your children have graduated from childhood, you can still benefit. Much of the research I share and the outline and prompts for the Parenting Plan can be applied to children of any age. When appropriate, I'll discuss how certain strategies in the book work for older children. Because I have a three-year-old and eleven-year-old, and support clients with children up to the age of eighteen, I'm well versed in each stage of child development. So, parents of grade-schoolers, tweens, and teens, read on, as this book will support you in crafting a customized blueprint for raising your unique humans. And remember, your Parenting Plan is a living document that can be revisited and revised as your family evolves.

1

DISCOVERING AND CLARIFYING YOUR PARENTING VALUES

TIGER PARENTING, HELICOPTER PARENTING, free-range parenting, attachment parenting, and so on. There are a comical number of parenting brands, and they're all accompanied by a subtle, and sometimes not-so-subtle, societal pressure to choose one and stick to it. But what if you resonate with only a few ideas from a few of those brands, or don't really connect with any of them? Well dear reader, all is not lost.

After I got my son through his first year, people started slinging questions about how I was going to deal with discipline, and hygiene, and communication, and socialization, and sleep, and all the other parenting stuff we explore in this book. My answer? "Um . . ." I must have been giving off a novice parent scent (a mix of sweat, dry shampoo, and pureed fruit), because holy moly, did everyone start laying the parenting advice on thick. I became an expert in the parenting styles and values of everyone from my in-laws to a crew of park parents, but I had no idea what *my* parenting values and style were. I was flying by the seat of my stretchy pants and working with a custom blend of ignorance, anxiety, hoovering tendencies, and heavy-duty bribery. Good times.

After numerous mini crises I knew I had to get my head straight. That was when I started exploring the ideas that became the class that became this book. Step one was clearing the slate. I had to wipe away everything, from the gems of wisdom to the straight-up wack advice I'd received from others and start from scratch. After scrubbing that slate, I had a clear foundation to build my Parenting Plan on.

The meditation at the following link will support you in clearing your own slate, so I highly recommend giving it a listen: https://www.baileygaddis.com/clearing-the-slate.

The first things I laid on that foundation were my parenting values. These values served as my guiding light as I built my Parenting Plan because they helped me clarify my parenting principles and standards of behavior. They also supported me in becoming a better mom and getting to know myself on a deeper level. Once I clarified these values, it was much easier to answer the prompts you'll journey through in the following chapters.

Why You'll Probably Judge Some of Your Values

The path to discovering my parenting values was fraught with self-judgment. For example, my frenemy Judgey came out to play when I realized that occasional bouts of excessive screen time, over-the-top birthday parties that drowned my home in wrapping paper, and an occasional dinner of cereal and ice cream didn't conflict with my personal values.

Judgey berated some of my more unconventional revelations because I was hardwired to believe that I needed to obey the culturally approved set of parenting values I'd been exposed to. Those revelations felt right to the real me but perverse to the me who wanted to fit in and please. This is one of the main reasons I'm adamant about clearing the slate before crafting the Parenting Plan. If we don't, we might unintentionally end up with a Parenting Plan that emulates the values of other parents, siblings, Supernanny, or others. The parenting beliefs that mirror their values could be so deeply entrenched in your mind that you don't have any space for new ideas. The result: if you have an instinct to value something your family of origin or community doesn't typically value, you might try to deny the value because it feels too difficult to fit it in with your societally prescribed values. For example, if your parents raised you to value formal education, you might face inner and outer resistance if your instinct is to value the school of life over pushing your children to get good grades.

As long as your genuine values don't harm others, there's nothing wrong with them. You have every right to stand tall in your values and allow them to be your compass. To support yourself in doing this, notice when you judge a value your instincts are pulling you toward. Instead of resisting it, uncover where the judgment is coming from. Are you judging it because it's something that truly feels wrong to you? Or, more likely, are you judging it because it conflicts with a value of someone who is a primary influence in your life? If it's the latter, I encourage you to summon your courage and empower yourself to forge ahead on your new, unique path. Yes, you might face temporary resistance from those you're veering away from, but the freedom and authenticity you'll realize will make the relational growing pains well worth it.

The "Good" Parent Myth

You might find yourself affected by what you think "good" parents do as you navigate this chapter, and this book as a whole. But what are "good" parents? The parents we see on sitcoms? Or our parents? Or maybe in-laws? I would say it's none of those, or all of those, depending on who you ask, because everyone has their own definition of "good." Our belief in the idea of this mythical "good" parent perpetually screws with our ability to live authentic, unique, satisfying lives as we raise or, more accurately, grow up with our kids. When we break away from the desire to mold our parenting behaviors to what's "good," a vast realm of possibilities opens. In this realm you get to define what kind of parent you want to be.

For me, the idea of being a "good" parent felt restrictive and dull. When I started exploring how I wanted to parent, I resonated more with the idea of being a weird parent. A curious parent. An empathetic parent. An ever-evolving parent. And that's just me. Everyone has the right to decide they want totally different ideals to guide them. I don't get to define what the universal "good" way to parent is, and neither do you, or your sister, or whoever.

Start at the Beginning

To help you begin pinpointing the parenting values you do and do not resonate with, I'm going to pull a Freud and take you back to your childhood. Whether you like it or not, your family of origin's values influenced you. This doesn't mean you're destined to hold identical values, but it does mean you should clarify what those values were. Getting this clarity can help you understand how various values look in practice and fine-tune your instincts as you craft your new or reimagined set of values.

To begin, answer the following questions.

- **How was I parented?**
  My answer: I was parented with patience and calm by my mother, and a large degree of flexibility, and then bouts of intensity by my father. Nature was highly valued, and we regularly skied and camped. My mom cooked healthy meals, but food wasn't a high priority; it was mainly viewed as fuel.
- **What did I like about how I was parented?**
  My answer: I knew I was loved and was told so often. I appreciate that friends and family were a high priority and that my parents exposed me to a variety of cultures through reading, live music, museums, and travel. I also deeply value that I was never shamed for fears or insecurities and my parents never used corporal punishment.
- **What did I not like?**
  My answer: When I was sad or hurt my father would often respond with anger—not necessarily at me, but the world at large for causing me pain. I didn't receive consistent discipline, which is something I carried into my own parenting and am actively working on.

If you have trouble answering these questions, listen to the meditation at the following link, as it supports you in opening your mind to memories that can help you explore the values that shaped your childhood: https://www.baileygaddis.com/memories.

After completing these prompts, review your answers and tease out the core values you were exposed to as a child. Write down those values and note which ones are influencing your parenting.

Going Deeper into Your Parenting Values

Now that you have a better understanding of the parenting values your caregivers exposed you to, you can go deeper into your core parenting values by exploring the following questions. I've included my answers again, not to coerce you into sharing my values but to provide a framework for how you might craft your answers. Remember, there's no right or wrong way to answer these prompts; let your mind be free to guide you to the responses that feel most authentic.

- **What does being a "good" parent mean to me?**
  My answer: Providing for my children's basic needs and then helping them feel free to explore and express their most authentic selves, instead of trying to shape them into the people I think they should be. Striving to remove hypocrisy from our interactions by exhibiting the actions and values I urge them to honor. Allowing exposure to the messier aspects of life, but in increments, and only at developmentally appropriate times. Fostering a desire to honor family and prioritize togetherness, while also learning how to be alone and value autonomy. Helping them feel safe to take unconventional paths if that's where they're drawn. Showing them my fallibility but also the stability of my love for them. Encouraging them to validate themselves instead of seeking it from others. Doing my best each day, while acknowledging that my best will look different each day.
- **How would I like others to describe my family?**
  My answer: They're a family that treats one another with respect and enjoys being together. They laugh often, travel regularly, and are conscious of the feelings of others. They can poke fun at one another but never in a mean-spirited way. They thoughtfully engage in difficult conversations. They're social but also take time to have family-only adventures. They do their best to

check in with one another every day and to be present during those interactions. Love is their compass.

- **How can I better parent myself?**
  My answer: By being consistent with the activities that improve my ability to thrive, like daily exercise, eating whole foods, putting the spoon away before reaching the bottom of the pint, and drinking water. Showing up to all my therapy sessions. Creating something every day, even if it's just a few sentences. Honoring my OCD tendencies without letting them rule me. Making time to have sex with my husband and forgiving myself for the fact that I have to schedule it. Stop pretending that I'm not ambitious. Stop obsessing over what other people think of me and beating myself up for all my foot-in-mouth moments. Realizing that anxiety isn't essential to my survival. Loving myself, as I am, right now.
- **What are my ultimate goals for my children and family as a whole?**
  My answer: To create a familial ecosystem that thrives on compassion, curiosity, and compromise. This ecosystem is a safe space for each family member to explore who they are and who they want to become, while also remembering that they are already whole and loved unconditionally. They then feel safe to venture into the wider world and take risks, foster positive change, and explore opportunities that give them a sense of purpose. We value our everlasting connection to one another and prioritize togetherness while also valuing independence. We challenge and propel one another, while also providing a haven where it is safe to rest, release, and recharge before continuing the adventure of life.

Your Parenting Mission Statement

Now it's time to review your answers to these questions and use them to create a parenting mission statement (or statements) that encapsulates how you want to parent. Don't stress too much about this as you can always add and revise.

Here's mine: I strive to weave love and respect into all interactions. I do my best to curb judgment and treat my family members as if it could be the last time we're together. I work with my family to make the world around us better through our words and actions. I value balancing dedication to work and education with travel, games, and time in nature. I support my family in following their passions and recognizing their innate value and purpose.

While there are few days that I live up to every facet of this mission, it is helpful having it as my North Star. It informs many of my actions and guides me back to equilibrium, especially when I'm in conflict with a family member or feeling like our paths are rarely intersecting.

If you've made it to end of this chapter and addressed all, or at least most, of the writing prompts, you are badass. This chapter is one of the most difficult to tackle because it deals with such a broad topic. I believe it's smoothish sailing from here, because now that you've begun identifying your custom parenting values, it will be easier to determine what feels right for you while navigating the parenting elements we'll explore in later chapters. So congrats, friend, you're one step closer to reclaiming the power to parent, and even just do life, in the way that feels most authentic to you and your family.

Guided Meditation

The meditation at the following link supports you in envisioning your greatest dreams for your family and digging even deeper into the parenting values you've defined in this chapter: https://www.baileygaddis.com/dream-family.

Writing Prompts

Here's a recap of the writing prompts from this chapter.

- How was I parented?
- What did I like about how I was parented?
- What did I not like?
- What does being a "good" parent mean to me?
- How would I like others to describe my family?
- How can I better parent myself?
- What are my ultimate goals for my children and family as a whole?

Parenting Plan

Parenting mission statement:

2

INVITING YOUR INTUITION ON THIS JOURNEY

YOUR INTUITION, YOUR INSTINCTS, YOUR SPIDEY SENSE, or whatever you want to call it, is key to living your most authentic, happy life, specifically in the realm of parenting. In my first book, *Feng Shui Mommy: Creating Balance and Harmony for Blissful Pregnancy, Childbirth, and Motherhood*, I write, "The first of the three elements of faith in Buddhism is intuition. Listening to this 'gut reaction' or 'sixth sense' is the first door that must be opened in order to access the other two core elements of Buddhist faith, which are reason and experience. When we unlock this voice of wisdom, the important questions we're being asked, or asking, will be answered."

Sounds lovely, right? Learning to live a life guided by our intuition instead of all the external noise is a revelation. And science backs this up. A groundbreaking study published in the journal *Psychological Science* found that intuition does exist and can be measured. The researchers also uncovered evidence that people can use their intuition to make decisions faster, more accurately, and with enhanced confidence. However, many of us resist the guidance of our intuition because it often has the big picture in mind instead of what will make the present easier. It's normal to want to take the path of least resistance, but when we remember that intuition is playing the long game, it can be easier to heed its guidance.

Another block some have with their intuition is that it can feel abstract and elusive. You might be like, "Bailey, how do I know that voice in my head is my intuition and not the voice of my overbearing mother?" Great question. In this chapter, we're going to dig into the subconscious mind, locate your intuition, and invite it to be your life coach.

The Three Types of Intuition

Researchers have identified three types of intuition: holistic, inferential, and affective. They believe holistic intuition uses various sources of information in a nonanalytical manner to provide feedback, inferential intuition provides automatic feedback based on past analysis and decision-making processes that are now automatic, and affective intuition bases its feedback on feelings.

For example, if you're in a tense social situation, holistic intuition will be clocking subtle cues, such as the body language and tone of voice of the people you're with, even if your conscious mind is oblivious to these cues. If you've been in similar tense situations, inferential intuition will quickly review all the information it's gathered in these past situations, particularly the strategies that were most effective at helping you navigate the tension. Affective intuition will focus on how your body is responding to this situation. They're a team, working together for your greater good.

Building a Trusting Relationship with Your Intuition

One of the simplest and most effective ways to pinpoint the voice of your intuition is by listening to the first message you hear and feel after asking yourself a question. It's the message you get before the mental chatter begins. It's best to start small by asking yourself what you want to eat or watch or say when you get a social invite. For example, if I receive an invite for a party and my initial reaction is to cringe, that's my intuition speaking. It speaks before my mind starts saying *Well, maybe you should probably go. You've been kind of a hermit lately and might forget how to speak full sentences if you don't start engaging with adults again. But what would you wear? Would it be ruder to RSVP and not go, or to not RSVP and show up last minute if you change your mind?* Enough! My intuition told me from the start that, in the words of Randy Jackson, "It's gonna be a no from me, dawg."

As you get better at noticing the input of your intuition, I encourage you to heed its advice. Start with low-stakes actions like eating the food your intuition told you to eat, or taking the route home it suggested, as this will help you build trust in your intuition's ability to make good choices for you. Building this trust will then allow your intuition to shine when you're faced with higher-stakes decisions.

I also want to note that listening to your intuition doesn't mean being impulsive. Just because your intuition is often the first voice you hear when faced with a question or situation, you don't have to act right away. But as you build the skill of tuning into your intuition and allowing it to rise above the noise, you'll have more clarity when engaging in critical thinking and be able to reach an informed decision faster. A study published in *British Dental Journal* found that when the dentists in the study were faced with a decision that had a pressing time constraint, was complex and ambiguous, and was based on a topic that lacked sufficient scientific evidence, using their intuition led to a better decision than if they'd utilized evidence-based decision-making. Those circumstances sound a lot like parenting, don't they?

Nurturing the Intuition with Information

Your intuition is birthed from the alchemy of knowledge you gather and information from your past experiences and conditioning. I also believe intuition contains a mysterious spark of magic that can never be fully defined (but that's for another book). A crucial piece of keeping intuition in peak shape is fueling it with fresh information and experiences—saying yes to life. Regularly expanding your knowledge also prevents your intuition from always guiding you toward what's most comfortable and known. When the intuition is consistently being refreshed, it's more likely to guide you into mysterious terrain that can lead somewhere extraordinary.

When faced with a nonemergency parenting situation, you have the opportunity to gather and assess a variety of information and then work with your intuition, and maybe your partner, to create a solution that's best for your family, not just one that will make you feel most accepted by your pack or unchallenged by newness. But how exactly do you do this? By applying the process of evolution, with a twist, to your decision-making: learning about the best available options, taking the pieces of each that make your intuition light up, and combining them into a one-of-a-kind solution. Here's an example.

Screen time used to be an ongoing, torturous struggle between myself and my son, Hudson. He was getting way too much of it, primarily because I was wary of the battle that would ensue when it was time to turn off the device. To allow the process of evolution to help my intuition find an answer, I asked two questions.

1. **What are the best available options?**
   After researching the many different ways parents limit screen time, my intuition was most drawn to the options of using a timer, slowly tapering down screen time over a few weeks, creating entertaining alternatives to screen time that didn't always involve my participation, curating the content, providing incentives for my son to help with this plan (aka bribery), and the hardest, holding myself accountable.
2. **What aspects of these options would work best for our family?**
   - **Timers.** Hudson would get really triggered when I was the one telling him to turn off the screen. Together, we decided the best option was to set automatic, password-protected time limits on his devices so they would automatically shut off when time was up. He was able to view a timer that showed how much time was left. I no longer had to be the enforcer.
   - **Tapering the time.** I knew Hudson didn't respond well to swift change, so I reduced his screen time by fifteen minutes each week until we got down to a reasonable amount of time.
   - **Screen time alternatives.** Every time I suggested super-cool screen time alternatives, Hudson gave me a thumbs-down. When I finally asked him for ideas, he suggested listening to audiobooks while drawing, creating an archery station in our yard, practicing math (ha, just kidding), and so on. Being the one to think up these alternatives gave him more ownership over the plan and made him less resistant to putting the screen away.

- **Curating the content.** Hudson would sometimes spend half his screen time just figuring out what to watch. Together we made a list of his favorite shows and games that my husband and I approved of, so he could choose one before screen time began.
- **Incentives.** To make the bitter pill of less screen time a little tastier, I promised to take Hudson out for ice cream each Sunday for the first four weeks of his screen time tapering if he didn't make the process a total nightmare.
- **Holding myself accountable.** Ugh. This part was the worst. As a writer, it's addictive to let my screen-loving child sit quietly behind that screen when I'm on a roll with a project. No messes are being made; all is quiet. *Maybe just fifteen more minutes?* But although there were a few slipups, I primarily stuck to the plan. Those aforementioned no-supervision-needed activities were helpful.

While it wasn't always smooth, this plan worked because it wasn't pulled straight from the brain of another person or a book. It was an amalgamation of knowledge gained through past experiences with my son and new information I gathered from various sources, picked apart, then pieced together based on what I intuitively felt would work for my family. In this situation, my son's intuition also came into play—something I'll discuss more soon.

Wow, that was a long example! And coming up with that plan was also a long process. The cool thing is, economists at the University of Bamberg and the Technical University of Munich have found that taking the time now to fuel your intuition with juicy information and hone your ability to listen to the feedback your intuition provides after processing said information will make the process go quicker in the future. And because you'll regularly dive deep into this process while crafting your Parenting Plan, your intuition will be a finely tuned, information-filled instrument by the time you're done with this book.

The Intuition Thrives on Curiosity

In addition to utilizing that extensive index of information you're constantly improving, your intuition also wants to cross-reference. This means that if, for example, you're trying to get your kid to eat more than toast, your intuition will analyze not only information about nutrition but also a range of other topics that could provide an inspired solution. For example, it might index information you've gathered while managing people at work, ideas from a tai chi class, and profound wisdom from that realty show you love.

One of the best ways to boost the informational health of your intuition is to stay curious. When you take your kids to the children's museum, pay attention to those signs explaining centrifugal force; when looking for a new book, take a break from the parenting books and read the memoir of someone you admire; when chatting with a friend, ask them about that horticulture workshop they took. In addition to helping your intuition thrive, this active curiosity will likely make life a lot more fun.

The Intuition Loves Mistakes

Another crucial component of fine-tuning the intuition is admitting when we make a mistake. Often, our egos do everything possible to convince us that a decision we made was the right one, even if all signs point to "not the right choice." But when we push past the discomfort of upsetting the ego and acknowledge that we would have been better served by a different decision, we're providing our intuition with a valuable helping of information. It's also important to sit with the situation for a while, not just acknowledging the mistake, but also brainstorming all the choices that could have resulted in a better outcome. In addition to building your intuition's intelligence, this is a powerful way to move through emotions like guilt and regret and get on with living a flawed yet fabulous life.

The Power of Observing Patterns

Actively observing life's patterns is yet another effective strategy for stoking your intuition with wisdom. The subconscious mind is hardwired to notice patterns, but the conscious mind often misses them.

When we actively look for and assess patterns, we enhance the impact of these observations. Our intuitive awareness, composed of a mix of physical, emotional, and spiritual awareness, will also help us pick up these patterns.

According to business researchers, top CEOs also rely on patterns, or what they call "rules of thumb," when making about 85 percent of their decisions. This intentional assessment of patterns can lead to *aha* moment after *aha* moment as you build on the wisdom your subconscious mind probably picked up on a while ago. This stealth gathering of information is one reason why intuition is sometimes referred to as *subconscious intelligence* and people report knowing something without knowing how they know. Each recognized pattern is like a puzzle piece, and the intuition helps you arrange the pieces into a full picture that is likely an effective solution to whatever you're dealing with.

For example, my client Chelsea was having the hardest time potty training her son Otis. Otis would pee in the toilet but poop in his underwear. I encouraged her to actively observe Otis's patterns over the next week. After that week she had an *aha*. "He always climbs under a table when he needs to poop!" she told me a week later. Her subconscious mind had registered this pattern, but her conscious mind had glazed over it. Now equipped with this knowledge of Otis's pooping pattern, Chelsea put tiny portable potties under the three tables in her house. It worked. Conscious observation + intuition = potty training win.

Gathering the Information, Then Letting It Go

We've covered a variety of ideas that employ the conscious mind, but because the intuition operates from the subconscious, it might be best to distract yourself after gathering all the information needed to make a decision. A study done by the University of Amsterdam found that research participants were more likely to come up with an effective solution for a complex issue if they did so while focusing on brainteasers, indicating that the subconscious mind made the decision. This might be why so many people have revelations when doing something like taking a shower or going on a walk; in these situations the conscious mind wanders off and the subconscious mind has space to serve up ideas.

So if you're faced with a tricky dilemma about how to support your child with social issues, for example, gather information on the topic, actively observe your child in social situations, then step away from it. Go for a hike or a swim, see a movie, work on an art project, or do anything else that redirects the conscious mind and lets the subconscious mind craft ideas.

How the Intuition Communicates Through the Body

Your intuition doesn't just work its magic from your mind; it courses through your entire body via your nervous system, hormones, neurotransmitters, factors that affect the immune system, and in my opinion, the spirit. So, when you're faced with a decision, your subconscious mind rapidly cycles through all the potential actions and outcomes. And according to a study published in the journal *Neuron*, your body often responds to this subconscious information before your conscious mind is aware of it.

Much of this response comes from your gut, or more specifically the enteric nervous system, which is two thin layers of more than one hundred million nerve cells lining your gastrointestinal tract. This system produces over thirty neurotransmitters and is so skilled at responding to subconscious information, it is often referred to as the "second brain." So as your subconscious analyzes information, your gut is providing almost instant feedback.

For example, if you're trying to decide whether to confront your mother-in-law about calling your child a crybaby right after she says it or after you've calmed down, your subconscious mind will quickly process all the potential outcomes of these two options. When processing what could happen if you discuss the issue in that moment, you might notice tightening in your stomach because your intuition knows that option probably won't lead to a productive conversation. When you think of discussing the issue after you've calmed your child and yourself, your stomach might soften, even though your anger is screaming at you to say something now. Stomach intelligence for the win.

You can utilize this additional layer of intuition by paying attention to the signals your intuition produces in your body. When you're thinking about moving forward with a certain decision, notice whether your body feels light and mind clear. Are they gently expanding, pushing toward that decision? Or is your body tight and heavy, and your mind jumbled and hesitant? Do you feel as though your body is contracting away from the decision? To gain skill in pinpointing the voice and often subtle feel of your intuition, visit the guided meditation link at the end of this chapter.

Using Your Intuition When Receiving Unsolicited Parenting Advice

My ego used to be the first thing that processed unsolicited parenting advice. It would scream *No! You're wrong. I know what I'm doing!* Often, it was right to push away the advice—but not always. Sometimes my ego caused me to miss parenting ideas that could have served my family. When I noticed my pattern of immediately becoming defensive and irritated about parenting advice, I became curious about what would happen if I received the advice with an open mind.

The first part of Operation Ego Check was acknowledging that I'm a pretty defensive person and probably always will be. Being honest about that helped me be less thrown off when my defensiveness was triggered. I also committed to replacing the sassy, dismissive remarks I wanted to spew with a deep breath. Then I would say, "Hmm . . . that's interesting. How did that work for your family?" This question would get the heat off me and allow the other person to focus on their own parenting and maybe share a helpful insight or two, or none. After the interaction I would then let my intuition chew on the given advice.

For example, when someone told me I should try "baby-led weaning," which is skipping pureed foods in favor of finger foods, I asked a few questions and later asked my intuition what it thought about that idea. Because I didn't know much about this idea but was intrigued, I researched it. In this situation, I ended up taking the advice and did baby-led weaning with both kids.

The more I used the strategy of breathing instead of immediately responding, turning the convo back on the advice-giver with a question, and then later considering and researching the idea, the better I got at gracefully receiving advice. My intuition also got speedier at determining if the advice was worth a try.

Telling the Difference Between Intuition and Harmful Unconscious Biases

There is a fine line between messages from our intuition and those from our unconscious, or implicit, bias that can easily blur, and sometimes should. We have biases about everything from the type of socks we like to how we take our coffee. Some of these biases are known and some unconscious, and largely they are harmless. It's also natural for these biases to influence our intuition. So what I'm discussing here is not all the unconscious biases we hold, but the ones that are based on inaccurate information and can lead to discriminatory behavior. Pretty much every human holds some unconscious biases of this nature, and even the most thoughtful, well-intentioned person can engage in discriminatory behavior they're not actively aware of.

Until we do the work to begin noticing and then removing layers of this variety of unconscious biases, they can have a strong hold on our beliefs and behaviors as they've been embedded in us from childhood. The seeds of unconscious bias are planted when a child's family, community, and society at large tell, or more often show, them what to believe and how to operate in the world. As the child ages, those biases continue, and unless they are able to recognize and deconstruct those that can be harmful, those biases will keep impersonating the intuition and leading to unconscious beliefs and behaviors the person likely has no intention of engaging in.

Luckily, harmful unconscious biases don't masquerade as intuition in many parenting decisions. For example, unconscious bias is unlikely to affect the bedtime routine you create for your family, or how you choose to navigate difficult emotions. But it can creep in when you're making decisions involving people outside your family and situations outside the home. For example, a more harmful unconscious bias might affect a parent's instincts when determining if they want their child to go to a school that has mostly White teachers or one that has teachers of many different ethnicities. If the parent can step back and assess if unconscious bias is impersonating their intuition, they might realize their bias is steering them toward the White teachers, even though the true voice of their intuition found the other school to be a better fit for their child.

It's also natural for parents to develop unconscious biases about their children, which can sometimes lead to unfair treatment. For example, if you've developed the unconscious bias that your middle child is your calm and obedient kid, you might have a bigger reaction to that child's intense emotional display than you would if your youngest child, the one you unconsciously label "the wild child," has a similar emotional response. You don't consciously want to treat one child more harshly than another, but that implicit bias can wreak havoc on your best intentions.

While this is a multilayered topic that I'm no expert in, I have found it helpful, in situations that don't require immediate action, to take a few moments to consider if my unconscious bias is coloring my reaction. This can be enough to support me in shifting course and tapping into messages from my intuition. Although these in-the-moment bias assessments can be effective, they're just baby steps in the journey of uncovering and deconstructing our unconscious biases. Luckily, there are now many helpful resources to guide us. Two that I've found helpful are *Biased: Uncovering the Hidden Prejudice That Shapes What We See, Think, and Do* by Jennifer L. Eberhardt, PhD, and *Anti-Bias Education for Young Children and Ourselves* by Louise Derman-Sparks and Julie Olsen Edwards.

Introducing Your Kids to Their Intuition

As you commit to the lifelong practice of infusing the wisdom of your intuition into your decisions, you can help your child do the same. Often, a child's decisions are made for them by adults or an older sibling, which can result in the child rebelling against those decisions or feeling like they need permission to make a decision. If we can instead create opportunities for our children to make intuitive decisions, research shows we can improve their outlook. This research, published in *Research in Organizational Behavior*, found a connection between the use of the intuition and a more positive mood and self-confidence.

I have not always properly employed this advice. When researching intuition, I realized I'd long been encouraging my son to use his intuition but wasn't creating many situations for him to do so. I would go on and on about how he should be curious, seek information, listen to his body, and do all the other things I've been telling you, patient reader, but then when he was faced with a decision, I often tried to make it for him. For instance, when I gave him the choice of having a birthday party or going to an amusement park, I urged him to use his intuition to make the decision. But instead of giving him time and space to do that, I started listing the benefits of the amusement park choice. I railroaded his intuition.

We obviously can't let our kids make all the decisions, but we can create situations where they can make a choice using their intuition. In these situations, it's important to set parameters to help ensure we don't have to shut down their decision. For example, if we simply ask, "What do you want for dinner?" our kid will probably request ice cream or that bag of old Halloween candy. However, if we ask, "Is your intuition telling you to have chicken and rice or avocado toast for dinner?" we're setting them up to make a decision we can honor.

One of the hardest parts about this is that many of us are hardwired to want our kids to think like us. And by teaching them to use their intuition, we might be empowering them to make choices that conflict with what we think they should want. This requires big-time letting go and figuring out how to be OK with the fact that our children are their own people. While it might serve our ego to have kids that think and do exactly as we do, pushing them into that way of being could stifle their ability to explore and express their authentic self. I regularly catch myself trying to coerce Hudson into sharing my interests and habits, and it breaks my heart when I realize he's trying to fit that mold just to please me. I even do this with my toddler, Grace. When I have the willpower to show an interest in and approval of what my kids are actually passionate about, which at this moment is coding and gaming for Hudson, and dinosaurs, shoes, and cardboard boxes for Grace, they totally light up. That light is a strong motivator to continue honoring where their intuition is leading.

Here are ideas to help your child connect to and trust their intuition.

- **Explain what intuition is.** If your child is unfamiliar with the idea of intuition, provide them with a simple, age-appropriate explanation. In my experience it's easiest for children to understand how the intuition affects their body. When I explained intuition to my son, he started nodding when I talked about the "gut instinct." "Yeah!" he said, "I know what that feels like! My stomach really hurts when I lie. When I tell the truth it gets better."

- **Create simple situations for your child to use their intuition.** Help your child begin learning the voice of their intuition by encouraging them to make low-stakes decisions throughout the day. For example, at bedtime you can ask if they want to read about an overindulgent caterpillar or a moonlit room filled with random stuff. You can then tell them to take a deep breath, close their eyes, and listen to what their mind and body is telling them to choose. If your child is old enough to discuss the Parenting Plan, you can ask them to use their intuition to help you fill in appropriate parts of the plan. This is especially helpful when working on the Family Values section.
- **Encourage your child to use their intuition in difficult situations.** As your child gets better at listening to their intuition, encourage them to utilize it in tricky situations, such as an altercation with a sibling or when facing the urge to lie. You can remind them to take a beat before acting and notice which decision makes them feel lighter. For example, when they have the choice to lie or tell the truth, their body will likely feel lighter when considering telling the truth, even though the lie probably seems like the easiest option.
- **Ask open-ended questions.** Help your child further explore and trust their intuition by asking them open-ended questions. If your child says they're bored, for example, you could ask, "If you had a magic wand, what would you do in this moment?" Their answers to this question could help their intuition lead them to a doable, boredom-busting activity. Essentially, we want to try to ask more and command less.
- **Use fun language.** When communicating with your child about intuition, think of how you can make the topic more engaging. When I began exploring intuition with Hudson, I would say

things like, "Let's work on listening to our intuition." His eyes would glaze over the moment I said "work." So, I started saying things like, "Let's play with our intuition." I also tried to find ways to relate the topic to his interests. I would sometimes sit with him while he played Minecraft and ask questions about how he knew certain actions were the right choice, and if he thought Creepers had an intuition.

- **Give the intuition time.** Many families are almost always rushing. This can make it tricky for a child to find their intuition. As parents, we can help by summoning that elusive patience when waiting for our child to make a decision. Without that space and time, it can be difficult for a child to hear and feel what their intuition is saying. In these situations, I have to remind myself that my son isn't taking so long to make up his mind because he's ignoring or trying to irritate me; he simply needs more time to cycle through the process of intuitive decision-making.
- **Share your intuitive moments.** As children often model what we do more than what we say, share what you're experiencing when using your intuition. For example, if you're driving them home from school and get stuck in traffic on the freeway, you can tell your child what your mind and body is experiencing as you decide whether you should stay on the freeway or take side streets. This can be especially potent when you feel like you made the wrong decision, as it's powerful for children to realize we also make mistakes and, most important, can admit when we do. You can talk them through why you think you made the mistake, what you learned from it, and what you might do differently in the future. You can also ask children those aforementioned open-ended questions when they make a mistake instead of simply telling them what they did wrong and what the lesson is. It will resonate more if they discover the wisdom on their own.
- **Explain unconscious bias.** When you feel that your child is old enough to understand the concept of unconscious bias, you can discuss how it can impersonate the intuition. Sharing examples from your own life is often one of the most potent ways to convey this concept. You can also share ideas on how to acknowledge

unconscious bias and loosen its grip on how you perceive and interact with the world. As this is a lifelong process, it can be an incredibly important, and fascinating, ongoing discussion to have with your child.

- **Share the "Quick Tools for Connecting to Your Intuition."** These tools, found at the end of this chapter, can help you and your child go on the life-changing mission of intuition-enhancing together.

Crafting Your Parenting Plan with Intuitive Ingredients

A study of chefs found that intuition was key when they were determining which combinations of ingredients they should test. The researchers discovered that the chefs' intuition was crucial in the process of idea generation and evaluation and the eventual creation of something delicious. In so many ways you are the head chef of your family, and as you journey through this book your intuition will help you source the "ingredients" that can transform your parenting life.

If you still feel that your intuition is elusive, know that the previously mentioned study in *Psychological Science* revealed that intuition improves over time and the mechanisms of intuition can be improved with practice. According to the researchers, people become better at trusting their intuition the more they connect to it and heed its guidance. So commit to trying the following tools while helping your child do the same, and trust that your intuition will help you craft an authentic and effective Parenting Plan.

Quick Tools for Connecting to Your Intuition

Here are some easy actions that help you forge a strong connection with your intuition.

- **Breathe.** Imagine that each deep inhalation pulls up your intuition from the recesses of your subconscious mind, and each exhalation allows the voice of your intuition to flow into your conscious mind. Do this as you contemplate each prompt in this book, and pretty much every decision-making moment in life.

- **Do a body scan.** A quick way to connect with messages from your intuition is to close your eyes and notice what you're feeling in your body, starting at the top of your head and scanning down.
- **Hypnotize yourself.** It's often easier for the intuition to communicate when you're in a light state of hypnosis, because hypnosis pushes the conscious mind aside and allows the subconscious to take over. You can get into this state by distracting yourself with a simple, repetitive activity. Walking outside is an especially effective option, as your conscious mind will be processing all the noises, sounds, sights, and smells while your subconscious mind and intuition go to work.
- **Do some free-flow writing or drawing.** Research has found an association between intuition and creativity. Free-flow writing or drawing can be especially helpful in encouraging your intuition to speak up, often through whatever it is you're creating.
- **Don't second-guess low-impact decisions.** Build trust in your intuition by allowing yourself to move forward with low-impact decisions it helped you make. While all the decisions won't be a win, many of them will. These wins help you realize the wisdom of your intuition.
- **Reflect on your best intuitive moments.** Occasionally, think about moments when your intuition gave a clear message and you listened. What was the result? You can also keep a list of your intuition's wins to help you remember its power.
- **Look at something blue.** Blue is a wonderful color to focus on when life seems chaotic and overwhelming, because it leads you back to your loving center and inspires a deep trust for the voice of your intuition.
- **Listen to this meditation.** The guided meditation at the following link will support you in becoming skilled at pinpointing the voice and feel of your intuition: https://www.baileygaddis.com /intuition.

Writing Prompts

- What part, or parts, of the body does my intuition speak through most often?
- What three actions are most effective at connecting me to my intuition?
- What is my intuition urging me to release?
- What is a big decision I've been struggling with? What does my intuition have to say about it?
- Can I commit to spending one day fully led by my intuition?
- What would it feel like to live a life almost entirely guided by my intuition?

THE NINE ESSENTIAL ELEMENTS OF PARENTING

You've done the prep work and are ready to get into the nitty-gritty of parenting and explore each chapter through the lens of your parenting philosophy and intuition. As you dig into the nine elements of parenting, you might have moments of overwhelm, confusion, and even panic because being a parent can feel super high stakes. It is, but it also has a lot of room for error—or what you might perceive as error. Kids are much more resilient than many realize, and your perceived errors are some of the best opportunities for growth for both you and your kid. So take some pressure off yourself! Know that you're never going to parent in a way that you, your kids, your partner, or anyone else considers perfect, and that's OK. They'll never achieve the mythical achievement of perfection either.

I also encourage you to view this journey as one that can be filled with ample and active curiosity, creative trial and error, and liberating, super-satisfying moments of *aha*. This isn't a journey meant to make you feel like a failure. It's a journey meant to add clarity, empowerment, and ease to your family life.

To get into the headspace of curiosity, creativity, and *aha*-ness, listen to the meditation at the following link: https://www.baileygaddis.com/creativity.

3

ELEMENT 1: CRAFTING A FAMILY COMMUNICATION PHILOSOPHY

Trying to communicate with a child can feel like having a conversation with a kitten. It's like your voice is a reminder to notice how fascinating the curtain pull cord is. And then when they accidentally hear something you say, they often have a natural inclination to object, sometimes by chucking a colorful piece of plastic at your face. Woe is us, fellow parents.

While kid communication commonly feels infuriating and perplexing, there are a plethora of tricks you can use to help both your kids and you artfully articulate thoughts, feelings, desires, and needs in a way that lands with the other. These tricks involve leprechaun tears, eye of Big Bird, unicorn placenta, and Nanny McPhee. Just kidding. You have way more powerful sorcery at your disposal.

Enter verbal and nonverbal methods of child-appropriate communication through the felt-senses, affectionate actions, clear and compassionate talking (and the weird voices kids live for), music, pretend play, and storytelling. We'll also explore how to use questions, pauses, and "good vibes" to meet your child where they are and help them feel safe to open up. Last, we'll look at how you communicate with yourself and express that self to your child. So, yeah, a full spell book of communication sorcery. We'll wrap it up with you crafting your own spells and putting it all together to create your family's customized style of communication.

Communication Is the Foundation of Relationships

Communication is one of the most crucial elements of relationships and, well, life, as it's tied up in almost everything. Each time we communicate with someone, including ourselves, we're gathering information that helps us answer questions like *Can I trust this person? How do they make me feel? Do I have anything in common with them? Do they understand me? Do I understand them?* This is one reason why the more you interact with someone, you either develop a friendship or decide that you just don't jibe. It's no different with our children. Each time we interact we're molding their impression of us and vice versa. So it's worth asking *What do I want my child's impression of me to be? How do I want them to feel around me? In twenty years, what do I want them to say when their therapist asks, "Tell me about your parents?"* Answering these questions and regularly revisiting them can make your interactions with your children more authentic and impactful.

Now let's pull back the lens. In addition to the above questions, I encourage you to ask *What is the purpose of communication? What are my primary goals when I communicate?* Pausing to explore these questions and define what this essential aspect of being human means to you will make it easier for you to customize the ideas offered in this chapter. These ideas will culminate in your bespoke formula for communicating with your family and will release a lasting air of ease, harmony, and understanding into your home before rippling out into the rest of your existence. It really is that powerful.

Letting Felt-Sense Guide Communication

Eugene Gendlin, the philosopher and psychologist who came up with the term *felt-sense*, described it as a physical, not mental, awareness of what's happening around you. Gendlin said felt-sense is like "an internal aura that encompasses everything you feel and know about the given subject at a given time—encompasses it and communicates it to you all at once rather than detail by detail." Essentially, felt-sense is another way of referring to our intuition speaking through the body. And just like feedback from the intuition, our felt-sense in a parenting situation doesn't often pop up fully formed; it needs time and space to come into focus. Not too much time, but at least the time it takes for us to breathe deeply and ask our racing mind to chill.

The felt-sense is a powerful tool when communicating because it lets us know if we're on the right track. Often, when our words aren't expressing what we're trying to communicate, the felt-sense will eventually tell us that we need to adjust course by providing uncomfortable sensations. When we register that feedback and try a different path, our felt-sense then informs us if the new path is working. For example, if you're trying to get your child to help you clean up their room and your words are becoming increasingly laced with irritation, your felt-sense may gift you a headache and tight chest. When your mind focuses on those sensations, it might say *What I'm saying isn't working. What else can I do?* You then put on music, start dancing as you throw stuffed animals into a basket, and say, "Wow! I'm having so much fun cleaning up!" This course correction causes your felt-sense to trigger a lightness in your stomach, especially if kiddo actually starts helping.

Often, the first new tactic you try after noticing physical discomfort won't immediately resolve the issue. It's normal to need to continue tweaking what you're doing or saying until you hit on the unique formula that feels right for you and your child. If you keep coming up against uncomfortable physical sensations, take another pause, or dance break, allowing yourself to exist in the discomfort long enough to hear what your felt-sense is urging you to try.

The felt-sense can also be effective when trying to decipher what your child is attempting to communicate. For example, if your child is upset, you can interrupt the regularly scheduled program by asking them, "What's happening in your body right now?" If they look at you like you've grown a second head, you can then get specific, asking, "How does your head feel? Your heart? Your tummy? Your fists?" If your child reports a funny feeling in their tummy, you can ask them what they think their tummy is trying to say. This inquiry into your child's felt-sense can do wonders for revealing what's actually going on for them.

When I regularly started asking my son how different parts of his body were feeling and what those feelings might mean, he began organically tapping into that and offering the information without prompt. Thanks to that, my now ten-year-old often says, "Mom, you're making my ears hurt and stomach twist." You're welcome, my sweet darling.

Something else that can help you and your child connect to the felt-sense is moving your bodies. Your toes tapping on the ground, your arms tracing an infinity sign in the air, your hips swaying back and forth can all help the two of you not only "hear" your felt-senses more clearly but also move out of the stagnation of anger, or irritation, or whatever it is you're trying to move through. This is one reason why dancing can be so powerful during tense situations. I dare you to randomly start dancing when in conflict with your child and note their reaction.

This awkward pausing and body moving can also break up the flow of the interaction and set it on a more productive trajectory. Most of us have set patterns we subconsciously follow when in various circumstances, especially when communicating with family members. When we break up those patterns, we open the door to change.

Speaking Through Actions

Ever heard the saying "Actions speak louder than words"? This little-known phrase is often the crux of communication with a child. They miss a lot of what we say, but they're watching us like a dog watches a person about to drop some bacon. The great thing about this is that it provides a super-effective method for communicating with kids, especially during challenging situations. For example, you can communicate that you're not a threat by crouching down to your child's level, relaxing your posture, and smiling. If they're struggling with a big emotion, you can open your arms, indicating that you're ready to give a hug, if they want one. Through these actions you're communicating that you're a safe harbor. If your child has moved through a big emotion, such as sadness, and is indicating they're ready to move out of it but need help doing so, you can use nonverbal communication, such as a silly face or dance, to help them make the transition.

The following are additional aspects of nonverbal communication that can strengthen the parent-child relationship.

Showing Your Child That You're Paying Attention

Nonverbal communication is an excellent way to help your child feel seen and powerful. For example, stopping what you're doing and turning your attention to them when they're trying to communicate does wonders for making them feel important. They also love mimicking. If you copy their movements when doing something like taking a walk, they'll likely delight in the fact that you're noticing how they move their body and they have the power to affect your movements.

Speaking of mimicking, remember that your child is going to mimic much of what you do, for better or worse. So if your partner leaves their dirty clothes on the floor but regularly asks your child to put theirs in the hamper, do you think your child is more likely to do what your partner does or says? This isn't to say we need to become obsessive about our actions around our children, but we should try to be aware.

Tip: If you're about to do something you really want your child to notice, capture their attention by making big, wacky movements before taking the action.

Nonverbal Family Language

You can make nonverbal communication specific to your family by working with them to come up with various hand signals, facial expressions, and body movements that have special meaning. For example, making a heart with your hands can be a nonverbal way to express love, wiggling your body can be your family's way of saying "let's lighten the mood," stomping your feet can be a way to show anger without saying something hurtful, shaking out your hands can be a signal that you're letting go of a tense mood, and putting your hands on your head can be a signal that you need those around you to be quiet because you have something important to say.

You can start this process by making a list with your family of messages you can convey with nonverbal signals. For example, you might write, "I love you. I need you to slow down. Please listen. You're hurting my feelings. I'm scared. I need a hug. I don't feel like talking. I need to be alone." Together, decide what action will correlate with each message. You can then add to the list whenever someone in the family sees a need for a new signal. As an added bonus, participating in the creation of the nonverbal family language helps your child take ownership of family communication and feel more "heard."

TIP: Before you begin creating this nonverbal family language, spend time noticing the nonverbal communication your child already uses so you can build the family language off it.

Emotion Drawer

You can also provide objects to help your child express themselves. You can make an "emotion drawer" where you store "angry paper," "sad fabric," "bored bubble wrap," "overwhelmed Play-Doh," or other go-to items your child can use when communicating and processing a certain emotion. For example, when they're angry they can go to the drawer and rip up a piece of angry paper, when sad they can rub a piece of sad fabric against their cheek, when bored they can pop the bored bubble wrap, when overwhelmed they can pound their fists into the overwhelmed Play-Doh, and so on.

To support your family in enhancing understanding of nonverbal communication, here are a few games to try.

- **Play charades.** This classic game helps you become more adept at communicating through your body and builds your family's awareness of the types of movements each person makes to convey certain information. You can adapt this game for young children by using picture flash cards showing simple actions or emotions.
- **Guess what the TV characters are doing.** Pop on your child's favorite show, mute it, and then work with them to figure out what's happening.
- **Tell a story without words.** Thrill your child by telling them a hilarious story without using words. Then have them do the same.

Primary Elements of Nonverbal Communication

Here's a breakdown of all the ways we speak without words.

Tone of Voice

"It's not what you said but how you said it," is something we've all heard, or said. Tone of voice is such a powerful communication tool that the same sentence can have a variety of meanings based on the tone of voice used to deliver it. For example, if you bumped into someone and say "excuse me" with a courteous tone of voice, you're conveying an apology. However, if you say "excuse me" with an annoyed tone of voice, you're conveying that you want an apology.

When talking to a child, it's important to tune in to what tone of voice would be most appropriate for the conversation at hand. For example, if your child is upset, using a low, calm tone of voice might be ideal. If your child is about to run into the road, a stern, loud voice would probably be best.

Paying attention to tone of voice is especially crucial when speaking to tweens or teens. They are hypersensitive to, well, everything, but especially the tone of their parents and siblings. A study published in *Developmental Psychology* found that teens are much more receptive to their parent's messages if they're delivered in an "autonomy-supportive" tone instead of a controlling tone. When teens were spoken to in this supportive tone of voice, they experienced more positive and fewer negative emotions, increased closeness with their parent, and willing engagement in the topic at hand. The opposite occurred when parents used a controlling tone.

With all that said, you might have noticed that it gets trickier to modulate your tone of voice when you're angry. But with practice you can adjust your tone even if Angel Bear uses your new duvet as a canvas for their permanent marker drawing, or their sister got home three hours after curfew and it's taking everything in you not to scream "WTF!" with a "WTF!" tone of voice.

You can practice by noticing your tone of voice when talking to your kids and toying around with changing it based on what you're trying to communicate. This can also work wonders with adults.

Facial Expression

Almost as important as tone of voice is what you're doing with your face when communicating. For example, if your eyes are wandering here and there and over to your phone when your child is talking, you're communicating that you're only kind of listening. If you have an animated expression as your child excitedly talks about the butterfly they saw, you help them feel like you're connecting to, and sharing in, their joy. If your child is nervous about riding a carousel, an encouraging smile can communicate your faith that the ride will be fun and safe. It seems like this would be a no-brainer, but so often our facial expression conveys not what we're trying to communicate to our child but what we're actually thinking—which isn't always good. And often, we're not consciously aware of what our face is saying.

To take control of your expressions, loosen your face by wiggling your jaw and moving your lips around. From there, tinker around with matching your facial expressions to what you're hoping to convey in each conversation. As any actor will tell you, you can have a full conversation with facial expressions alone.

Body Language

Our bodies say so much about what we're paying attention to, how interested we are, and if we're relaxed or tense. They can also be intimidating to a child, which is why getting on their level, turning your body toward them, and relaxing your posture and hands is such an effective way to make them feel comfortable enough to communicate. It's also important to notice whether your child wants physical space. For example, if you lean in to talk and they lean away, their body language is communicating a need for space.

Touch

Children are incredibly sensitive to all forms of touch. An adult tightly gripping their shoulder, for example, can trigger anxiety or fear, while a gentle hug can melt away grief. You can convey that your full attention is on your child when communicating by gently placing a hand on their arm or holding their hand. And, of course, a hug is one of the greatest communicators, if your child wants one.

The Art of Communicating with Short, Simple Sentences

Less is more. Remembering that can transform communication with children, as they typically have an attention span of three to six minutes. This short period of attention means that no matter how interesting they find your soliloquy on the merits of not squishing peas into the dog's ear, they're going to tune you out pretty fast. Because of this, parents have to be quick and clear when communicating. And verbal communication is arguably the least favorite type of communication for most children, because, um, boring.

Here are some of the many benefits of keeping it short and sweet.

Builds Vocabulary

Speaking to your child concisely can support them in learning to speak in sentences and in building their vocabulary, as they're more likely to absorb your words. You might think that we'd want to use those fancy words our eighth-grade English teacher put on the vocabulary test, but no. A child is best able to develop a robust lexicon when caretakers gradually add in new words when speaking to the child and make those words more advanced as the child ages.

You can further enhance your child's vocabulary by repeating their sentences using the correct grammar and pronunciation. For instance, if they say, "Me want wawu," you can then say, "Oh, you want water?" This strategy is often much kinder and more effective than saying, "No, little dude, that's not the right way to say that. No water for you, you illiterate bed wetter."

Challenges Your Mind

While speaking in simple, short sentences might sound easy, it's not for most of us. People like me who love a long ramble find it difficult to speak simply, as it requires careful thought about how to say something in the simplest form possible, and then restraint to not continue talking.

A great way to practice is to ask yourself, *What is the one thing I'm trying to say right now?* Then, say that one thing and stop! If there are additional, truly essential thoughts you need to share with your child, leave space between each. For example, if you're getting Darling Sweetie Pants ready for school you might first say, "It's time to put underpants on." Before saying, "And put your pants on," wait until the underpants are on. Then continue on in such a manner with the other getting-ready activities.

This get-to-the-point style of speaking is also effective with teens, as most are so busy with school or peers that they're rarely around, or they're just savants at tuning out their parents' voices. Keeping things short and simple can also help you avoid the dreaded act of lecturing.

Tip: Using a silly voice, when the situation allows, increases the chance of your child listening to you. It can also help lighten your mood when feeling tense.

The Magic of Musical Communication

While kids often tune out spoken words after a few minutes, they typically have a much longer attention span for songs. A silly, made-up-on-the-spot ditty based on what's happening in that moment can capture a child's attention and potentially shift their mood, if that's your intention. Musical communication can also light up areas in the child's brain that support the following:

- Reading, language, and speech perception
- Social skills of empathy, trust, and cooperation
- Mental alertness
- Motor skills
- Long-term memory
- Spatial temporal learning, which is the brain's ability to mentally move objects in space and time to solve multistep problems

In addition to firing up an assortment of mental territories, communicating through music can cause neurogenesis, which is the production of new neurons that support neural plasticity, brain homeostasis, and maintenance of the central nervous system. You can amp up all these benefits by encouraging your child to sing their responses to you, hum a tune while playing, or attend a music class.

Another benefit of musical communication is that it can make an unpleasant message easier to stomach. For example, if you're telling your child it's time to leave Grandma's house, the message might be less distressing if you're singing it to the tune of "Take Me Out to the Ballgame." While your child might still protest, you can thwart a major tantrum by shaking up the exchange and singing your responses to their protests. It's a really fun, eccentric way to communicate.

TIP: Pull out a classic lullaby when your child is distressed, as this type of mellow music has been found to slow down the heart rate. You can also sing one to yourself when needing a dose of Zen.

If you're not in the mood to sing, you can play music that can help your child express thoughts and emotions that might be difficult to convey with words. For example, when your child is happy you might play the song "Happy" by Pharrell Williams. The song "Shake My Sillies Out" by Raffi can accompany a silly mood, and "Into the Unknown" by Idina Menzel can help a child move through nervousness. As you help your child build up their "emotions playlist," they can communicate their mood by simply requesting the song that correlates with it.

I recommend revising this emotion playlist as your child ages and their musical tastes evolve. This might mean that you end up listening to punk rock when your teen is excited, or heavy metal when they're angry, but you'll score major cool points by not complaining or, gasp, turning it down. This is why earplugs and noise-cancelling headphones were invented. But you could also choose to rock out with them, even if their tunes aren't your jam.

Children can also use instruments, or even household items like a wooden spoon and empty coffee canister, to "play" emotions. For example, if your child wants to express anger, they can bang on a drum. Feeling playful? Tickle a windchime. Feeling sad? Press some minor keys on a keyboard. The movement required when playing instruments can also help children produce endorphins and flush out stressor hormones.

TIP: If your child shows an interest in learning an instrument, encouraging this skill can enhance their mathematical learning and self-esteem.

Accessing Your Child's Inner World Through Pretend-Play

Because it can be difficult for some children to communicate through traditional conversation, they often communicate through play. For example, when my son was four, I saw him pretend that one of his stuffed animals was yelling at another. As I listened, I realized he was playing out an argument my husband and I recently had that we assumed Hudson hadn't heard. But, yeah, he was listening, and it stressed him out. After realizing Hudson was communicating through play, I paid more attention to it. This helped me discover that he was afraid a snake was going to swim out of the toilet and bite him if he sat on the toilet to poop, dairy sometimes hurt his stomach, and so much more.

In addition to paying attention to Hudson's play, I started engaging in some of it in an effort to gather specific information. For instance, when Hudson started preschool, I would ask him how his day was, and he'd just say "fun." So one day I grabbed a toy dinosaur and asked Hudson if we could set up a preschool for it. Through our dino preschool play I discovered that Hudson's favorite part of school was riding tricycles, that he felt scared and sad when it was resting time, and that he was having a hard time sharing.

Pretend play is also prime time for parents to share information, as most children are actively listening to what's being said during this time. If you need to convey information about table manners you want your child to adopt, for example, you can recommend playing restaurant or get out a tea set. You can then slip in subtle teachings, and when you later sit down for dinner you can say something like, "Remember how your doll kept her napkin in her lap during tea? That's also a plan for us at the dinner table." Covert lessons for the win.

Procuring and Processing Information with Storytelling

Sharing stories is an amazing way to explore tricky ideas with your child, encourage them to open up about topics they might struggle to share without the cloak of story, and help them process the happenings in their world.

Here are some ideas for weaving story into your communication plan.

Storytelling Recipe

A simple storytelling recipe is character-setting-problem-solution. You start by telling your child about a character you feel they'll connect with. If they have a favorite stuffed animal or doll, you could make the story about them.

Next, tell your child about the setting of your story and how the character interacts with it.

Then, explore the problem the character is facing, how the problem affects that character, and the many ways the character tries to solve it.

Finally, share how the character solved the problem.

You can use the same formula to tell the story of something that happened in your child's life, or something that will happen in the future. A study published in the journal *Current Directions in Psychological Science* found that children whose parents regularly tell them stories about the past in a detailed, emotional, and collaborative way have stronger autobiographical memory, language, and socioemotional skills than children whose parents don't engage them in this elaborative reminiscing.

Before I learned the art of folding boring parenting messages into a story, my son rarely heeded my requests to stop eating sand (or boogers), licking the window, or sticking dried oak leaves in his ear (ouch). Sure, he might listen for a few minutes, but then he would go back to the offending activity. This pattern would repeat until I gave up or got upset, and then made him upset. Storytelling is what helped me and many of my clients break through this issue.

For instance, when my client Liz's daughter Olivia was three and her son Liam was ten months old, Liz noticed Olivia was being rough with

Liam. Liz kept telling Olivia not to hurt Liam, but she'd rarely listen. Liz then told Olivia a story about an alligator who was really rowdy with her baby brother. Throughout the story Olivia expressed concern for the baby alligator and anger at the sister alligator who was being so rough. While thinking about the sister alligator's actions didn't totally eradicate Olivia's own rough behavior, it significantly reduced it.

Unearthing Insights

In addition to using stories to convey messages, you can use them to draw information out of your child. For example, if your child has been having a hard time going to bed but you can't determine what the issue is, you can tell a story about a teddy bear dealing with the issues you suspect your child might be navigating, such as a fear of the dark or monsters in the closet. As you tell this story, you can ask your child questions about how the teddy bear might be feeling, as their answers can provide insights into the root of their fear.

Finding the Gems in Your Child's Stories

Paying attention to the stories your child tells can open a window into their inner world. Often, the stories they tell reflect what's top of mind—what's exciting, worrying, or confusing them. When your child wants to tell you a story, you can help them feel safe to do so by practicing active listening and providing the reactions you think they want at different parts of the story. You can also express engagement by asking questions when your child comes to a stopping place. This interest can help you mine more insights while also making them feel important and skilled in communicating. And while it's tempting to correct things like grammar and pronunciation, avoid these corrections as they can block the flow of creativity.

Piecing Together the World Through Story

An additional benefit of all this storytelling is that it helps children make sense of the world and their place in it. Life bombards children with new information, often cuing more questions than answers. Sharing stories can answer many of their questions and provide a safe space to explore topics your child is curious about but doesn't know how to ask about. Feel free to mix in wacky stories whose only purpose is to help you and your child laugh together. I could argue that a shared laugh with your child is one of the most potent ways to connect.

TIP: You can make your story a "choose your own adventure" by asking your child questions about what decision they think the character should make.

Artful Discourse

Carry the stories you and your child tell into a new medium by offering opportunities to use items like crayons, watercolors, or Play-Doh to craft elements of those stories, or new stories. Art is often the special sauce that allows humans to express our innermost, abstract, and sometimes messy emotions and ideas. It lets us pull pieces of worlds out of our mind and build them on paper, in clay, or using whatever medium we're working with. It allows us to express inner states that can't be described with words.

While your child's art might look like a hurricane of scribbles, it means something to them. Because of this, ask questions about their art.

- Are there characters in your art? If so, what are they doing? Or trying to do? How do the characters feel?
- If your art were a book, what would it be called? Would you like me to write the title on your art? Are there any other words you want me to add?
- How did you come up with the idea for this?
- What's your favorite part of this creation?
- How did you feel when you were making this?

TIP: Create an art space with few limitations. For example, instead of setting up watercolors in an area where your child has to be careful not to get paint on the carpet, have them sit on the patio, or on top of a splat mat in the kitchen.

Questions Are the Way

A common theme in many of the ideas I've covered is asking questions, as that is one of the most potent ways to show your child that you're focused on them and encourage them to continue communicating. When you respond to something your child says or does with a "how cool," or "that's interesting," and stop there, you're unintentionally shutting down communication. When you instead ask a question, you're showing interest and creating a path your child can follow to what they really want to express.

For example, if a child says after preschool pickup, "We read a story about a cat and a boy today," it would be normal for a parent to say, "That's nice." But if the parent instead asked, "What happened to the cat and the boy in the story?" the child might say, "The cat died, and the boy was sad." By continuing to ask questions, the parent might eventually discover that the story made the child worry about their pet dying, or curious about death. Essentially, asking questions about seemingly innocuous things children say can lead to illuminating conversations, and help children feel safe sharing.

You can further support your child in understanding the world and feeling safe communicating by answering the many questions they ask you, then asking a follow-up question. For example, if your child asks, "Why are we going to the grocery store?" you can say, "Because we need to buy healthy food for our bodies. What kinds of things do you think healthy food helps our bodies do?" This strategy can open the door to interesting conversations and help prevent every parent's favorite phenomenon of the child asking "why" every time we say something. We're taking that "why," shaking it up, and serving it back to them. Bon appétit, kids.

Embrace the Pause

As I considered what one thing would make all these communication ideas easier to apply, I kept thinking *pause*. If you just remind yourself of that one word, and then do it regularly when communicating, you'll create time and space to welcome in all the juicy communication ideas you want to weave into your life. When you pause, you don't just say the thing your ego wants to spit out, but you give your intuition time to access all your wisdom and craft a response that is true to you and your values.

These pauses also create time to really absorb what the other person is saying. Most of us miss about half of what other people say because we're busy thinking of what we want to say next. If you know you're going to pause before responding, you'll feel freer to really tune in to what the other person is saying, and they'll feel it. They'll sense that you care and want to understand them. You'll likely find that the more you pause, the more you forge deep connections and develop more interesting, expansive ideas, because you're opening yourself to fresh perspectives, even if you're just having simple convos with a two-year-old.

If you're thinking that all this pausing will lead to awkward social interactions, know that the pause doesn't have to be crazy long. Even just a few seconds can give space for your wisest self to speak. But when you're talking with family or close friends—people you likely don't feel as much pressure being "normal" around—take longer pauses and let them know why you're doing it. And if they take your pauses as an opportunity to keep talking, stop them and let them know you need a moment to think about what you want to say. This will initially feel strange, but you'll get used to it. Doing this with children can be magic because through your actions you're teaching them that it's OK to slow down and be thoughtful about what they say to others.

Focusing More on Understanding Than Being Right

My ego hates that I'm writing this. It's like, "No! Being right is everything!" And yes, being, or at least feeling, right is intoxicating. It helps affirm our view of the world and makes us feel superior. Because of this, it's often the subconscious motivation many of us have in conversation. But the high of being right quickly fades, and the price for that high is, well, high. When our goal is to prove that we're right, or at least more knowledgeable, we're more focused on forming a solid argument than listening to what our convo partner, or sometimes more accurately opponent, is saying. This is such a bummer, because instead of connecting with and learning more about the other person, and likely the world, we're just regurgitating information that's already been bubbling around in our brain. We don't leave the conversation any richer.

This innate desire to prove our rightness is often most pronounced when speaking with kids, as the idea that adults know more than kids has been hammered into most of us. Often, we don't even consider that the child or teen could have an idea that's as good as, or even better than, our own. This can result in us stopping them midsentence to let them know that "No, no, no, we adults know what's best. This is how it's going to go." It also prevents parents from developing a deeper understanding of their child and conveys the message that the child's ideas don't really matter. Obviously, there are plenty of times when parents don't have time to listen to a child's point of view, such as when they're crossing a busy street, shoving their hand in a cake, or, for a teen, watching inappropriate content. But when we're not in situations that require prompt action, we can slow our roll and focus on understanding our child instead of proving how right we are.

When your child enters tween- and teen-dom, you'll also encounter their fierce need to be right, which can be oh so triggering. Many teens develop an unshakable belief that they know *everything*, especially when it comes to what they should be allowed to do. This can create an intensity in the teen that makes efforts to instill logic seem futile. Being wrong can also feel threatening for teens as their self-esteem is often shaky at this age and being negated can feel devastating. This certainly doesn't mean parents have to just agree with everything the teen says and wants, but listening to their side can at least help us understand the strange land they are coming from.

Tip: When your child, or anyone, says something you know (or at least you think you know) is incorrect, don't interrupt them to make a correction. While this is incredibly hard for most of us to do, it injects the conversation with enhanced patience and compassion. And when that incorrect thing is said, you certainly don't need to pretend that you agree, but you also don't need to retort. Think about the times when someone has stopped you midsentence to correct something you said. This probably broke your train of thought and might have put you in a more defensive frame of mind. If you had been allowed to fully share your thought, and the correction was provided later, you might have been more receptive to it. Above all, consider if proving that you're right is more important than the fracture it might cause in the relationship.

Listening Our Way Through Conflict

Many of my clients and I had the past misconception that actively listening to our children when they were asking for something we knew we couldn't give them gave them false hope. But focusing on understanding your child doesn't mean you're going to give them everything they want; it just gives them the respect of being heard, of getting a chance to state their case without being shut down. It can also have the surprising result of your child being more amenable to solutions you propose.

For example, when Hudson was three, he would cry every time we left the park. When he'd protest, I'd always cut him off and say, "No. It's time to leave. That's the plan. Let's go." One day, I decided to listen. Hudson said, "Just five more minutes." I asked why he wanted five more minutes. He said he needed to go down the slide three more times. I asked him why. He said because he liked when the wind pushed his hair back. I asked him if I could pick him up and show him something. When he agreed, I swung him back and forth so air rushed through his hair. He laughed, and I asked if that was as fun as the slide. He said no. But I could tell he was kind of lying. I then told him that we still had to leave but promised I would remind him to start with the slide next time we were at the park, so he got plenty of slide time. I also told him he could fly like an airplane in my arms to the car, and at home when he wanted his hair to fly. He said OK. We left the park without tears. This process took time, and didn't work every time, but it reduced our conflicts by at least 50 percent.

What If Kids Hold the Secrets of the Universe?

As you focus on understanding your child, you might be surprised by how often they offer compelling arguments that shift your view of a situation, or even the world. For example, Hudson once said, "I don't always like to be alone with my own self, but I need it." He also told me there were solar systems and galaxies in his body and "bwain." Then he shared that his penis has a banana face and turtle poop looks like butter. These are the moments that remind us that children are much more profound than many of us realize. What if they have just as much to teach us as we have to teach them? The only way we can learn the answer is to listen.

TIP: When talking to your child, shift out of the mindset of "I'm an adult talking to a child" and into the mindset of "I'm a human being trying to compassionately connect with another human being."

What's Your Vibe Saying?

Most of us have had the experience of picking up on someone's negative or positive vibe even if that person wasn't doing or saying anything obviously negative or positive. I believe this vibe, or the energy a person emits, reverberates from our thoughts and feelings. This idea might sound woo-woo, but it's worth considering. You can be saying loving words to someone, but if those words aren't channeling through the heart, if you're not really feeling them, they won't have the same impact. This is especially true when communicating with kids, as they're masters at reading energy and knowing when a message isn't being channeled through the heart.

So how do we pump up those positive vibes? For me, a positive vibe originates with envisioning a golden, loving light flowing from my heart into the heart of the person I'm communicating with. If I'm not communicating with a particular person, I envision that light filling the area I'm in. Take a moment to think of times when you radiated good vibes and consider what thoughts and feelings were percolating in your mind and heart.

Because no one is a "good vibes only" guru robot, you're probably not always shining with that golden light, and that's OK. But as you grow more attuned to the vibe you're serving, you can become more skilled at shifting that vibe, if you feel that's necessary, and being cognizant of how your vibes are impacting others. If you just can't kick a bout of dark vibes, you might choose to go to a private space and give your full attention to your feels, instead of trying to hide them from others. When you can't access privacy, you can be transparent, even with your kids. Putting words to your energy by saying something like "I'm feeling a little sad right now" can do wonders for relieving the tension of the energy you're exuding. When telling your children about your more challenging moods, it can be helpful to offer reassurance, such as, "I'm feeling sad, but you don't need to worry. I won't be sad forever."

Overall, I encourage you to start tuning in to the vibe, energy, mojo, aura—or whatever it is you want to call it—that you're broadcasting. Once you notice it, play around with turning its volume up or down, or changing the channel. Claiming responsibility for this energy will have a powerful impact on your relationship with your child, yourself, and even the world.

Tip: Before communicating with your child take a moment to notice not only your vibe but also theirs. Are they broadcasting a sad vibe? Maybe they have that goofy mojo going? Noticing this can help inform how you approach them.

Sharing Yourself

While it might seem that children are raging egomaniacs only interested in themselves (often they are, and that's normal), they frequently are curious about the people around them, specifically their parents and siblings. When appropriate, communicating your emotions and thoughts on a certain topic can help your child develop a deeper understanding of who you are and fortify your bond with them. You can begin forging this intimacy by, for example, telling your child some of the interesting things that happened during your day, what you're looking forward to, and something that's making you feel nervous, or happy, or curious.

Because children are also curious about the idea of the past, present, and future, you can show them photos from your past and share simple stories about it. To integrate the future, you can daydream with them about fun things that might happen during an upcoming trip, or even just tomorrow. We often forget that we are one of the most fascinating elements in our child's life. Leaning into this can do wonders for your relationship.

How Do You Talk to Yourself?

Most of us spend a lot of time thinking about how we communicate with others but little time exploring how we communicate with ourselves. You can start giving yourself the thought and attention you're so worthy of by writing down some of the things you say to yourself during the day and then analyzing what you wrote. Are you always putting yourself down? Offering compassionate messages? Making excuses for yourself? Keeping yourself so busy you don't have time to connect with yourself? If you realize there's room for improvement, you can shift your self-talk into a more loving, honest, forgiving space by pretending that you're talking to your child.

It's also important to explore how your family, teachers, peers, and others influenced your inner voice as a child, and what aspects of that, good or bad, are still influencing you. This review is crucial because the messages your inner voice absorbed in childhood might have become so ingrained that you don't even realize their impact. To gain clarity, write down the messages from childhood you remember having an impact. Maybe they're messages you heard often, or something that was just said to you once but really stuck. You likely won't remember these messages verbatim, so just write down the gist, how it influenced you, and if it's something you want to hold on to or release by reparenting yourself. This reparenting can be as simple as considering what you would tell your child if they were given the message you want to release.

This analysis of childhood messages can emphasize the impact of everything we say to our kids and ourselves. It might seem like they're always ignoring us, and sometimes they are, but often they're actively listening for information that helps them determine what others think of them, their parents in particular. When I was a child, I once overheard an important adult in my life say about me, "She should have a butt whooping." While this message might seem insignificant, I've never forgotten it. Until I did reparenting work around it, I let it cause me much shame and make me hypervigilant about not breaking any rules or "ruffling feathers."

My challenge for us is to try the communication tools I outline in this chapter, and tools we discover from other sources, not only with our children but also with ourselves. And before you say anything to yourself, ask if it honors the pre-communication mantra you're about to create. If it doesn't, edit your thought.

Pre-Communication Mantra

The Buddhist faith teaches that anything you say should honor the following tenets: "It is spoken at the right time. It is spoken in truth. It is spoken affectionately. It is spoken beneficially. It is spoken with a mind of good-will." This is a beautiful example of a pre-communication mantra, which is a filter through which you run everything you want to say before speaking.

Creating this mantra with your family can be one of the most effective and simple ways to ensure your communication reflects your family values. So read over your family philosophy and values and pick out ideas that would be appropriate for your pre-communication mantra. Maybe your values lead you to adopt some version of the Buddhist tenets, or maybe your family wants to add in things like being concise and clear, or humorous and free of unsolicited advice. It can be whatever your family wants it to be.

If your child is too young to participate in the creation of this mantra, they'll organically learn to adopt it by witnessing you and other family members utilizing it.

When Communication Breaks Down

Despite best efforts, communicating with our children will sometimes feel like a living nightmare, as no amount of patience and clever tools will prevent the occasional breakdown of communication. When that happens, forgive yourself and your child, or whoever you had a verbal tussle with, and reset. It's like a healthy eating plan—just because you spend a day gorging on cheeseburgers and ice cream doesn't mean your health is ruined. You forgive yourself for the indulgences and recommit to healthy eating tomorrow, or even an hour after you saw the bottom of that pint of mint chip. Reach for growth, not perfection.

Make It Your Own

While every variety of communication mentioned in this chapter likely affects your family in some way, there are probably a few that resonate more than others. For example, maybe you're a musical family that feels comfortable communicating by song, or maybe you're all about expressing yourselves through art, or maybe you all love a loud, lively conversation. The good news is there's no one "right" way to communicate. Every family is unique in what works for them, and what their communication goals are.

To begin customizing the information you received in this chapter and filling in the Communication section of your Parenting Plan, allow everything that doesn't seem relevant to your family fall away, at least for now. What's left? What ideas do you feel will support the type of communication you want to foster in your family? Is there a communication style, or certain words or phrases, you feel would enhance your family's communication? Is there anything you would change about these ideas? The writing prompts that follow will further support this inquiry.

After clarifying which ideas could be a good fit for your family, you can explain them at a family meeting, incorporate the family's feedback, then request that everyone practice two or three of the agreed-upon tools for a few weeks. You can then evaluate how those tools are working before exploring the introduction of additional ideas.

Guided Meditation

The meditation at the following link helps you to reflect on how your family currently communicates and then to envision your family communicating in a way you view as effective, loving, and harmonious. The goal is to help you continue piecing together the ideas you resonate with from this chapter and unearthing your unique ideas. Visit https://www.baileygaddis.com/communication.

Writing Prompts

- What does communication mean to me? What are my primary goals when communicating?

- After spending a week observing my family's communication, what do I feel is working? What isn't working?
- What are the main things we communicate in our family? What do we want to communicate more? And less?
- What types of communication nourish my family? What types of communication cause suffering in my family?
- What is our family's pre-communication mantra?
- Do different family members have different communication preferences, skills, and limitations we need to honor?
- What communication ideas from this chapter do I want my family to try? Is there a communication style, or certain words or phrases, I feel would enhance my family's communication?
- What type of language is not allowed in our family? Are there specific words or phrases we agree to not use? Are there any other communication guidelines we want to honor?
- How can I create a more loving, heartfelt vibe when communicating with my child, and the rest of my family?
- How can I help my child effectively communicate with others?
- How do I want my communication with my child to evolve as we age?
- How often will we have a family meeting to communicate about important topics?

Parenting Plan

Pre-communication mantra:

Communication tools we're implementing:

Off-limits words and phrases:

Words and phrases to use more:

Facial expressions and hand and body movements we'll use to convey certain messages:

Topics we want to communicate about more:

How often we plan on discussing the state of our family communication:

Plans for working through topics that are hard for us to discuss:

4

ELEMENT 2: NAVIGATING ALL THE EMOTIONS

CHILDREN'S EMOTIONS CAN BURST OUT OF THEM like fireworks. Sometimes it's dazzling, and sometimes it hurts your ears. They hold nothing back. But as they age, they're conditioned to manage their emotions primarily so they don't make other people uncomfortable. And this can be good in certain situations. When I'm on an airplane, it's probably best that I keep my massive anxiety quiet. When a friend hurts my feelings, it's probably best that I don't start crying and raging on the spot. While emotion-based social norms are occasionally beneficial, they can also stunt our emotional growth and ability to process emotions in a way that's authentic to our unique needs.

A result of being conditioned to believe that emotions should be subtly expressed is that many of us parents are seriously triggered when our children are loudly expressing them. We then get more triggered when we try to get our children to conform to "normal" social protocol and they scoff at us, probably thinking it's absurd we would even suggest they tamp down their emotions. But there's a middle ground, a space where you can support your child and self through big emotions while fostering harmony in your family and nudging you and your child into the amazing, uncomfortable space where emotional intelligence blossoms.

The first steps on the path to that lovely field of emotional intelligence are exploring the science of childhood emotions, the effects parents' emotions have on children, and a feast of ideas for making emotional fireworks less destructive and more liberating, informative, and even fascinating.

The Science of Emotion Regulation in the Early Years

A child's brain is a beautifully constructed, ever-evolving structure whose foundation is developing a combination of different social competency skills, including motor control, thinking, communication, and emotion regulation. Unfortunately, emotion regulation often receives the least amount of attention, as it's not as easily tested and quantified—but its development is just as crucial to the foundation as the other aspects of social competency. Healthy emotion regulation skills include the ability to identify and understand feelings in oneself and others, constructively navigate big emotions, regulate behavior triggered by emotions, develop empathy for others, and establish and sustain relationships.

Researchers have discovered that the prefrontal cortex plays an important role in emotion regulation, as this area of the brain undergoes significant change related to synaptic density and myelination during childhood. Synaptic density refers to the number of synapses, or points of contact between neurons where information is passed from one neuron to the next. The number of synapses indicates how well the central nervous system is developing and functioning. Myelination is the process of myelin wrapping around axons, which are the threadlike parts of a nerve cell that send impulses from one cell to another. This process affects how fast neurons can communicate, as axons coated in myelin send messages faster than those lacking it. These neurological changes support the development of the ability to suppress an impulsive response. They also help to develop working memory, which temporarily holds new information in the brain and connects it with other information, so someone can keep track of what they're doing and have more cognitive resources available when navigating a challenging situation.

In addition to happenings in the prefrontal cortex, a study published in the journal *Infant and Child Development* found that the development of social and emotional skills in the early years is heavily influenced by the family environment and parenting, specifically emotion-related parenting practices. Not surprisingly, how the people a child is regularly around express emotions, talk about emotions, and show acceptance of emotional displays strongly affects how the child will navigate emotions. These are all elements we'll soon explore, so let's prepare by journeying further into the science of emotional development and regulation.

Evolution of Emotion Regulation from Birth to Preschool

Children's early emotional experiences "literally become embedded in the architecture of their brains," according to a paper published by the Center on the Developing Child at Harvard. These emotional experiences are deeply influenced by the stage of emotional development the child is negotiating, as throughout these stages a child discovers what feelings and emotions are, and how and why they happen; recognizes feelings in themselves and others; and eventually learns effective tools for regulating emotions.

In the first year of life, children are incapable of modulating their emotions and express distress when they have an unmet need and positive emotions when their needs are met. This is when children begin experiencing basic emotions like joy, anger, sadness, and fear. Things get more complex as babies become young children, as they now have the capacity to interpret their personal experiences and assess others' actions and feelings, and how that relates to themselves. During this time children also develop a more comprehensive understanding of the full rainbow of emotions, such as shyness, surprise, elation, and empathy, and start dipping their toes in the waters of emotion management. At around two years of age, children begin identifying and utilizing emotion regulation strategies such as trying to distract themselves, expressing their emotion to a caregiver, or attempting to change the situation that's causing them stress.

By preschool, children who have been supported in developing emotional intelligence have a greater capacity to adeptly traverse social landscapes and develop healthy relationships. Researchers at Harvard report that by this age, children have added pride, shame, guilt, and embarrassment to their emotional repertoire, which are helpful in becoming a contributing citizen of the world. This is also the age when children have a firmer grasp on using words to communicate emotions, a variety of methods to thwart a tantrum, and self-restraint when tempted to express emotions in a way that might be inappropriate for a certain setting. At this stage, thinking begins to have a greater impact on children's emotions, and they tend to be more in tune with their feelings and those of others.

How Empathy Affects Emotion Regulation

In a child's early years, developing empathy is a crucial step on the journey to emotion regulation, as a child with healthy emotion regulation skills is better able to shift their attention from their own emotions to those of others. According to the psychologists who authored the *Handbook of Emotions*, there are three levels of empathy development in early childhood.

The first level, *emotional contagion*, is the stage most children are in for about the first year of life. Emotional contagion consists of the child essentially "catching" another person's emotions, as the child has not yet learned to view themselves as separate from others.

Around their first birthday, children typically shift into the next level, *attention to others' feelings*, which also involves the developing ability to understand that others exist separate from themselves. During this stage children might start showing concern for another's emotions and attempt to regulate their reaction to those emotions.

Children often develop the third level of empathy, *prosocial behaviors*, around age two. This involves the child's ability to understand the mental states of others and engage in prosocial behavior, such as giving someone a hug or gently touching their cheek if the person seems sad.

Researchers have found that in addition to age, the development of a child's empathy is connected to their verbal ability and their primary care provider's emotion socialization style, which is essentially how this person teaches the child about emotions.

Emotion Regulation Can Vary Wildly

Humans differ in how they experience and express emotions, even if they're at the same stage of development. Some people feel so much that it consumes them, while others seem to effortlessly bat away big emotions. One cause of this is genetics. The COMT gene can affect how sensitive someone is to emotional stimuli, as it's associated with the prefrontal cognitive processes of emotion regulation and working memory. Two additional sources of differences in emotional temperament are the social environment in a child's family and the other environments they frequent, and the physiological processes influenced by the health of the parasympathetic nervous system. These are prime reasons a person's temperament doesn't change much as they age, though how they regulate that temperament can change.

The Role of the Child's Unique Temperament

As you navigate the journey of nurturing your child's emotional intelligence, one of the best things you can do for your sanity and theirs is to find love and acceptance for their distinctive emotional temperament, as there's no way to completely rewire how they naturally experience emotions. However, you can help them develop tools for navigating those emotions when they arise.

To gather information about your child's emotional temperament and what kind of support and tools they might need, explore the following questions.

- How does my child initially respond to stimuli like new people, environments, foods, or changes in routine? Do they jump into the newness, or are they hesitant?
- After my child's initial reaction to a change or new situation, how do they adapt?
- Does my child typically have high or low intensity when responding to a situation?
- How active is my child? Are they always moving? Are they slow and methodical? Do they fidget a lot?
- Does my child follow regular patterns for physical functions like eating, sleeping, and pooping?
- What is my child's typical demeanor or mood? For example, are they usually friendly and chatty? Or quiet and cautious?
- What is my child's typical attention span? How easily are they distracted?

- What amount of stimulation is required to get my child to respond? Do they seek or avoid high levels of stimulation? (For example, does your child readily respond when you're whispering to them? Or do you need to make eye contact and use a loud, clear voice to get their attention?)

The emotion regulation ideas from this chapter you end up using or adapting will be influenced by your answers to the aforementioned questions, as they offer insight into what your child might best respond to. And while it's common for children to be placed into a category such as "easy," "slow to warm up, or shy," or "difficult or challenging," I encourage you to create your own label for your child, such as "curious and animated," "thoughtful and careful," or "vocal and confident." Or, you can choose to not label your child and just view them as a unique character who has the exact temperament they're meant to have for the unique life they're meant to lead.

How Big Emotions Shake Up the Mind and Body

Emotions have a major impact on the mind and body, specifically the neural, cardiac, and neuroendocrine systems. When an emotion is triggered, neuropeptides, or chemical messengers released by neurons, are produced, and their configuration is affected by the emotion. These neuropeptides then connect to receptors on cells, and when those cells eventually divide, the new cell will have more receptors for the type of neuropeptide it was commonly exposed to. For example, if a person feels joy more than anxiety, they'll produce more cells inclined to attach to "joyful neuropeptides" than "anxious neuropeptides." Positive emotions beget positive emotions.

In addition, the mind thrives on emotions like joy, pride, and awe and responds to them in a variety of ways.

- Positive emotions can boost levels of the neurotransmitter serotonin, which stabilizes emotion by carrying feel-good messages between nerve cells in the brain and throughout the body.
- Positive emotions cause the brain stem to produce dopamine, known as the "pleasure chemical," and create heightened neural

sensitivity in the medial prefrontal cortex, which is an area of the brain connected to creative thinking, learning, focusing, and decision-making.

- Happy feelings carve pleasing pathways deep in the brain, specifically in the ventral striatum, which is below the cortex.
- A positive emotion tells the brain it's safe to interact with a new environment or stimulus, thus making it easier for us to try new things or interact with new people.
- Positive emotions can enhance a person's resiliency, focus, cognition, creativity, efficiency, open-mindedness, and ability to integrate a variety of information. These emotions can also build lasting physical, intellectual, and social resources.

Regarding the body, positive emotions pump up the health of the immune system, regulate blood sugar, and help to prevent obesity and diseases. They also lower blood pressure and improve heart health, flush out stressor hormones like cortisol, and can even prolong someone's life. In addition, positive emotions help the body return to a state of equilibrium after it experiences the stress of a negative emotion, which supports the cardiovascular system in recovering from stress. And, according to a study cited in the book *Emotion, Social Relationships, and Health*, children who consistently experience positive emotions with their parents have a lower chance of having accumulative "wear and tear" on the body as they age.

Then we have negative emotions. A study published in the journal *Biological Psychiatry* reported that negative emotions can impair thinking, as the development of emotion and cognition (thinking) are intertwined and rely on complex neural circuits in the prefrontal cortex, limbic cortex, basal forebrain, amygdala, hypothalamus, and brainstem. The neural circuits related to emotion regulation are especially interactive with circuits connected to executive functions like planning, judgment, and decision-making. Essentially, emotion regulation and problem-solving are knotted together, so when a person learns how to regulate emotions, their problem-solving skills improve. In addition, negative emotions can significantly narrow someone's attention to one thing, typically the situation or thought that triggered the emotion.

Another area of the brain tied to emotions is the hippocampus. According to a study published in the journal *Developmental Psychology*, the size of a person's hippocampus largely affects their capacity to understand, connect to, and sensitively respond to someone else's emotions. Not surprisingly, the hippocampus doesn't reach peak volume until a child is around nine to eleven years old. However, young children reach an important milestone in hippocampus development between eighteen and twenty-four months, as this is when the hippocampus, prefrontal cortex, language areas, cerebellum, and two hemispheres of the brain become pros at communicating with one another.

The amygdala is another piece of the brain puzzle affected by emotion, anger, and anxiety in particular. This part of the brain is responsible for the fight-or-flight response, which triggers the release of adrenaline and cortisol. In this state it's common for heart rate, blood pressure, and breathing to increase, body temperature to rise, sweating to occur, and a flushed face to form. In addition, muscles often tense and the hands or the jaw clench. When young children experience the fight-or-flight response, they're typically most aware of their racing heart and a fluttery or clenched sensation in the stomach.

When the amygdala triggers this response, it stresses the hippocampus by impairing something called long-term potentiation (LTP) in this area of the brain. LTP is a process that strengthens the communication between neurons and is an important part of neuroplasticity, or the ability of the brain to change and adapt in response to our experiences. While the typical levels of stress experienced during childhood are unlikely to have significant impact on a child's neuroplasticity, especially if they're receiving consistent emotional support from a caregiver, chronic stress can weaken neuroplasticity and potentially cause life-altering mental and physical issues.

An additional aspect of stressful emotions is that they can influence how certain genes are expressed, or turned on, specifically genes affecting the limbic system, which is the system of nerves and networks in the brain involved in behavior and emotional response.

Not All Stress Is Bad Stress

If I've now made you stress about stress, let me ease your concern and provide insight into the three categories of this phenomenon: positive stress, tolerable stress, and toxic stress.

Positive stress occurs when a child experiences emotions that cause a brief increase in heart rate and stress hormone levels. The brevity of the stress response is typically due to an empathetic caregiver supporting the child through the stressful situation. For example, when a child falls and scrapes their knee, their stress response will likely be brief if a caregiver is there to provide comfort. This type of stress response is crucial to healthy emotional development.

A tolerable stress response often occurs from a more serious situation that could potentially cause stress for a prolonged time, such as the death of a loved one or a natural disaster. Negative effects from this heightened stress response can be buffered by the consistent support of a caregiver.

Stress becomes toxic for a child when they experience intense, frequent adversity, such as neglect or abuse, without ample support. Toxic stress disrupts brain development, increases the chance of cognitive impairment and stress-related disease, and can even lead to organ damage. However, intervention from a compassionate caregiver can counteract this harm.

Creating Space for Big Emotions

Now that we've explored the science of emotions, let's consider what we can do when they arise. Have you ever noticed that when somebody has a big emotion, the energy from it seems to fill the room? When a child is the one having that big emotion, it can feel like the power of it could shatter the windows and reverberate into the bowels of the earth. When we try containing that energy, we often just agitate it, making it bigger. For example, if a restaurant doesn't use the right ratio of cheese to pasta in a child's mac and cheese, that child might quickly turn that joint into Hell's Kitchen. Depending on how all-consuming the dissatisfied little food critic's emotion is, a parent's attempts to calm them might only feed the energy of the emotion. When a child is swirling in a hurricane of emotion, one of the only effective things to do is help them safely ride out the storm.

Upstairs and Downstairs Brain

In the book *The Whole-Brain Child,* Daniel J. Siegel and Tina Payne Bryson describe the brain as having an upstairs and downstairs. The upstairs is a complex and nuanced "floor" containing the cerebral cortex and is responsible for more sophisticated processes like thinking, forethought, imagining, assessing, problem-solving, and decision-making. When the lights are on upstairs, it's easier to regulate emotions, control the body, experience empathy, and review consequences before acting. This "floor" is under construction until a person's mid-twenties, and maybe even longer.

The downstairs contains the brain stem, limbic region, and amygdala and is responsible for creating strong emotions; controlling basic functions like breathing, blinking, the beating of the heart, and so on; and triggering innate responses like fight, flight, or freeze.

With a parent's support a child can learn to strengthen the "staircase" that helps integrate information between the upstairs and downstairs. This integration allows the upstairs and downstairs to work together and accomplish things like brainstorming what to do after an action results in guilt, or self-soothing after moving out of the apex of an experience like fear. Speaking of the apex of an experience, when a child is experiencing the full strength of an emotion like anger or fear, the amygdala, located downstairs, can sometimes lock the "baby gate" and trap the child downstairs.

Moving to a Private Space

When your child is trapped in the downstairs brain, one of the most effective strategies is calmly bringing them to a safe, private space where they can't hurt themselves or others. You can then be a loving, quiet presence as your child moves through the apex of their emotion.

This simple relocation offers the following benefits:

- **Protects your emotions and regulates your reactions.** Moving you and your child to a private space during one of their emotional displays can help you avoid the embarrassment, frustration, or guilt you might experience if you're in the presence of others.

This can be helpful because these emotions might cause you to respond to your child unauthentically. For example, if your child has a meltdown in front of your mother-in-law, embarrassment might push you to respond in the manner your mother-in-law would approve of, instead of doing what you truly think is best.

- **Prevents an escalation of emotion.** Children are very sensitive to the energy of others, so when onlookers have reactions to your child's emotions it can be even harder for them to work through it. Avoid the emotional distraction of all those rubberneckers by getting your tiny hurricane out of there tout de suite.
- **Provides a powerful coping mechanism.** Helping your child take a beat in a private space teaches them a lifelong coping strategy. Removing oneself from a situation when feeling the rising urge to do something regrettable can prevent overwhelming emotions from causing irreparable damage.

After your child winds down and the "baby gate" to their upstairs brain opens, you can guide them through the emotion-coping tools I provide in this chapter, and the customized ones you'll create while working through the Parenting Plan writing prompts.

TIP: Preemptively create space for big emotions. As you probably have a sixth sense for when your child is about to erupt, you can begin transport to the private space before they get locked in their downstairs brain. This preemptive relocation might even thwart the emotional overflow by providing your child a break from whatever is triggering their emotional response.

How Emotions Affect Action

When my son was three, his preschool teacher told me that he'd gotten in a tussle with a friend over a tricycle. Fists were thrown. I felt so embarrassed upon hearing this and feared my child had anger issues. What I wish I'd known is that in many situations the behavior a child takes in reaction to a certain emotion is almost purely instinctual, especially for young children. This stems from evolution, which has caused humans to tend to take a particular action when experiencing a certain negative emotion. For example, fear causes us to want to take flight, anger causes an urge to fight, and disgust makes us want to throw something (or someone) away. This is also why the body responds to emotions in different ways—it's preparing us to take the action the emotion is pushing us toward.

Positive emotions also evoke an urge to act, but in a broader sense. The broaden-and-build theory of positive emotions created by Barbara Fredrickson proposes that unlike negative emotions, positive emotions can serve a diverse platter of options regarding what we do or don't do when feeling a certain way. For example, joy has been found to create the urge to play, push limits, and be creative, and interest triggers the instinct to explore and take in new information and experiences. These positive emotions can also increase a person's repertoire of physical, intellectual, social, and psychological resources.

Learning to Regulate Emotion-Triggered Responses

A major developmental goal of early childhood is finding a balance between acting on instinct when there's a true threat, like a snake on the trail, and utilizing forethought before acting when a situation that isn't life-threatening triggers an emotion like anger or fear. The good news is most children naturally develop this behavioral balance as their attention control, language abilities, memory, and reasoning skills improve. However, it is up to us to help ensure our child's actions don't harm them or others as they learn the fine art of self-regulation. We'll explore ideas on how to do this shortly.

Helping Children Understand Emotions

One of the greatest ways to nourish your child's emotional intelligence (EQ) is helping them understand those emotions. Understanding emotions means that a person can identify and name emotions, especially explaining how those emotions affect them, noticing the potential cause of an emotion or even predicting it, and using tools to regulate their emotions. This socioemotional competence minimizes the confusion and overwhelm a child might experience when having intense thoughts and physical feelings for which they have no frame of reference. Not surprisingly, this knowledge also supports the health of a child's relationship with their self and others.

Caregivers can nurture a child's socioemotional competence by providing examples of healthy emotional expression, regularly having discussions about emotions, and teaching that it's natural to have emotional displays, even the negative ones. Research has found that children in families who often talk about emotions have an increased chance of developing academic success, healthy friendships, fewer infectious diseases, and the ability to deftly handle difficult social situations. It's crucial to begin this education in a child's early years as this is when their brains are most flexible and able to eat up all this yummy emotional wisdom.

Developmental Stages of Emotional Understanding

When a child is about two years old, they typically begin describing their desires and emotions and are able to tell the difference between their desires and emotions and those of others. Between the ages of three and four, children start mastering the ability to recognize the facial expressions that commonly communicate emotions like happiness, sadness, or anger, and understand that situations and desires can affect emotions. During this stage children also develop an understanding of the beliefs that can contribute to varying emotions, and that people can have different beliefs about the same situation. For example, they might understand that while they love a carousel, another child might be scared of it. A child's emotional vocabulary is also more extensive by this age.

By a child's sixth year, they're able to follow simple rules and directions, develop social skills such as giving compliments and apologizing, begin to place a greater emphasis on peers, and understand that people can hide emotions, for example, pretending to feel happy when actually feeling sad. Development from age six to eight involves deeper exploration and understanding of relationships and morality, the ability to take on more responsibility, and the building of more complex coping skills. From eight to eleven, peers take on a greater importance in a child's life, and children experiment with being independent from their families. This is also the time when a child's self-esteem and sense of competence begins growing, both of which become more intertwined with success in school and extracurricular activities. As they near adolescence, children start experimenting with riskier behaviors in an attempt to better understand more complicated emotions, and they continue to develop emotion regulation skills.

Adolescence, the period from age twelve to eighteen, can be an intense time both emotionally and physically as adolescents are navigating rapid change while also figuring out who they are, who they want to be, and how they fit into the world, especially outside the home. They seek greater independence as they prepare for early adulthood, and grapple with more nuanced emotions, such as rejection, self-criticism, romantic desire, and stress.

The Emotional Understanding Toolbox

There are a number of simple activities and conversations you can engage in with your child to lay a sturdy foundation of emotional understanding. As you weave this emotion education into your days, prevent it from feeling like yet another chore by having fun with it and making it your own.

- **Naming emotions.** Being able to verbally name emotions is so important, because it supports the awareness of emotions in oneself and others, can reduce the intensity of a negative emotion and the amount of time it sticks around, and makes it easier to use emotion regulation strategies. A great way to help your child begin naming emotions is to the share the name of an emotion after they experience it. You can also talk about the emotions others seem to be experiencing in real life and in books or other sources of media. Hanging up a poster that depicts common emotions in your child's bedroom is another helpful tool.
- **Recognizing how emotions affect the outside of the body.** As children learn the names of emotions, they'll also begin recognizing the facial expressions and body language that typically signify various emotions. A fun way to explore this is to make emotional faces in the mirror together. You can also have your child guess which emotion corresponds to the face you're making, and vice versa. In addition to facial expressions, you can

explore the various ways people hold their body when feeling certain emotions. For example, you might explain that people often slump their shoulders when feeling sad, push out their chest when feeling angry, or bounce around when feeling joyful.

- **Recognizing how emotions affect the inside of the body.** Understanding how emotions affect things like breathing, heart rate, and sensations in the stomach can help a child understand why their body has reactions such as sweating and red cheeks when embarrassed or nervous, for example. You can help your child develop this knowledge by talking about what was happening in their body soon after they've mellowed from a big emotion. You can also share how your body reacts to various emotions.
- **Becoming an emotion-trigger detective.** Emotions rarely spring up out of the blue; they are typically triggered by a thought or situation. You can help your child become an emotion-trigger detective by asking them what they think caused a person in real life, or a book or movie, to have a certain emotion. Discussing these emotion triggers conveys the message that it's often necessary to discover the cause of a person's emotion to fully understand what they're experiencing.

  You can also share that many emotions are triggered because a person had a desire that was met or unmet. Some example desires you can discuss are independence, celebration, connection, cooperation, empathy, inclusion, peace, reassurance, and safety. This detective work builds a child's knowledge of cause and effect, which can inform how they behave in various circumstances.
- **Describing desires.** Learning to clearly understand and state one's desires can prevent, or minimize the intensity of, a negative emotion, as the child or their caregiver may be able to fulfill the desire once they understand it. If the desire can't be fulfilled in that moment, the caregiver is still equipped with valuable information they can use to help the child navigate any emotions the unmet desire triggers.

  As your child works on understanding and naming their desires, you can help them out by clearly stating the desire you think they're having when it comes up. And not just the surface-level desire, but the deeper one. For example, a child wailing when their parent makes them hold hands when crossing the street doesn't just have the desire to walk across the street alone, they have the desire to experience independence. This understanding can allow a parent to then find a safe way to give their child a taste of freedom.

- **Discovering that emotions don't have to control behavior.** A crucial aspect of understanding emotions is learning that we don't have to let them control our behavior. You can remind your child that while it's always OK to feel an emotion, it's not always OK to do the thing the emotion makes you want to do, such as scream at or kick someone.

  A fun way to absorb this idea is role-playing situations that typically trigger your child. You can make it even more fun by letting your child play the parent and you the child. For example, you can pretend that it's time to brush your teeth and you really don't want to. You can pretend to be really mad and throw an invisible toothbrush across the room. Your child will likely be thrilled to then reprimand your behavior. Next, you can act out a less destructive way of expressing your emotion, such as stomping your feet, shaking out your body, stating how mad you are, taking a few deep breaths, and then brushing your teeth.

  We'll unpack tools for supporting children in regulating responses to emotions later in the chapter.
- **Learning there's a place for all emotions.** While it's common to label emotions as negative or positive, having a certain emotion doesn't make someone a "bad" or "good" person; it just makes them a person. In addition to explaining this to your child, you might also choose to share how everyone feels a range of emotions and we never need to feel shame or embarrassment for them; they are a natural part of being human. This is also a good time to share that your parent-child relationship is a safe space to express and explore emotions.
- **Understanding that emotions are temporary.** Piggybacking on the idea that there's a place for all emotions is the teaching that

emotions don't last forever, even when they feel red-hot and all-consuming. Understanding the transitory nature of emotions can provide immense relief, especially if a child can hold that nugget of knowledge in the back of their mind when having an uncomfortable emotion. And knowing that a positive emotion won't last forever can help us remember to lean in and enjoy it.

- **Calling out positive emotions.** Because of our pessimistic friend negativity bias, it's more common for humans to call out and talk about negative emotions than positive ones. You can support your child in having more awareness for the positive by acknowledging when they, you, or anyone is having a positive emotion. For example, "Wow! You seem so joyful right now! What does that feel like?" Or, "I feel so loved when you give me a big, cozy hug. That makes my heart happy, and my stomach feel light and warm."
- **Overcoming the upper limit problem.** In the book *The Big Leap*, psychologist Gay Hendricks describes a phenomenon called the upper limit problem, which is essentially a person's tendency to inject themselves with negativity after reaching a certain level of positivity. Gay suggests that we each have an "upper limit" for our tolerance of positivity and subconsciously bring ourselves down when we reach our upper limit of feeling good. We self-sabotage our positive vibes by thinking or doing something that creates negative emotions.

  I don't share this to minimize anyone's pain, as I understand that there are plenty of times when a negative situation slams into us and produces a slew of challenging emotions. What I'm exploring are those times when we're having a good day and suddenly start talking ourselves out of our positive emotions.

  While young children might have difficulty wrapping their head around this topic, you can begin teaching it through modeling. For example, when you reach your upper limit of good feelings, you can tell your child, "I'm feeling really good, but my mind is trying to convince me to start feeling bad. To keep feeling good I'm going to think about all the things in my life I'm happy about, like you!"

When to Discuss Emotions

While it's tempting to dive into an emotion talk right after a big one has occurred, a study by researchers in the Developmental and Educational Psychology department at Universitat Autònoma de Barcelona found that it's better to discuss emotions when a child is in a calm, happy headspace. Discussing emotions during story time can be especially effective, as books offer a natural entry point to the conversation.

Here's an example of an "emotion processing" conversation I had with my son.

> ME: "How do you think Little Critter feels when his grandma says he can't play hide-and-seek in the clean sheets?"
>
> HUDSON: "Mad!"
>
> ME: "I'll bet he does feel mad. Is that how you felt yesterday when I said you couldn't climb into the washing machine?"
>
> HUDSON: "Yes."
>
> ME: "How did that make your body feel?"
>
> HUDSON: "It made me feel like I was lava, and my tummy was a rumble."
>
> ME: "Do you remember what it made you think?"
>
> HUDSON: "That you were mean, and I wanted to be with someone else."
>
> ME: "Why do you think you got mad?"
>
> HUDSON: "It was fun in the washing machine and not outside the washing machine."
>
> ME: "I get that. It doesn't feel good when someone wants us to stop doing something fun."
>
> HUDSON: "Yeah!"
>
> ME: "Why do you think I didn't want you to get in the washing machine?"
>
> HUDSON: "Maybe I would get tummy ache if I spun around in it."
>
> ME: "Totally. Do you remember what you did after I asked you to get out of the washing machine?"
>
> HUDSON: "I hit the washing machine. It hurt my hand."
>
> ME: "It did. Do you think there's something else you could have done to show how angry you were?"

Hudson: "I could have hit my angry pillow! Pow pow! And say I really mad."

This conversation continued for a while, and almost every page of *I Was So Mad* by Mercer Mayer inspired a new emotion discussion.

The time it takes to have these discussions pays off, as the more parents engage children in these talks, the more willing children are to chat about emotions, and their emotional intelligence blooms.

Acknowledging and Validating Difficult Emotions

There is something so powerful in another human simply bearing witness to our suffering with little judgment. When someone sends the message that it's OK to have a difficult emotion and this emotion is valid and not an inconvenience, much of our resistance to the emotion fades, and often we're able to move through it sooner. This is true for all ages. We all want others to accept our emotions, so we then have permission to accept our emotions. This cycle of acceptance can be life-changing.

Only after acknowledging and validating our child's emotions can we begin the process of helping them feel better and problem-solve ways to resolve the issue that triggered the emotion.

You Don't Have to Think the Emotional Reaction Is Legitimate

Helping children feel secure when having big feelings increases their ability to regulate emotions. The two most important steps in helping a child develop that security are acknowledging their emotions and treating them as a legitimate reaction to a distressing event. The second step is easier said than done.

I'm often able to acknowledge my child's emotion but then quickly try to talk them out of it because *I* don't think the emotion is a legitimate reaction to whatever triggered it. But the thing is, I don't have to believe their emotion is a legitimate reaction because I'm not the one experiencing it. Just because I wouldn't have had the same reaction to the emotion trigger doesn't make my child's emotions less valid. The simple fact that they're having the emotion makes it legitimate. Taking our personal beliefs out of the equation can simplify the process of supporting our child through an emotion, as we no longer have to waste time and mental resources figuring out if we agree with their reaction.

Don't Rush to Resolution

When a child experiences a difficult emotion it's common for parents to want their child to feel better *now*. We attempt to create quick resolution by telling our child all the ways the situation can be resolved and all the things they have to be happy about. We might even throw in some bribes, such as, "I know what will make you feel better. Ice cream! Let's go get ice cream!" But when we do all this, our unintentional subtext is *You're wrong for feeling this way*. This often makes the child either burrow deeper into their emotion or feel shame for it. This in turn can make them feel emotionally insecure with us or pretend to feel better just to please us.

Instead of rushing the child's emotional relief, we can lean into their emotion by being a silent source of support. If they seem receptive to talking, you can empathize with what they're going through. For example, say, "It seems like it really hurt your feelings when Maddie took your toy. I can understand that. It looked like you were having fun with that toy, and it's disappointing that you're no longer playing with it."

Encourage the Emotional Reaction

While children typically freely express emotions, they occasionally suppress them. This suppression is appropriate in certain settings, but often a child's emotional suppression isn't occurring because they don't want to be loud at their sibling's school concert, for example, but because they're feeling shame about the emotion. In those situations, encouraging the child to express the emotion can be like sprinkling magic on their emotional development.

For example, if your child seems like they're holding back tears after scraping their knee, simply telling them it's OK and helpful to cry after an injury can help them understand that crying doesn't make them weak but helps them effectively process a distressing situation. Or, if your child is holding back anger over another child getting the last swing at the park, instead of ignoring the simmering anger, you can ask if they want to go to a private space and let out that anger. These situations support your child in understanding that all emotions are valid, and we can almost always find a way to fully express them in a way that doesn't physically or emotionally harm ourselves or others.

Clear the Emotional Slate

Even when we're actively encouraging the full expression then release of emotions, remnants of those emotions can linger. To clear the emotional slate, it can be helpful to do a daily emotional cleanse by engaging in activities that help lingering pieces of difficult emotions flow out of us. Activities I do with my kids include yelling into a pillow and then giving the pillow a few whacks, and busting out our wildest dance moves to a favorite song. Laughing for no reason is also a winner. Just start laughing; because it's contagious, your child will start laughing and you'll both continue to laugh because laughing is funny.

Helping our children learn to trust and normalize their emotions is a gift that will touch almost every aspect of their life. And bestowing this gift on your child also bestows it on you. If you're like me, you often question your emotions and wonder if they're an overreaction or an indication that you're weak. Sadly, this is a more common reaction to emotions than acceptance and validation. But we can change that. We can set up future generations to have a loving and productive relationship with emotions, while also healing our own relationship.

Reveling in Good Feels

Have you ever found that when your child is expressing heightened excitement you eventually ask them to calm down? I certainly have. It's like I'm conditioned to think there's an acceptable amount of time to express excitement, and then it must stop. What's up with that? It's such a bummer. I'm sure this has something to do with the upper limit problem I previously mentioned. I can only handle so much good energy within and around me until I have to tamp it down. But I can change that!

If you too can only tolerate the expression of mega excitement in your child (or self!) for a finite amount of time, consider if you'd be willing to allow them to ride that wave of excitement until it naturally ebbs. During that time you can even choose to revel in your child's excitement. This reveling can counteract the unfortunate phenomenon of disconnecting from that pure, youthful joy as we age and can help prevent our children from falling victim to the same affliction. Let the kids reteach us how to feel excitement on such a deep, visceral level that it's nearly impossible to extinguish it with pessimism.

Tools for Moving Out of Difficult Emotions

Now that we've explored many of the trails weaving through emotions, let's explore tools that can help your child step off the trail. After your child has moved past the peak of their emotion and regained the ability to comprehend what you're saying, you can guide them through clearing the emotion by reminding them that emotions aren't permanent and teaching them the following strategies.

- **Deep breathing.** This coping technique is such a cliché because it works. Various studies have shown that deep breathing can reduce pain, anxiety, depression, and stress and return the mind and body to a state of equilibrium. You can help your child understand the concept of deep breathing by telling them to pretend that they're smelling a flower, then blowing up a balloon.
- **Counting.** The soothing, repetitive nature of counting from one to ten over and over again with your child, or repeating the ABCs, can reset their brain and calm their nervous system.
- **Screaming.** That's right, screaming. Grabbing a pillow and filling it with the loudest, mightiest roar can help a child notice, express, and release a big emotion such as anger. According to traditional Chinese medicine, yelling might even cleanse the energy that supports the liver. However, we obviously want to set parameters for where and when the yelling can occur.
- **Moving.** Jumping jacks, dancing, whacking a pillow, running around the backyard, and other types of physical exertion can force out the lingering energy of an emotion and replace stressor hormones with endorphins.
- **Encouraging crying.** If your child seems like they're holding back tears, remind them that it's OK and even healthy to cry.

Crying has been found to flush out stressor hormones, trigger the production of oxytocin and endorphins, and calm the nervous system.

- **Melting the emotion with golden light.** Ask your child to close their eyes and tell you where they feel the emotion in their body. You can then gently place your hand on that area and tell them to envision a golden light shining out of your hand and melting away the discomfort of the emotion.
- **Calling on the five senses.** Bring your child back into their body by asking them to describe what they see, hear, taste, touch, and smell.
- **Releasing emotion through art.** As emotions can sometimes feel confusing and hard to describe, even for adults, it can be helpful to ask your child to draw their emotions. These drawings will probably be pretty abstract, and that's fine. The process of creating the art can help the emotion move through and out of the body while the mind is able to make more sense of it. A study published in the journal *Frontiers in Psychology* found that drawing can also elevate a child's mood.
- **Giving the emotions nicknames.** Emotions can feel overwhelmingly powerful at any age, but especially in childhood. You can help your child take some of the power away from challenging emotions by giving them silly nicknames. Here are some my son came up with.
    - Fear: Captain Pooty Pants
    - Sadness: Senorita Pickle Butt
    - Embarrassment: Smelly McStinks A Lot
    - Nervousness: Fluffy Wuffy Booty Bear
    - Anger: Doctor Doody

  When a difficult emotion eventually pops up, you can encourage your child to talk to the emotion by name, describe how it's affecting them, then eventually ask it to go away. "I can feel you in my tummy Fluffy Wuffy Booty Bear. It feels like you're made of lots of butterflies . . . OK, that's enough. Later, Booty Bear."
- **Tapping.** Also called Emotional Freedom Technique, tapping is an amazing strategy for resetting energy and rewiring the brain. The process consists of thinking of what's bothering you and

how intense the resulting emotion is, then resetting your energy around that issue and emotion by tapping on specific points on the body while reciting a positive affirmation. When describing this to a child, you can make it more fun by telling them that each point they tap is like a magic button that helps them feel better. I have a video on YouTube demonstrating the technique: https://www.youtube.com/watch?v=k3TTGzSi1DY.

As you try out these tools, adapt them as you see fit and notice what works best for your child. You can then start using the same set of tools each time your child needs help coping with and then clearing an emotion. This repetition can result in your child summoning these tools on their own and having the skills to reverse some of the genetic damage of stress.

Detaching When the Child Tantrums

Just as important as guiding our child through emotion-coping strategies is having our own strategies when the child is going nuclear. While many of the tools just shared can also benefit parents, one of the most effective things to do during a child's tantrum is to lovingly detach. This detachment doesn't mean you ignore your child, it just means you put up an energetic shield so you can experience your child's feelings with empathetic objectivity and have the mental and emotional clarity to provide effective support. When a parent doesn't detach, they're at risk of being triggered, which can lead to frustration and often escalation of the tantrum. Before I started detaching, many of Hudson's tantrums would result in mutually assured destruction.

Here are some ideas for detaching.

- **Remember that you don't have to be the fixer.** The natural inclination for most parents is to fix their child's problem ASAP. But because it's often impossible to immediately dissolve a child's suffering, you get to take the pressure off yourself. Remind yourself that your only responsibilities are providing quiet comfort and staying curious as you eventually work together to problem-solve.

- **Refill your well of patience.** A big piece of loving detachment is patience, which needs regular refilling. In the morning, I'm often pleased with myself as I calmly navigate my children's intense emotions. But as the day goes on, my well of patience gets lower and lower, then bam! Patience gone. Emotional 180 commence. To avoid this, I have to refill my patience by taking blips of alone time (aka toilet time) to close my eyes, take a few deep breaths, and envision patience (which to me looks like millions of tiny stars) pouring into a well in my mind.
- **Pop in some headphones.** If you find it nearly impossible to detach when your child is screaming, discreetly pop in earplugs or headphones. While you of course want to hear what they say when they calm, you're not going to miss much if they're in wailing mode.
- **Stay cool when watching something suspenseful.** Train your brain and body to detach from stressful stimuli by watching a suspenseful show and staying calm even when you know something surprising is about to happen. You can summon this calm by taking deep breaths, relaxing your body, and reminding yourself that it's safe to stay in a calm, neutral state.

An added benefit of all this emotion regulation is that it's been found to rub off on children, supporting them in developing their own emotion regulation skills.

The Magic of an Apology

Despite our best efforts, we sometimes blow our lid. When this happens, we might say or do something regretful, and that can feel really yucky. Apologizing is one of the best ways to wash off the yuck. This is easier said than done for many adults, as we've been conditioned to believe that adults shouldn't apologize to children because it shows fallibility and weakens our position of authority. But what if instead of weakening our authority, apologizing to our children after treating them unfairly strengthens our bond and builds trust? Apologizing can also help children realize that parents aren't demigods but mere mortals who also make mistakes.

It's OK to Not Always Like Your Kid

Your child's emotional displays, or maybe just some of their habits, might result in you not always liking them. And that's OK. While I think it's safe to assume you will always love your child, it's totally normal to have moments where you'd rather be at jury duty than deal with your offspring. This doesn't mean you're a horrible parent, it just means that you and your child are different people with unique sets of annoying habits, pet peeves, and triggers. Sometimes you're going to bug the hell out of each other.

When you think, *Can I trade in little Lucas for a puppy?*, remind yourself that these thoughts are normal and fleeting. Your sweet-cheeked-mini-muffin will likely do something a few minutes later that melts your heart.

The Art of Processing Your Emotions in Front of Your Children

Not surprisingly, witnessing how their parent regulates emotions informs how a child regulates emotions. This is especially true of anger, as research has found that children who regularly see a parent respond to situations with anger develop the same tendency. Because of this parental influence, it's essential for us to model how to be comfortable with big emotions, and process and express them in a way that doesn't take those around us hostage.

The idea of modeling emotion regulation in front of children seems odd to some, especially people raised by parents who hid most of their emotions, often with the exception of anger. Those parents probably thought they were protecting their children, but the emotional secrecy likely only served to limit emotional education.

To provide your child with a more well-rounded emotional education, try the following.

- **Telling your child how you feel.** While parents often think we're so great at hiding emotions, kids can usually see right through us. So when a parent isn't acknowledging an emotion that is radiating off them, a child can become nervous, maybe assuming the situation is more dire than it is. In such a situation, you can ease your child's discomfort by telling them how you're feeling, in an age-appropriate way. For example, "I'm feeling sad right now because one of my friends is sick." Or, "I'm feeling irritated right now because of something that happened at work." You can provide further relief by answering their questions about your emotion.

- **Fostering social intuition.** Social intuition is a person's ability to make primarily nonconscious decisions about another person's emotions, attitudes, and intentions based on things like body language and other nonverbal cues. Humans not only make regular judgments about others based on these cues but also unconsciously communicate their own inner state through nonverbal cues. While a person's social intuition naturally improves from childhood to adulthood, we can help it along by intentionally paying attention to, practicing, and reflecting on the nonverbal cues of others and our self.

  To do this with your child, notice and call out your nonverbal cues, and theirs, when experiencing an emotion. For example, when irritated you might say, "I'm noticing that when I'm irritated, I sigh a lot and tense my shoulders." Or, "When you're nervous, you often tap your fingers and chew on your lip."
- **Asking for advice on coping with an emotion.** Children love being asked for advice, as it feels like a novelty. You can gift them with the role of problem-solver by asking if they have ideas for how you can manage an emotion. They might then recommend coping tools you often suggest, such as a hug, deep breath, or drinking a glass of water.
- **Being an emotional-response role model.** We can take a dose of our own medicine by asking *What would I tell my child to do in this situation?* when faced with an emotion-triggering circumstance. When I started doing this, I realized my natural responses, such as countering a rude remark with a rude remark, were not what I'd encourage my children to do. If I want them to develop emotional maturity, it has to start with me.

As you navigate the exploration and regulation of your emotions with your children, remember that your attention to this is making frequent deposits into their well of emotional intelligence.

What to Do When Emotions Significantly Affect Quality of Life

While big emotional displays are par for the course with kids, you might find that your child's emotions seem much more intense and distressing than the emotions of other children. In this situation it's often wise to consult with a pediatric mental health specialist, who can help you determine if your child has an emotional difference that requires expert support. Many parents are surprised to discover that children can have serious mental-health challenges, such as anxiety disorders and depression. Studies have even shown that children with more serious mental-health issues often have the same kind of brain changes seen in clinically depressed adults. The good news is that seeking professional support for your child as soon as you suspect a mental-health challenge can provide them, and you, with the tools to manage this issue.

Sprinkling Your Magic on These Ideas

Now that you've received a massive helping of information on emotions, I encourage you to step back and notice what stands out. What ideas seem most relevant to your family? What piqued your interest? What fresh ideas are you having? No two readers will answer those questions exactly the same, or craft identical plans for managing emotions. Some families thrive on big expression while others require gentler ways of journeying through the feels. And one way isn't better than the other.

Before you answer the following prompts, sit with the general idea of emotional expression to clarify what it means to you. How are emotional expression, processing, and regulation woven into your life? What impact do emotions have on your personal and familial life? This contemplation can help ensure your unique perspective heavily influences the Emotions section of your Parenting Plan.

Writing Prompts

- How did my parents express emotions? How did they influence my relationship with emotions?
- How does each family member typically respond to challenging emotions? What aspects of these responses are working? What's not working?
- Do I feel like a family member needs professional support in navigating emotions?
- In my ideal world, how would I, and each member of my family, navigate difficult emotions?
- What is my family's formula for processing and clearing emotions?
- What daily practices can my family use to reset emotions and clear the slate for a new day?
- What are my family's parameters for emotional expression? For example, is it OK to hit the couch but not the wall? Is it OK to scream into a pillow but not at a person?
- How will my parenting mission statement inform how my family navigates emotions?

Parenting Plan

Nicknames for difficult emotions:

Formula for processing and clearing emotions:

Daily emotion reset practices:

Parameters for emotional expression:

5

ELEMENT 3: BUILDING HEALTHY BOUNDARIES

Ever feel like you and your child are fully enmeshed? Like their emotional and physical experiences are yours, and vice versa? If so, you're a candidate for boundaries, something most parents are in the market for.

When I was introduced to the concept of parental boundaries, I scoffed, thinking, *Of course I don't have boundaries with my kids. If I could stick them back in my uterus, I would.*

When I finally tried setting boundaries, I felt so selfish, like I was abandoning my son in favor of my own needs. Like I was withholding affection and attention. Like I was, dare I say it, a "bad mom." But as I trudged past that initial discomfort, I realized the value in boundaries. I realized those boundaries were helping me feel less depleted at the end of each day, and more myself. And my son was blossoming, developing new friendships and an enhanced sense of confidence and resiliency. He would also finally poop without me sitting in the bathroom with him. This all resulted in us developing a less strained, more dynamic relationship that allowed us to be two autonomous people who could lovingly stand up for our own needs, while also really enjoying time together.

So, what exactly are boundaries? In the realm of relationships, boundaries are guidelines a person has about their interactions with others, regarding things like physical touch, communication, time management, and anything else they have a preference about. Glennon Doyle, in her podcast *We Can Do Hard Things*, says, "Part of being human is deciding who and what you will allow in your life and then holding the line. And it is my right to hold that line." These boundary lines are based on a person's unique values and priorities, which is why everyone in your family will likely have slightly varying boundaries. For example, you might be totally fine with getting hugs from your child as often as possible, while they might determine that they will deny a hug request if they're not in the mood. Or, your partner might be totally comfortable with loud, intense arguments, while your boundary dictates that you will not continue a discussion if it gets too heated or voices are raised. Getting clear on your boundaries, and helping your family do the same, can work wonders for the health of relationships with self, family, and all the other humans out there.

When setting boundaries, it's important to consider if the boundary only dictates what *you* will do in a certain situation, not what you demand someone else do. For example, a healthy boundary might be, "If you yell at me, I will not continue the conversation." What would not be a boundary is, "You cannot yell at me when we're having a conversation." The idea is that, ultimately, we cannot control the behavior of anyone but ourselves. Setting boundaries empowers you to care for and protect yourself in a way that no one else can. Boundaries often end up adjusting the behavior of others—not because you demand it but because they decide to make the shift. In this way, setting boundaries is one of the most considerate things you can do for yourself, and those around you.

Benefits of Developing Boundaries

As people discover and communicate their boundaries, their level of self-respect often increases, as they're acknowledging that what feels important to them really matters and is worthy of respect. This exploration of boundaries also makes it easier to discern and honor other people's boundaries and offers a treasure trove of additional benefits.

Fosters Autonomy and Confidence

When parents, and hopefully others, regularly honor a child's boundaries, they experience what it means to be respected and come to expect and advocate for that respect. This respect through boundaries supports children in being more grounded, developing a deeper knowledge of themselves, and having a greater sense of confidence, competence, and self-reliance.

Minimizes Micromanagement

Boundaries often protect parents from our instinct to hover and micromanage our child's life. Many of us do all we can to shield our children from failure, disappointment, and frustration, but as you probably know, allowing them to experience these challenges, within reason, is essential to their growth. Getting clear on boundaries in this area can help ensure you stick to your plan when everything in you is begging to fix a situation you think your child needs to fix on their own.

Cultivates Mutual Respect

One of my favorite outcomes of my family creating boundaries is that my son and I have developed a deep, mutual respect. We both have a clear understanding of the other's boundaries and try to respect them as much as possible, often through compromise and compassion. It's like we're in this parent-child dance that I'm often leading but that also provides ample opportunities for him to lead. Creating boundaries has woven friendship into our relationship. We now have really weird, interesting conversations and love spending time together.

Protects Against Toxic Relationships

As you and your child become more secure in setting, and standing up for, your boundaries, you'll both have less tolerance for people who don't respect them. This can transform your life by weeding out relationships that aren't supportive of your well-being, or at the very least limiting interaction with a certain person until they start honoring your boundaries. For example, my client Sasha's mother would call her multiple times a day and leave long, intense voicemails if Sasha didn't pick up. This caused Sasha considerable stress, so she set a clear boundary, telling her mother, "I will call you on Monday, Thursday, and Sunday night, but only if you stop calling me." While it was incredibly difficult, Sasha stuck to her boundary and would not call her mother at the agreed-upon times unless her mother had honored the boundary. When her mother eventually shifted her behavior, it created a positive ripple into the rest of their relationship.

While your child hopefully doesn't yet have any toxic relationships, learning to set clear boundaries at an early age helps ensure they won't tolerate any form of relationship that doesn't involve mutual respect.

Lowers Anxiety

One of my favorite parts of boundaries is that they imbue life with predictability and stability, which can seriously reduce anxiety. For example, my client Frances used to get anxious before seeing her in-laws because she was afraid they'd give her parenting advice, she'd get irritated, and they'd end up in an argument. When it got bad enough, Frances told her in-laws she needed them to stop sharing their opinions on parenting, her parenting in particular, and that she would remove herself from their presence if they crossed this boundary. "They were totally shocked when I said this," Frances said, "but they eventually stopped giving me their whack advice when I stuck to the boundary by excusing myself every time they said, 'Well when our kids were little . . .'" Frances no longer gets anxious before spending time with her in-laws because her boundaries created more predictability and stability in that relationship.

The predictability boundaries provide is also a major relief for children. If they know how to protect themselves when someone breaks one of their boundaries (a topic we'll get into soon), they'll feel more relaxed, especially in new situations. Your child will also likely feel more secure in their relationship with you as they learn your boundaries and how you'll respond if one is broken. This parental consistency increases the chance that your child won't break the boundary, as they'll no longer be curious about what your reaction will be.

Let's say that you've told your child that your closet is a private space and they're not allowed to play in it. If you then find them in your closet, you might decide that the most appropriate reaction is to calmly remind them that it's not a plan to play in your closet and inform them that you're going to pick up their body and move them to a space they're allowed to play in. If you have this calm reaction every time, instead of sometimes saying, "Eh, whatever, just play in there for a bit," or, "I have told you so many times that you can't play in here! Go to your room!" your child won't be confused about what will happen if they play in your closet. That knowingness and trust in the cause and effect of your relationship will likely be an immense comfort.

Improves Efficiency

Boundaries often streamline life and can gift you more time. When you're clear on what you expect from others and have a plan about how you'll respond if they breach one of your boundaries, you save time and effort. This is especially true in your relationship with your kids, as they'll likely stop causing your "mad alarm" (as my son calls it) to go off as much because they now know what triggers it. When they do occasionally trigger the mad alarm, you won't waste time arguing with them about how to resolve the situation because you already have a plan for what to do if a certain boundary is breached. And the same time-saving benefits are garnered from your child's boundaries.

Sample Boundaries

Following are categories and examples of boundaries that could help you and your child discover yours. As you read, jot down the boundaries you or your child might resonate with and specify how they relate to your needs.

- **Physical**
  - Privacy
  - Personal space
  - Personal belongings
  - Public displays of affection
  - Private displays of affection
  - Roughhousing
  - Nakedness
  - Food

- **Mental and emotional**
  - Dishonesty
  - Saying no
  - Communication during arguments
  - Topics of conversation and personal questions
  - Oversharing
  - Joking around
  - Labeling
  - Responsibility for emotions/blame
  - Gossip
  - Advice
- **Spiritual**
  - Negative or positive energy
  - Spiritual rituals
  - Unkind judgments of personal beliefs
- **Daily rhythm**
  - Time management
  - Finances
  - Sleep
  - Work
  - Home care

Using Your Lens for Your Boundaries

While many people have boundaries for issues such as personal space and time management, the specifics of those boundaries differ from person to person. It's important to acknowledge from the start that the only person who has to agree with your boundaries is you. They have automatic validity the moment you discover them. I make this point because as you and your child, and hopefully the rest of your family, discover personal boundaries, I don't want the lens of someone else to blur your boundaries. For example, if you're creating a boundary around hugging, but you were raised by a touchy-feely mom, you might hear her voice saying, "A boundary on hugging? Well, that's just silly. Hugs should be given as often as possible." Being affected by this lens might cause you to not set a boundary that's important for you.

Children are especially vulnerable to the lens of others when setting boundaries, and they'll look to you for validation. While we'll discuss what to do when boundaries conflict with family rules, such as locking bedroom doors in the name of privacy, I urge you to do your best to be an objective guide as your child outlines their boundaries. This is an important step in the process of viewing your child as an autonomous human who is allowed to have beliefs and preferences that vary from your own. And your child will discover that they can trust you and be their authentic self with you.

Discovering Your Boundaries

While you've probably thought up a few boundaries, let's walk through ideas that can help you clarify what boundaries will set you up for more secure, authentic, and respectful living. As you go through this exercise, write down the boundaries that come to you, as this makes them more concrete and ensures you won't forget them.

- **Pay attention to when you feel uncomfortable.** Discomfort is one of the clearest signs that a boundary is required. For example, if you get uncomfortable when your children are constantly touching you, you might need boundaries around touch. Or if it hurts your feelings when your partner teases you, you might need a boundary for how you receive this type of "playfulness."
- **Consider what or who you avoid.** Take a deep breath, commit to being super honest, then write down the people, situations, or topics you avoid. This list will present additional areas of your life that require boundaries. For example, if your list reads, "Mom, parties, teasing, Cousin Pat, and religion," you can work on crafting boundaries around those people, situations, and topics.
- **Ensure your boundary is respectful.** As you create boundaries, make sure they won't breach the boundaries of others, or unintentionally manipulate them. The key to this is considering if a boundary would require something to happen to another person that they might feel uncomfortable with. For example, my friend Gemma's partner told her, "To feel more secure in

this relationship I need you to kiss me more," but Gemma felt uncomfortable with too much physical contact. In this situation it wouldn't be fair of Gemma's partner to ignore her needs in favor of his, and vice versa. So, they made a compromise, agreeing that the partner would ask for a kiss and Gemma could let him know if she was comfortable kissing in that moment. She also requested that he not become passive-aggressive when she did occasionally say no to kissing, as this signaled that her boundary wasn't worthy of respect.

You can spot boundaries that might not be respectful of others by considering how you'd feel if someone presented you with the same boundary.

Discovering Your Child's Boundaries

While boundaries are incredibly important for young children, it's a topic that can be hard for them to navigate. If your child is at a stage where they can reflect on situations and people that make them uncomfortable, you can go through the list of sample boundaries and help them reflect on each category. For example, with the category of personal belongings, you can ask if your child has items they don't like other people to touch. If they say, "My dollhouse," you can deduce that one of their boundaries is that others don't touch their dollhouse. You can then support your child in this boundary by moving the dollhouse out of reach when they have friends over or a sibling is in their room.

If your child cannot yet clearly discuss the cause of their discomfort, you can uncover their potential boundaries by reflecting on past situations that seemed to make them uncomfortable and paying attention to their future discomfort. For example, if your child seems uncomfortable when their grandparents tell them to give everyone hugs, your child might need a boundary around personal touch. You can then help them advocate for this boundary by letting others know that your child will provide hugs only if they feel comfortable doing so. As your child grows, your positive example of boundary setting and advocating can organically lead them to do the same.

Here are some things to keep in mind when exploring your child's boundaries.

- Don't assume your child's boundaries are the same as yours. While it's natural to believe others feel the same way we do about various topics, this can blur a parent's vision when helping their child set boundaries. For example, if you need alone time for a certain period each day, you may assume your child would also benefit from that alone time. However, if your child is an extrovert who thrives on being with others, alone time might feel like punishment. This doesn't necessarily mean they couldn't still benefit from alone time, but it does mean it probably isn't an important boundary for them.
- Keep boundaries within the parameters of family rules. As you help your child outline their boundaries, you can let them know they can't contradict your family rules. For example, when my son said he needed his bedroom to be a private space, he asked if he could start locking his door. Because a locked door went against our rules, we decided that an acceptable alternative would be placing a sign on his door requesting others to knock before entering.
- Set the boundary of emotional responsibility. A boundary all humans can benefit from, but especially a parent and child, is *I am only responsible for my own emotions*. This boundary can support you and your child in taking accountability for your own emotions and developing a healthy sense of autonomy.

This is especially helpful for children who often misbelieve they're responsible for their parents' emotions. For example, my son used to try really hard to cheer me up whenever I was sad. While the sentiment was sweet, his fixation on and sense of responsibility for my emotions caused him to also become sad if I didn't quickly move out of the emotion. This wasn't healthy for either of us. I felt guilty whenever I had challenging emotions, and he didn't know how to protect himself from my emotions. Our mutual work to understand the boundary *I am only responsible for my emotions* freed us from becoming entangled in the other's emotions. While we're still working on the instinct to try to fix the other's challenging emotions, we no longer absorb the other's emotions. At least not as much.

Setting Boundaries with Yourself

While it's common to think of boundaries only in the sense of how they affect your relationship with others, it's interesting to consider the benefits of setting boundaries with yourself. After all, you are the person you're with the most. One of the easiest ways to pinpoint your internal boundaries is to review your list of boundaries for your interactions with others. For example, if you have the boundary *I will not accept the labels others try to put on me* or *I will only continue conversations with those who speak to me with respect,* you can create the self-boundaries of *I will not label myself* and *I will speak to myself with respect.*

As you help your child uncover internal boundaries, you can ask if they notice a voice in their head. If they're able to identify that voice, you might reshape their world by informing them that, with practice, they can gain a lot of control over what that voice says. For example, you can tell them that when that voice is saying mean things, they can tell it, "That's not nice and I'm not going to accept your unkind words." Or when the voice is telling them to dump out a giant bin of toys, they can tell themselves, "I will not participate in dumping out all those toys, because it will be hard to clean up."

When Inner Voice is breaking boundaries, your child can envision a huge gate dropping down between them and it. They only lift the gate when Inner Voice is ready to play nice.

Highly Sensitive People Need More Boundaries

People who have sensory processing sensitivity (SPS) experience greater sensitivity and responsiveness to their environment and social stimuli and are deeply affected by the moods of others. They also have stronger activation of brain regions involved in awareness, empathy, and self-other processing. While SPS can be an advantage in many situations, it can also be exhausting and lead to feelings of instability. Because of this, highly sensitive people often need more boundaries than those who aren't as sensitive.

Boundaries are helpful for highly sensitive people because they help them conserve energy and feel more secure, especially when interacting with others. It's like boundaries are a shield, protecting them from the energetic missiles of others.

If you feel that you or your child is highly sensitive, you might end up with a long list of boundaries. This isn't a sign of weakness or fussiness; it's a sign that you're getting to know yourself on a deeper level and summoning the courage to advocate for your true self.

Independent and Collaborative Boundaries

As you categorize your boundaries, you'll notice some can function without much discussion, while others need to be crafted collaboratively to effectively function. Independent boundaries, such as only being touched with your consent, or not accepting others calling you hurtful names, are straightforward boundaries you can set without input from others. No one has the right to tell you that a boundary that fits into the independent category needs amendment.

Collaborative boundaries are trickier, as they require discussion and often compromise. For example, one of my husband's boundaries is that he needs to continue speaking until he has said everything he wants to say. But because he can talk for a considerable length of time without pausing, his boundary can cause me to feel unheard. We compromised by saying we will place a finger on our nose when we have something to contribute to the conversation. This allows my husband to finish his thought while ensuring he doesn't dominate the conversation.

Determining if a boundary is independent or collaborative can provide realistic expectations for what needs to occur for a boundary to be honored.

Signing a Boundary Contract

When we express a boundary to another person, it's like we're presenting a boundary contract. We're letting them know that if they want a relationship with us, they need to "sign" our contract, or in the case of a collaborative boundary, provide revision requests to the contract before signing. You can make this a tangible experience for your family by actually writing and signing boundary contracts.

Sitting with your family and listing each person's boundaries gives everyone a chance to ask clarifying questions and discuss potential alterations to collaborative boundaries or those that conflict with family rules.

Here are some examples from my boundary contract.

- I need to be able to say no to some requests without becoming the "bad guy."
- I will not accept blame for the emotions of others.
- I will remove myself from a conversation if I'm being yelled at or mocked.
- When I'm upset, I will go to a private space and require time alone.

Sharing Boundaries with People Outside Your Family

You're now ready for the hardest part: sharing your boundaries with people you don't live with. When I first researched boundaries, I saw many boundary-setting formulas along the lines of, "I don't like it when you do *x*. It makes me feel really *y*. I need you to stop doing that. If you can't honor that, I'll do *z*." Such examples made me resist setting boundaries because they sounded harsh, and I could envision the receiver of those statements shutting down.

However, I'm a people pleaser and have a hard time being blunt with anyone who did not grow in my uterus or help put humans in my uterus. Because of my allergy to harsh talk, but determination to be a boundary setter, I use what I feel is a gentler boundary-setting formula. I've found this formula dissolves the defenses of the other person and hasn't yet led to any serious arguments or a downright refusal of a boundary. However, if you don't have my people-pleasing affliction and want to get straight to the point, feel free to use a more direct formula.

Boundary-Setting Formula

1. **Express your appreciation for the relationship.** Help the other person be more receptive to your boundary request by starting the talk with a genuine expression of gratitude. This gratitude

lets them know why you enjoy having them in your life and why you're motivated to put effort into the relationship by setting clear boundaries. For example, I once told a friend, "I want to start by saying how much I appreciate your friendship. You are so thoughtful and easy to be with, and I look forward to continuing to grow our relationship."

2. **Clearly state the boundary.** Next, you can outline your boundary and share if it's a boundary you would apply to any relationship, as this conveys that it's not personal. During this phase of the discussion with my friend I said, "Because I value our friendship so much, I need your support in keeping our kids from wrestling when they're together. This is a boundary I've had to set in many relationships because the roughhousing often ends in injury or argument."
3. **Ask if they'd be willing to honor that boundary.** To ensure the person understands your boundary, straight up ask them if they understand and if they'd be willing to honor it.
4. **Explain how you'll protect yourself if the boundary is breached.** Unfortunately, some people won't take your boundary seriously unless they know what will happen if it's breached. In my situation I said, "If the wrestling doesn't stop, we'll have to start hanging out without the kids."
5. **Tell them that you trust in their ability to honor the boundary.** You can reiterate how important the relationship and boundary are to you by thanking the person for their willingness to hear you out and sharing that you trust they will commit to honoring your boundary.
6. **Ask what their boundaries are.** As boundaries often serve to strengthen a relationship, you can use this opportunity to ask the person if they have any boundaries they'd like to share. To keep the convo in a positive space, take a deep breath and do your best to not be defensive if they then set some boundaries.

TIP: Practice your part of the conversation out loud so you become comfortable speaking and hearing the words.

Why Sharing Boundaries Can Be Hard

It's hardwired in most of us, from a very early age, to do whatever we can to make others comfortable. This often leads to us dishonoring our boundaries for the sake of someone else. When you eventually start advocating for your boundaries, you might feel really uneasy, thinking, *Why are my needs more important than this person's comfort?*

As I've already shared, everyone is responsible for their own emotions. It's not your job to make people around you feel a certain way. Sure, it can be good to be kind, open-minded, generous, and all those other nice things, but not when it causes you physical, mental, or emotional harm. You have the right and responsibility to be your staunchest advocate. An unpopular view in polite society is that you should focus on your own comfort before the comfort of others. If everyone started doing that through advocating for their boundaries (not by being jerks), there might just be more calm, content, and well-adjusted people in this world.

Sharing boundaries can get even trickier when you receive pushback, which is almost guaranteed. If someone who is used to you accepting certain behavior is told you will no longer accept that behavior, they might be offended, or baffled, and try talking you out of your boundary. In these moments everything in you might scream, *Retreat! Backtrack! Make them comfortable! Make them like you again!* But standing your ground will help your self-esteem and self-respect flourish. Eventually, that person will get used to your boundary. And if they don't, you can choose to distance yourself.

As your child ages they will also receive pushback when asserting boundaries. This might result in them losing some friends or having difficult social moments, which hurts for both of you. But the two of you pushing through all this inner and outer resistance will help you blossom into people who know their worth; have more authentic, respectful relationships; and inspire others with your integrity. Your child might even become your guide in how to advocate for boundaries, as the habit of shirking one's own well-being for the sake of others is not yet firmly embedded in most kids. They can be bold in their boundaries.

I now need to admit that I'm preaching what I aspire to, not what I am. I have a lot of codependent relationships and still have a knee-jerk reaction to make those around me comfortable. I also really don't want people to think I'm rude, or (gasp!) not like me. I've been working on this for years, but it wasn't until I created the Boundaries section of my Parenting Plan that I finally made strides toward change. And oh wow, that change has been so hard. I've shaken up relationships, had uncomfortable conversations, and left interactions thinking, *That person doesn't like me right now, and I'm dying to fix it.* I still have a long way to go, but all the struggle is outweighed by the boost in self-respect, confidence, and emotional resiliency I gain from advocating for my boundaries.

Making Breached Boundary Plans

Look at your list of boundaries and brainstorm strategies you can use if someone violates one. Pinpointing these strategies increases the chance that you'll actually advocate for your boundaries, as it's easier to act when you know what you need to do.

So go wild, write everything that comes to mind, and hopefully uncover creative ideas for boundary advocacy.

Here are examples of boundary-breaching plans my clients have created.

- Ask the other person to pause right after they say something disrespectful and let them know I can't continue the conversation if they don't use respectful language.
- Take three deep breaths before I say anything. My self-advocacy won't be as effective if I'm angry.
- Pick up my child and take them out of my bedroom when they come in during my alone time. I'll calmly tell them that we'll spend time together when I'm done in thirty minutes. I also need to remind my partner to honor my alone time boundary by keeping the kids entertained.
- When someone tries to talk me into something after I say no, I'm going to say, "I hear that this is important to you, but I need you to respect my no."
- My daughter has decided that when her friends are saying mean things about someone, she is going to say something nice about

> that person. She will keep doing that until her friends get the hint and stop their unkind words.

TIP: As you brainstorm, consider responses for boundary breaches depending on the type of relationship you have with the boundary breacher. Because let's be real, the way you'd respond to your child breaching a boundary will likely be different than your response to a friend.

Regarding young children, you'll likely need to support them in advocating for themselves when their boundaries are breached. This support will help them learn valuable tools for self-advocacy that they'll likely start organically applying as they age. It's also helpful to share your child's boundaries with their other caregivers and let those caregivers know how they can support your child when their boundaries are breached.

You can also help your child understand boundary advocacy by sharing a metaphor provided by psychiatrist M. Scott Peck in his book *The Road Less Traveled and Beyond: Spiritual Growth in an Age of Anxiety.* Peck suggests imagining you live in a castle surrounded by a moat, and there is a drawbridge that grants others access to your castle. You and you alone control that drawbridge. You can encourage your child to imagine pulling up their drawbridge when one of their boundaries is breached. The piranha-filled moat then cuts off the offending party from the castle until they're ready to honor the boundary and treat your child with respect.

Boundaries Work Both Ways

A primary ingredient in the magic elixir of having your boundaries honored is seeking and honoring the boundaries of others. We all know people who are really good at advocating for their own boundaries but have little interest in the boundaries of others. Needless to say, these people often have challenged, unbalanced relationships.

Also, make sure that you adhere to your own boundaries when interacting with others. For example, if Diana has the boundary *I will not engage with anyone who is calling me hurtful names*, but she uses hurtful names when speaking to others, it becomes difficult for others to respect Diana's boundary.

In addition to showing others the respect you expect, you can infuse harmony into your relationships by actively seeking out a person's boundaries. While it would be easiest to just ask someone what their boundaries are, many people aren't consciously aware of their boundaries. Because of this, you might have to discover this information through observation. For example, if you notice that a friend stiffens when hugged, you can switch to another form of greeting when you see them. This will likely be a huge relief to them. But be forewarned: the better you get at uncovering peoples' boundaries, the more popular you'll become, and the more popular you become, the more social gatherings you'll be invited to.

TIP: Help your child learn to decipher the boundaries of others through nonverbal cues by telling them when you notice someone's cues of discomfort. You can then discuss what that person's boundary might be in that particular situation.

Boundaries Need to Harden Before They Soften

A tricky thing about boundaries, especially for highly sensitive people who have a lot of them, is that they can create such a strong shield that it's difficult to have relaxed interactions with others. It can also be tricky for the people on the other side of that thick boundary shield, as they probably feel like they're always walking on eggshells. This social discomfort isn't worth betraying your boundaries for, but it is worth eventually softening your boundaries for. Let me explain.

My client Tatiana is a highly sensitive person with a lot of boundaries. She spent many years, and exceptional effort, transforming from someone who let others walk all over her, as she said, into a strong woman who stands up for herself no matter how uncomfortable it makes others. But once Tatiana became firmly embedded in her boundaries, she developed social anxiety. "I get so nervous being around anyone but my immediate family," Tatiana said, "because I'm sure someone will breach one of my boundaries, and it will create an uncomfortable situation. My kids also say they don't like going out with me because they're embarrassed by how I react to others."

Tatiana eventually alleviated her anxiety by softening her boundaries. This softening meant that instead of reacting to every minor boundary breach, she would take some deep breaths and envision her energetic shield softening. She said, "I see it as this free-form sphere of light that protects me, but is also flexible enough to gently adapt to the energy and actions of others."

Tatiana developed the ability to soften her boundaries in certain situations only because she first put in the time to foster their strength. This process is different for everyone. For example, people who are inherently confident and comfortable being direct will likely harden their boundaries a lot sooner than people pleasers like me who feel that advocating for boundaries will cause the world to loathe and reject them, then banish them to the sewers.

Tools for Ensuring Common Parental Boundaries Are Met

While your boundaries are just as important as your child's, I'll bet you often sacrifice some of yours in favor of pleasing your child. But with a little planning, you can help ensure everyone in the family gets their boundaries met.

Creating Safe Spaces for Solo Play

While most parents crave some daily alone time, it's tricky to implement this boundary if you feel it's not safe to leave your kid unattended. An ideal solution is having another adult watch your child while you savor some free time, but that's not always an option. Another solution is setting up a fun space that's safe for solo play. Then, each day let your child know they need to play in that space for thirty minutes, for example, while you do you. You can also set up a video baby monitor so you can keep an eye on them without going into the room.

If you feel like screen time is the only way to keep your kid from getting into something potentially dangerous while you have a chill-out, whip out that screen, buddy.

Finding Daily "No Touch Time"

Most kids touch their caregivers a lot, and it's important that they not feel rejected in their pleas for physical affection. But sometimes a parent needs their body to themselves for a hot minute. Because of this, you can set the boundary that no one touches you for a certain period of time every day. (Most parents yearn for this in the evening, after they've had a day full of touch.) You can make this touch-free time easier for your child by setting a timer and letting them know that until the timer goes off, they need to pretend that there's an impenetrable force field around you. And if you think the request to not touch you is going to make your child want to touch you even more, engage them in a distracting activity like drawing or Play-Doh tinkering during this time.

Having Agenda-Free Togetherness

Increase the chance that your child will honor your boundaries by engaging in "wants nothing" time with them. During this time you want nothing from your child and have no agenda; you're simply present with them as they play. This all-in period of connection helps fulfill a child's need for attention and often makes it easier for them to give you cooperation or space later in the day.

Protecting Your Energy

A helpful tool when you're with anyone, but especially family members, is envisioning a golden light around you that protects you from the emotions of others. It's like this light dissolves any negative energy brought into your sphere of awareness. This energetic protection doesn't make you cold or unfeeling but instead makes it easier for you to offer empathy and be an objective support for the person struggling.

This idea is especially important in the parent-child relationship where parents often live by the adage, "I'm only as happy as my least happy child." But if we absorb our child's emotions, our capacity to be a strong support is diminished and the child's suffering is often magnified. Instead, consider the taboo idea that it's OK for you to be happy even if your child is sad, or mad, or whatever. You're certainly not happy because your child is going through a hard time, but your ability to energetically separate from them allows you to experience positive emotions.

In addition to these ideas, you can fold other activities into your family schedule that help ensure your boundaries are met.

Guided Meditation

The meditation at the following link will support you in discovering your boundaries, envisioning what life might be like when those boundaries are met, and fortifying yourself with the courage and self-respect to advocate for them. We'll also explore your child's potential boundaries and how your family dynamic will shift for the better as boundaries are woven in. Visit https://www.baileygaddis.com/boundaries.

Writing Prompts

- What are my boundaries? Which boundaries are nonnegotiable, and which are flexible?
- What do I think my child's boundaries are? How can I support those boundaries?
- How can I teach my child to recognize and honor the boundaries of others?
- How will I respond when my boundaries are breached? How will I support my child when their boundaries are breached?
- What are core boundaries that could serve my family? What boundaries would be a natural fit with my parenting mission statement?
- Do I want to create boundary contracts with my family?

Parenting Plan

Family definition of boundaries:

Core family boundaries:

My personal boundaries:

My child's boundaries:

Formula for sharing boundaries with others:

Boundary breach plan:

Daily boundary-support activities:

Boundary contracts:

6

ELEMENT 4: EXPLORING THE MESSY ART OF DISCIPLINE

One of the most unsavory aspects of parenthood, with the exception of wiping poop off tiny butts, is disciplining. It's essential to engage in this unsavory act if we don't want our offspring riding roughshod, but it's really difficult to do in a way that doesn't shame or blame our child or result in them just ignoring us. It's like walking a tightrope between correcting disruptive behavior and preserving a healthy, trusting parent-child relationship. Enter a disciplining plan, which serves as a balancing pole as we walk that tightrope.

Note: As you navigate this chapter, you might find that behavior I suggest needs correction isn't something you feel is important to discipline, or you might feel that the disciplining ideas I present aren't strict enough. And I agree with you either way. Trust your instincts and craft a disciplining plan that stays true to your values and expectations. At my son's school they talk a lot about how different families have different plans. So if one child talks about being allowed to stay up late while another shares that their bedtime is 7:00 PM, they are reminded that one family plan isn't better than the other. They are learning to explore and celebrate differences, which is one of my primary goals of this book, but especially this chapter.

Examining Your Current Disciplining Plan

You're probably already engaging in discipline practices, so let's start there. Reflecting on what you're doing that works, what you'd like to edit, or what you're ready to throw out provides a personalized foundation you can build on as you read this chapter.

To protect your insights from dissolving as soon as thoughts of dinner, and that meeting, and that stain on the carpet, and so on and so on, pop into your head, record your answers to the following prompts.

- What disciplining strategies have you used recently that worked well? What could work better if it was adapted? What didn't work, or didn't feel right to you?
- Where did the disciplining strategies you currently use come from? Your parents? Friends? A book?
- Which of your child's disruptive behaviors do you not know how to effectively discipline?
- What disciplining strategies interest you?
- What disciplining strategies are a hard no for you?
- In your ideal world, how would you and your child feel after you apply discipline?
- What are your overall goals for disciplining?

Keep your answers to these questions handy as you read the rest of this chapter so you can refer to them when questioning whether certain ideas align with your disciplining beliefs and goals.

How You Were Disciplined Affects How You Discipline

For better or worse, influences from childhood weave themselves into adult actions, typically as knee-jerk reactions. For example, if one of your primary caregivers always yelled when they were angry, you might be programmed to yell when angry. Or, if a primary caregiver would calmly explain that they needed to take away a privilege because of a disruptive behavior, that might be your go-to method when disciplining. It's also common to rebel against the way you were raised if you had a negative experience. This could result in you consciously doing the opposite of what your parents did.

To review how your childhood might influence your disciplining beliefs, we're going to do some regression therapy to help you relive your worst childhood memories. Kidding. But I do encourage you to skim your childhood memories and reflect on the disciplining techniques your primary caregivers used. As you do this, make a note of which techniques you're utilizing with your children, and how those techniques made you feel as a child.

If your childhood instilled disciplining beliefs that resonate with you, great! You can build upon those in this chapter. If these disciplining memories make you cringe, the good news is you can reprogram the related disciplining beliefs, replacing any you feel were harmful with beliefs that reflect your current values. For support in clearing unhelpful disciplining beliefs from your repertoire, listen to the guided meditation at the following link: https://www.baileygaddis.com/reset-old-beliefs.

The Three Cs of Cooperative Discipline

My heart smiled when I first heard about cooperative discipline. Before that, I was inconsistent with disciplining because I didn't have a go-to formula I found effective and compassionate. Cooperative disciplining was what I'd been looking for; it's composed of a formula of three Cs: clarity, consistency, and calm. Ideally, the caregiver strives for clarity when explaining behavior expectations and the consequences that result if they're not met, has consistency in reactions when expectations are not met, and utilizes calm resolve when enforcing the consequence.

The three Cs made sense to me and actually made me excited for my son to push boundaries so I could practice. While this excitement for boundary-pushing didn't last, my love of the three Cs did, and eight years later it's still the foundation of my disciplining plan. I love this concept because it's fairly broad and can be applied in many different ways, meaning you can adapt it to your unique disciplining philosophy. It's so adaptable that the three Cs are utilized in a range of environments from workplaces to classrooms.

Here is a breakdown of each C.

Clarity When Explaining Expectations and Consequences

While it seems like a no-brainer that a parent would clearly explain expectations for their child's behavior before the child engages in disruptive behavior, this usually doesn't happen. Often, the explanation of expectations comes *after* the indiscretion, when the emotions of parent and child are heightened. These heightened emotions can make it harder for the parent to clearly communicate, and for the child to absorb the message. But with forethought we can break this habit and provide our children with much-needed clarity.

To determine what your expectations are for your child's behavior, make a list of the environments and situations they're commonly in. For example, breakfast, playtime at home, riding in the car, park play, going to the grocery store, naps, dinner at Grandma's, and so on. Then, write down your expectations for your child's behavior in each situation. These expectations can be based on what you think is reasonable for your child, your values, and other dynamics you deem important.

In addition to clearly outlining a rule, or expectation, you can tell your child why you do or do not want them to do something. The old adage "because I said so" often just confuses children and doesn't motivate them to meet your expectations. If you instead give them a clear, logical explanation for your expectation, they will be more likely to understand your message. For example, if you need your child to clean up their blocks when they're done playing, you could say, "I need you to pick up the blocks so no one steps on them and hurts their feet." This helps the child understand that you're not asking them to pick up the blocks to make their life boring but to prevent others from getting hurt. You can make this a positive conversation by assuring them that you're confident in their ability to meet expectations and that you're there to offer support.

After communicating expectations, and the reasoning behind them, calmly explain the consequences for not meeting expectations. You might say, "It's a plan to be gentle with the dog. If you pull on her ears, I'm going to pick you up." This ensures the child understands the stakes of taking a certain action and doesn't feel blindsided when you swoop in with all your consequences.

Help your child engage in the conservation by asking if they have any questions, and if they think the expectations and consequences you explained are fair. If they don't think they're fair, you can discuss potential alternatives, with the caveat that while you're open to their ideas, you are the one who will make the final decision.

Because it can be difficult for children to remember everything you say, give them a quick review of the relevant expectations and consequences before entering a situation. For example, before getting out of the car at their sibling's soccer game, you can remind your child that it's a plan to hold hands in the parking lot and not run onto the soccer field, and that they'll need to stay in their chair if they can't meet these expectations. These reminders set your child up for a positive experience, as your expectations will be fresh in their mind.

You can also encourage your child to meet expectations by mentioning the positive results of that behavior. For example, you could say, "It's a plan to drink water when we're at the park. If you don't drink water, you could get really hot, and we'll have to go home early. But if you drink water every time I offer, you can play for a full hour!"

Consistency in Parental Reactions

It's important to have a consistent reaction when your child engages in dangerous or disruptive behavior. Your child knowing what your reaction will be often increases the chance that they'll meet expectations, as it's not as exciting to push boundaries when the outcome is known. Parents also often find relief in this consistency because their reaction to their child's behavior is no longer based on their mood, but instead on a clear plan of what to do if certain behavior occurs. The guesswork for parent and child is removed.

A potential roadblock with this consistency is the temptation to make consequences incredibly undesirable to encourage children to meet behavior expectations. However, when consequences also create an undesirable situation for us parents, we're more likely to veer off course. This was my biggest struggle with consequence consistency. For example, if I told my son we were going home if he engaged in certain behavior at a party, but I wouldn't actually take him home if that behavior occurred because

I didn't want to leave the party, I was sending confusing messages. If I had first considered what consequence I'd actually carry out, that consequence would have been some quiet time with me in a private space.

Another roadblock is the child's other caregivers not being on the same page about consequences. For example, if Mom takes Henry back to bed when he comes into the living room after bedtime, but Grandma lets Henry stay up and watch TV with her, Henry isn't receiving a clear message about what happens when he gets out of bed after bedtime. In chapter 11, we'll discuss aligning caregivers with your disciplining plan.

Calm Resolve When Applying Consequences

One of the surest ways to make disciplining an opportunity for growth instead of shame is staying calm when implementing consequences. This is easier said than done because most parents get angry, or at least irritated, when children do something they were asked not to do. While this is an understandable response, it's not productive because the parent's heightened emotions can make the situation more about them than the child, and the child's emotions and self-esteem might be shredded in the process.

For example, after my son dumped out the box of eight billion Legos I asked him not to dump out, I went ballistic, saying, "I literally just told you not to do that! I seriously don't understand why you made that choice. Now, instead of starting dinner I have to help you pick up all these Legos. I'm so tired, and this really isn't what I want to be doing right now. I need you to start listening to me. And I need to get rid of some of these Legos—there are way too many in this house." And I went on and on, with my sweet boy's face looking more and more defeated with every word I spat.

When another Lego dump occurred the following day, I took a deep breath and willed myself to stay cool. This time, I said, "Oh wow, that's a lot of Legos! I'm wondering if you heard me when I asked you not to dump them out? If you did hear me, can you share why you decided to dump them out anyway?" Then, Hudson told me that he can't find the Legos he wants to use unless he dumps out the container. My response: "It seems like it's overwhelming for you to have so many Legos in one container. Should we separate them into smaller containers? Yes? Great.

We can do that now as we clean them up. After we do that, it's only a plan to dump out one container at a time. If that doesn't feel like something you can do, I'll have to put the Legos away." This calmer me put the focus back on my child, helped my brain stay in problem-solving mode, and resulted in my son feeling relieved instead of shamed.

You can make your consequence delivery even more Zen by lovingly connecting with your child before and after implementing a consequence. A great way to do this is with a compliment sandwich. For example, when applying a consequence after your child runs into a parking lot, you could say, "I really appreciate that you stopped running and returned to the car when I called your name. Because it's not a plan to go into a parking lot without a grown-up, I'm going to put you in the stroller. You have such a great memory, so I'll bet next time we're in a parking lot you'll remember to stay right by my side." This "sandwich" shows them that in addition to noticing the behavior you do not allow, you're also noticing their "good" behavior.

As we don't live in Pleasantville, even the chillest of consequence deliveries can still result in your child being upset. In these moments, remind yourself that your child's reaction is pretty standard for young children (and all people experiencing unwanted consequences) and is not your fault. If you checked off the boxes of the three Cs, you did all you could to thoughtfully apply discipline. How your child responds is their thing—you're not the keeper of their emotions.

Tip: When disciplining your child, pretend they're the child of one of your friends, and that friend is watching. This always does the trick for me, as I'm much less likely to lose my calm with my friends' kids because I don't want to be seen as a bad parent and don't want to piss off my friend. So in this case, my fragile ego and need to be liked work in my favor!

Using Productive Consequences

All consequences are not created equal; some are productive, some are neutral, and some are potentially damaging. Productive consequences are the jam as they not only encourage children to not repeat certain behaviors but also make more sense and help them learn about themselves and how the world typically operates. This category of consequences also prevents you from having to preach to your child, as the consequences communicate why the child should avoid certain behavior in the future. There are two types of productive consequences, natural and rational.

Natural Consequences

These are the consequences that the laws of nature apply if your child is engaging in certain behavior. All you have to do in this situation is not fix the consequence. For example, if you give your child an ice cream cone and say, "It's a plan to sit down while eating this so the ice cream doesn't fall on the floor," a natural consequence occurs if your child then runs, and the ice cream falls on the ground. In this situation you would support the natural consequence by not giving your child more ice cream. Instead, you'd comfort them as they grieve the loss of their scoop. The one obvious caveat to natural consequences is we can't use them if they'd put our child at risk.

Rational Consequences

Another type of productive consequence is a rational follow-up to a certain behavior. For example, a rational consequence of a child running around a pool would be leaving the pool and going to a location where it's safe to run. Another example would be putting away finger paints and getting out Play-Doh if the child uses the family pet, instead of paper, as a canvas.

When applying a rational consequence, it's important to do so soon after the offending behavior so the child can connect the dots. Waiting too long to apply such a consequence can confuse and frustrate the child, because they've likely forgotten about their earlier behavior and might feel like you're disciplining them for no reason.

Unproductive Consequences

Neutral consequences aren't damaging but lack opportunities for learning. An example is not giving your child dessert if they didn't help clean up their toys. As dessert and playing with toys are unrelated, the only thing the child learns from this consequence is that their parent follows through with applying consequences. If the consequence is that the toys that were not cleaned up cannot be played with the next day, the child learns that their parent follows through with applying consequences *and* that they lose the privilege of playing with certain toys if they don't help clean them up.

Damaging consequences are those that shame or physically harm a child. These consequences can result in the child not repeating a certain behavior, but not because the child has learned why the behavior is not beneficial—they only stop the behavior out of fear of emotional or physical pain.

What Science Says About Corporal Punishment

I often get asked about the long-term effects of corporal punishment, specifically from adults who experienced it as children. So, I went deep into research mode and discovered some interesting points. Here's an overview of that research.

- An analysis of seventy-five studies on spanking, published in the *Journal of Family Psychology*, reported that "non-abusive spanking" is not more effective than other forms of disciplining in adjusting a child's behavior. Researchers also found that spanking negatively affected children's mental health and relationship with their parents.
- According to a study published in the journal *Child Abuse and Neglect*, children who were disciplined with corporal punishment were more likely to use physical force, such as hitting, when attempting to resolve conflicts with peers and siblings. The study also revealed that when these children became parents, they were more likely to use corporal punishment with their children, creating an intergenerational cycle of this form of disciplining. However, parents who experienced corporal punishment are certainly capable of breaking this cycle.
- A study conducted in twenty of the largest US cities found that children who were spanked more than twice a month had an increased risk of mental health disorders and cognitive problems.

The study suggests that each spanking episode reinforced the last episode, resulting in a negative cycle.
- A study published in *Neuroimage* found that harsh corporal punishment (HCP) during childhood could reduce prefrontal cortical gray matter volume and performance IQ. The researchers also noted that HCP could increase the chance of antisocial and violent behaviors, depression, suicidal behavior, substance abuse, and psychiatric disorders like PTSD. In addition, they found that HCP could obstruct social cognition, as a child could have difficulty reconciling a parent's loving and gentle behavior with the intentional harm they inflict.
- Physical punishment can create short-term stress that accumulates over time and affects the brain's stress hormone production.
- Spanking can alter a child's brain function in ways similar to severe forms of maltreatment. The areas of the brain affected are responsible for emotion regulation and threat detection.
- While many mental health professionals used to suggest spanking as an effective form of disciplining, surveys show that the majority of mental health professionals, physicians, and child welfare personnel no longer support the use of physical punishment.
- Parental use of corporal punishment has been banned in over fifty countries.

Encouraging Behavior You Value

Now that we've looked under the hood of the types of consequences parents apply when undesirable behavior occurs, let's explore how we can promote desirable behavior. One of the easiest ways to do this is acknowledging when your child engages in desirable behavior, such as brushing their teeth after only being asked once or putting their dirty clothes in the hamper. Each word of affirmation a child receives is like a star being born in the constellation of their self-esteem. The birth of each star motivates the child to engage in more of this positive behavior.

While lighting up the constellation of a child's self-esteem sounds like a no-brainer, most of us are programmed to primarily comment on a child's disruptive behavior and let the positive behavior pass without a word. Changing this habit can have a significant positive impact on children, as a study published in *Scientific World Journal* found that positive behavior recognition promotes a child's identity formation and cultivates a variety of social skills, such as moral reasoning and the ability to infer and evaluate others' perspectives.

There are many ways to weave positive behavior recognition into your relationship with your child.

Offering Thoughtful, Specific Words of Affirmation

When parents do comment on a child's positive behavior, it's often an offhand "good girl" or "atta boy" instead of a thoughtful acknowledgment. What if we put as much effort into crafting our affirmations as we do our criticisms? The recipe for a thoughtful affirmation includes why a certain behavior is positive and how it makes you feel. For example, a parent would say, "Wow, I noticed how gentle you were with your baby sister. Being gentle with her is so important because it helps keep her safe and teaches her that she can trust you. It makes me really happy seeing the two of you gently playing together."

Praising Effort Instead of Outcome

You can cultivate your child's intrinsic motivation for continuing a positive behavior by praising their effort more than the outcome of their effort. For example, instead of saying, "I'm so proud of you for winning the soccer game!" you could say, "I was so impressed by how focused you seemed during the game and that you kept passing the ball to your teammates. And I loved seeing how much you were smiling!" Focusing on the effort the child made during the game instead of just the win helps them look below the surface of the outcome of their behavior and consider internal motivations for committing to the sport, such as building teamwork skills and having fun.

Seeking "Yes" Situations and Avoiding "No" Situations

In addition to noticing naturally occurring positive behavior, you can set your child up for affirmations by creating situations that are likely to elicit positive behavior. For example, if your child loves organizing, you can have them help you put away forks and spoons, as this will present an opportunity for you to comment on how helpful your child is. Or if they are great with animals, you can both volunteer at an animal shelter.

Then we have activities that are likely to provoke a "no," such as eating at a formal restaurant or being in a crowded public space. While it's impossible to avoid all situations that could lead to a no, you can at least steer your child away from these situations whenever possible. For example, if one of your children is in a play but you know it will be difficult for your other child to sit through it without fidgeting or talking, you might opt to have them stay home with a sitter.

Tip: When you can't avoid a "no" situation, you can swap the "don'ts" and "no's" with affirmative guidance. For example, if your child is kicking the seat in front of them on a plane, you could say, "It's a plan to keep our feet off the chair in front of us. If you need to, you can put your feet in my lap." Instead of boxing your child in with disapproval, you're opening a door to nondisruptive behavior.

Offering "But-Free" Affirmations

When I was a kid, I always expected a "but" after someone said something nice to me. "You're so clever at writing, but your math really needs some work. You have a great sense of humor, but your laugh is kind of annoying." Every "but" cancelled out the kind words, often leaving me feeling less-than.

A common belief among human services professionals is that conditional affirmations can lead someone to view themselves negatively, while unconditional positive regard and acceptance create ideal conditions for personal growth. Specifically, unconditional positive regard and acceptance can trigger people's fundamental tendency to develop their abilities and explore their potential so they can become the best version of themselves.

Pointing Out Your Positive Behavior

While children learn more by example than by telling, they learn even more if that example is *paired* with telling. Because of this, it can be helpful to point out when you engage in a behavior you're trying to get your child to adopt, such as closing the door quietly, putting the toilet seat down, or rinsing off a dish. You might say, "I'm making sure to close the door right now so mosquitos don't get into the house," or, "Oops! I almost forgot to put the toilet seat down. It's important I do that so the dog doesn't drink out of the toilet." Adopting this habit was doubly good for me because it helped me realize when I was being a hypocrite about things like turning off the lights when leaving a room, not interrupting others, or having too much screen time.

Considering Rewards for Positive-Behavior Milestones

An additional option for positive-behavior encouragement is a reward such as a tasty treat, toy, or fun outing. For example, you could promise your child a trip to the toy store if they remember to put their dirty clothes in the hamper every day for a week. However, this is a parenting tactic that inspires ample debate. One side says, "Rewarding desirable behavior encourages more of that behavior," while the other side says, "Rewarding desirable behavior only encourages children to engage in that behavior for an external reward, not the internal satisfaction they receive from engaging in the behavior."

I agree with both sides. Promising rewards has been one of the most effective tools for helping my son adopt certain positive behaviors. This is why giving kids a piece of chocolate every time they poop in the toilet is such a popular tactic. But I've also had to work with my son to not expect a reward for every positive behavior and find intrinsic motivation for engaging in activities such as brushing his teeth and eating healthy food.

To be effective at promoting both extrinsic and intrinsic motivation, a reward should be proportional to the behavior. For example, a proportional reward for remembering to feed the dog every day for two weeks might be a new stuffed animal. A disproportional reward for this behavior would be a trip to Disneyland.

Like all the other ideas in this book, whether you promise rewards for certain behavior will depend on if you think it will be effective for your kid, and if it fits with your family philosophy and values.

When We Unintentionally Encourage Disruptive Behavior

I am guilty of unintentionally encouraging disruptive behavior by labeling my son as "wild," doing the things I ask him not to do, giving him more attention when he's having a meltdown, and bribing him to calm down. If you also feel like you unintentionally, occasionally, kinda sorta encourage disruptive behavior, here are some things to consider.

Labeling

Humans tend to label everything and everyone: "That person is smart, that dress is chic, that woman is beautiful, this cheese smells like feet." This habit comes from an innate need to categorize in an effort to find order in life. However, childhood development specialists advise against placing negative labels like *difficult*, *bossy*, *crybaby*, *manipulative*, *troublemaker*, *overly sensitive*, and so forth on children, as these labels can affect a child's developing identity and adversely affect their decision-making, behavior, and relationships. These labels also affect a parent's perception of their child and can influence how they relate to and communicate with them.

Children tend to live up to the labels placed on them, because the labels stick them in a box that limits their ability to "try on" other traits. For example, if Sammy needs time to warm up to new people and is regularly labeled *shy*, he might start to embody that label and could have even more difficulty forming new relationships. If this label wasn't placed on Sammy, he would have more freedom to adjust how he operates in social settings.

Labels can also lower a child's motivation for adjusting certain behaviors. If a child is labeled *aggressive*, they might become more comfortable being aggressive, as it's what people expect of them. On some level the child thinks, *Everyone already thinks I'm aggressive, so I might as well live up to that expectation*. The child could also start believing that there's no use in trying to adjust their behavior because the label is firmly embedded in how others perceive them.

The impact of negative labels ties into the Golem effect, a psychological phenomenon in which low expectations placed on a person by a superior, such as a teacher or parent, lead that person to fulfill the expectation of substandard behavior. It's like the low expectations are a self-fulfilling prophecy. On the flip side is the Pygmalion effect, or Rosenthal effect, in which high expectations trigger better performance in a person, especially in a specific area. So if a child is consistently told they're a fast runner, they'll probably run faster than they would if others didn't have that expectation. But positive labels aren't always positive.

While positive labels are lovely on the surface, they can have the unfortunate effect of making a child believe that certain traits are innate and not a result of positive mental processes and actions. If a child is always told how smart they are, for instance, they could eventually reduce the effort they put into learning because they believe it should just come naturally. If the child then starts doing poorly in school, they could feel devastated, as being smart has become such an important part of their identity. Or the child could shy away from intellectual challenges, as they don't want to engage in anything that could contradict their *smart* label.

An alternative for using a positive label is acknowledging the effort and behavior that leads to a certain positive label. For example, instead of calling a child smart, a parent could say, "I'm noticing that all the time you're spending looking at your alphabet cards is helping you understand the alphabet." This reframing puts the emphasis on a child's actions and has a better chance of motivating similar positive action. Psychologist and Stanford University professor Carole Dweck calls this the "growth mindset," which helps a person see effort as something that propels them forward, challenges them, and offers opportunities to develop new skills. Growth mindset becomes even more powerful when a child's parent has this mindset about both their child and their own self.

Giving Children More Attention When They're Being Disruptive

Imagine a child gently tugging on a parent's arm, requesting that they stop what they're doing to play. The parent then says, "In a minute," for many minutes. When the child eventually starts screaming, the parent gives them their full attention. But of course, it's not positive attention, it's are-you-freaking-kidding-me-right-now attention. Sound familiar? It does to me.

When Hudson was four, I was traveling a lot for work and often busy working when I was home. During this time, he had tantrums almost every time we were around other people. Each time, I'd take him to a quiet space and support him in working through his emotions. What a wise child. He realized that the only time he got quality time with me was when he had a public tantrum, so he started having more public tantrums. The solution: give him one-on-one time before we were around others. That's the key—figuring out how to honor a child's need for attention before they go nuclear.

Disciplining Behavior, Not Emotions

It's easy to confuse a child's behaviors with emotions, and vice versa. For example, when a child is angry and kicks the wall, we want to discipline the wall-kicking behavior, not the anger. The wall-kicking is a reaction to an emotion, and something that discipline can effectively adjust. However, an emotion, which is a natural and instinctive state of mind triggered by a situation, mood, or relationship, is not something that should be disciplined, because it's healthy and normal. So the parent of the wall-kicking child saying it's not appropriate to get angry isn't effective because emotions can't be disciplined. The discipline might cause the child to hide certain emotions, but it won't cause them to not experience them.

It's critical to communicate the distinction between emotions and behavior to yourself and your child because it helps you both understand that emotions are never wrong, but that there are limits to what a person can appropriately do when having those emotions. I first discussed this with Hudson after he became upset about a friend giving him a birthday gift he already had. He pushed the gift away, crossed his arms in frustration, and yelled, "I already have that! I want a different gift!" I was mortified, but instead of going with my instinct of bribing him to calm down and say thank you, I took him to his room so he could move through his emotions without continuing his disruptive behavior. After a good cry he was more receptive to talking, and I told him his feelings were normal and understandable, but the behavior of pushing the gift away and not thanking the friend was not a plan. When he then apologized for getting upset, I reminded him that I wasn't concerned with him getting upset, only about his resulting behavior. Many years later he and I are still working on differentiating our emotions from behaviors and reminding one another that our emotions are always valid. My therapist is great, but Hudson's advice is often the best.

TIP: Regularly remind yourself that it's developmentally normal for young children to push boundaries and experiment with disruptive behavior. While this behavior certainly requires consistent disciplining, it's not usually a sign that your child has behavior issues. On the contrary, it often means they're undergoing the healthy development of autonomy. However, if you're ever concerned about your child's behavior, it's wise to consult with a pediatric mental health specialist.

Validating Emotions Doesn't Undermine Discipline

Many of my clients have asked if comforting their child after applying a consequence undermines the consequence. My answer is always a firm no. Let's say you take your child to sit in the car with you after they pinched a child who took their toy at the park. If you hug them and say, "I can see that you're really upset, and I'm going to sit here with you while you move through that," you're not undermining the consequence for pinching but simply communicating that you understand their feelings and are there for them no matter what. On the flip side, ignoring a child's feelings post-consequence sends the message that their emotions are a further indiscretion and not valid. This message can result in a child feeling shame for their emotions and becoming conditioned to suppress them to the detriment of their mental health. I don't think there's ever a bad time to offer your child a hug and loving words.

Another piece of this is the concern that patience communicates permissiveness. Luckily, this is another parental worry we can release. Practicing patience as our children learn to adjust disruptive behavior communicates that we don't expect perfection. While it's frustrating to feel like you're always disciplining a certain behavior, many children need time and lots of trial and error as they learn to meet your behavior expectations. Practicing patience during this process is one of the best gifts parents can give.

Creating a Safe, Cozy Space for Processing

Being disciplined can provoke a swirl of frustration, anger, and confusion, even if the discipline was applied with the compassion of Mother Teresa and Zen of the Dalai Lama. It can be tricky for children to process this swirl of emotions when they are still in the environment where the disruptive behavior and discipline occurred. It can feel like the space is still thick with challenging energy. This is why it's often helpful to have a special space you can take your child to if they're upset after being disciplined.

There are various factors to consider when creating this safe space.

Nurture the Five Senses

After working with your child to determine where to set up this space, consider how it can nourish the five senses, as this can help your child come into the present moment and reconnect with their "upstairs brain." Here are some ideas for how to stimulate each sense:

- **Sight.** A picture of a beloved friend, family member, or fictional character; artwork your child is proud of; or a collage of your child's favorite things.
- **Sound.** A portable speaker or headphones your child can use to listen to soothing music or their favorite songs. I recommend creating a playlist with your child that you can play when they're in this space. You can also include things like a wind chime or singing bowl in the space.
- **Smell.** A scented eye mask or kid-safe room spray to activate a child's sense of smell while also promoting relaxation.
- **Touch.** A cozy blanket, pillow, stuffed animal, sweater, or robe; or a stress ball, sensory toys, or other items that can busy your child's hands.
- **Taste.** Flavored honey sticks, a favorite healthy treat, and of course water to help flush out those stressor hormones.

Because movement can help children process emotions, you can also keep items like a jump rope, yo-yo, or yoga ball in this area.

On-the-Go Emotion Processing Kit

When creating this space in your home, also create an on-the-go emotion processing kit you can store in your car. If your child frequents other locations, such as daycare or a grandparent's house, plan with those caregivers on how to create an emotion-processing zone in those locations.

Sacred Space

Make sure everyone in your family understands that this is a sacred space where nothing but comfort and support are provided. Parents aren't allowed to bring a child to this space and continue discussing why the child's behavior was disruptive; rather, the parent is a calm, mostly silent, source of support. The idea is to make this an area where the child feels safe enough to let their complicated emotions pour out and create space for more soothing emotions to flow in.

Name the Space

Last, ask your child to help you name the space. Ideas my son came up with for his processing-space include Cuddle Corner, Cozy Wozy Wonderland, and my favorite, Mean-Free Mommy Zone.

Staying Cool When Kids Resist

We have now reached one of the hardest parts of disciplining: keeping our ship together when the kids aren't meeting our behavior expectations. It can sometimes feel like the effort to stay cool sucks the life force out of us and leaves us a deflated shell of our former jolly self. Or it can feel like all calm has left the building and we're meeting our children where they are: the charming town of Irritationville.

While it's understandable to lose it every now and then, doing so often leaves us and our children feeling like close-minded adversaries. So, what do we do? I suggest tinkering with the following tools to discover if any support you in reaching that elusive state of calm when your kid is screaming in the face of discipline.

Crisis Calmer

When you're triggered and can't access the part of the brain where your well-thought-out disciplining plan lives, you might feel the only tools at your disposal are a raised, irritated voice and frustrated words. To get back to equilibrium, try the Crisis Calmer: take three deep breaths while massaging your jaw, then shake out your arms and hands. This takes a whopping twenty seconds.

These simple steps will get you out of fight-or-flight mode and reconnect you with calm, clarity, and all the amazing custom ideas you're crafting as you work through this book. If you're retriggered, just repeat the Crisis Calmer mid-conversation.

Another interesting thing about the Crisis Calmer is that it will probably throw off your kid. When I started doing the Crisis Calmer, my son often paused his resistance because he was confused by my goofy, unexpected behavior. Sometimes, this pause helped him reset. He eventually started doing the Crisis Calmer with me, and it transformed the tone of our disciplining encounters.

Objective Observer

It's easy to take our kid's behavior personally. When they start wailing when another child gets a balloon before them, for example, we might start spiraling into thoughts like *Why are they doing this? Were they ignoring me every time I've talked about waiting for your turn? Other parents are probably judging me right now. What am I doing wrong? I must be doing something wrong.* None of these thoughts are fair to us or the situation, and they reduce our capacity to use our disciplining tools.

To avoid taking your child's behavior personally, pretend that you're not their parent but a kind stranger tasked with supporting this child in distress. Or, envision yourself floating above the scene and becoming a calm, objective observer who is able to make sound recommendations based on what you see. Above all, remember that at that moment there are likely hundreds of thousands of parents around the world also dealing with an unruly little human.

The Behavior Is a Puzzle Instead of a Problem

I love me a good puzzle. It fires up my creativity and problem-solving skills and scratches my need for a hint of mystery and adventure. Because of this, I've found it incredibly helpful to view Hudson's or Grace's difficult moments as puzzles instead of problems. This simple reframing makes it easier for me to remain objective, stay calm, and pull from my toolbox of resources when my kids do all the things I don't want them to do.

Sure, sometimes it feels like they're two-thousand-piece jigsaw puzzles with each piece hopping away when I try to grab it. But when I remember that even the most challenging situations have a solution, I'm able to have some fun with my perplexing, captivating, and ever-changing little puzzle people.

Teamwork Makes the Scheme Work

When our kid screams no and chucks their shoe across the room, it's second nature for most parents to go into boss mode and set our subordinate straight. But when that subordinate also thinks they're the boss, the situation can quickly escalate.

When we dissolve the hierarchy and view ourselves and children as teammates, the way we respond and communicate shifts. If your team member does something you don't feel is effective, or might even be harmful, you wouldn't shame and punish them but would instead support them in figuring out a different way of operating so the team can thrive.

Keep Returning to Love

I'll bet that even in those moments when you'd rather be doing your taxes than dealing with your child, you still have unconditional love for them. Returning to this love when they're decimating boundaries helps motivate you to use tools like the Crisis Calmer and protects your child's self-esteem from being bulldozed by the disapproval you might be radiating. Shifting into a vibe of love almost immediately changes the energy of the situation and sends the nonverbal message that your love is not conditional on your child's behavior. It's like you're saying, "Even when you're bugging me, you're still loved and accepted."

Schedule Dates with Your Child

Having a standing one-on-one date with your child can be one of the most potent ways to reset the relationship and deeply connect with them. The shifts this deepening connection can create might even organically adjust your child's behavior for the better. But ideally, you go into these dates with no agenda other than getting to know your child better and enjoying your time together. You'll probably start relishing this time, as it will likely lead to a healthier, more nuanced relationship.

Here are some ideas for making these dates a success:

- **Stick to the plan.** While life might feel like you're playing whack-a-mole with to-dos, a dedication to not rescheduling these dates can help your child feel important and develop enhanced trust in you.
- **Embrace silence.** Sometimes kids want to talk about everything, and sometimes they don't. Give yourself permission to lean into silent moments that allow you and your child to just be together without any pressure to perform and that help you both develop the skill of being comfortable with silence.
- **Let your child choose the activity, within reason.** You can amp up your child's excitement for your date by letting them choose the location, as long as it falls within parameters such as, "the destination has to be in our town and not cost more than *x* amount." This offers them a taste of power and helps them feel seen by you, as you're showing that their interests matter.
- **Focus more on connection than discipline.** During parent-kid dates, I've found it's helpful to give myself permission to not be a stickler for discipline. When I adjust my focus from upholding rules (which is, of course, important most of the time) to just having fun with my kid, there is a subtle but powerful shift in the relationship.

Understanding Why Kids Rebel—And Anticipating the Behavior

Pam Leo, author of *Connection Parenting*, says, "A hurtful child is a hurt-filled child. Trying to change her behavior with punishment is like trying to pull off only the top part of the weed. If we don't get to the root, the hurtful behavior pops up elsewhere." Every behavior is in service of meeting a certain need, and sometimes the pursuit of that need blurs common sense, which can lead to disruptive behavior. But when we figure out how to meet our child's root needs before they use undesirable behavior, we can organically dissolve the behavior instead of trying to force it out of the child.

To begin digging up the roots of disruptive behavior, make a list of the needs you think your child is trying to meet when "acting out." Here are examples from my clients.

- Mabel screams when we're leaving her friends at the park, maybe because she's communicating a need for more outdoor play and community.
- On hectic mornings Violet resists everything from getting dressed to getting in her car seat, maybe because she's communicating a need for a slower pace and more consistent routine.
- Teo refuses to walk next to me when we're out in public, maybe because he's expressing a need for more independence.
- Ella always picks a fight with me right before it's time for her to go to her dad's house for the weekend. It feels like she's trying to make our temporary time apart easier to handle. She might be expressing a need for more reassurance and emotional support from me when she's at her dad's.
- Trevor starts telling really inappropriate jokes, and acting totally wacky, whenever his older brother is home from college, maybe because he's expressing a need for more approval and attention from his brother.

While these parents were just guessing at what needs their kids were trying to meet when exhibiting various behaviors, it gave them a place to start.

After making your list of disruptive behaviors and the needs you think they might be masking, create another list that includes ideas on how you can meet the needs before they lead to disruptive behavior.

Here are examples from my clients.

- To meet Mabel's need for more outdoor play and community, we'll join an outdoor music and movement class, make our backyard a more inviting space for play, and plan more playdates.
- To meet Violet's need for a slower pace and more consistent routine, my mom is going to come over on weekday mornings to help Violet slowly get ready for daycare and then drop her off an hour later than I usually do. We're also making a chart of each thing that needs to happen in the morning and letting her choose the order of that routine.
- To meet Teo's need for independence, I'm giving him "big boy" responsibilities, such as retrieving our mail by himself, selecting his own outfits, and making his own snacks. Out of the house, I will let him help me retrieve various items at the grocery store, insert the credit card into the terminal when paying, and press the pedestrian push button before we cross a street.
- To meet Ella's need for more reassurance and support when she's at her dad's house, I remind her that she can call or text me at any time and try to nurture her ability to connect with her dad by reminding her of all the fun things they'll likely do together. I came to these ideas by straight-up asking her why she picked these fights and gently offering my theory.
- To meet Trevor's need for more approval and attention from his brother Chase, Chase and I agreed that he would have a one-on-one outing with Trevor twice a month.

If your child continues the disruptive behavior you were attempting to dissolve with need-meeting, brainstorm additional needs that could be at the root of their behavior. This is a fluid process that will likely require frequent observation, brainstorming, trial and error, and, for older children, potentially challenging conversations. To support you in this expedition into the root of your child's needs, here are some common needs that can trigger disruptive behavior.

- **Rest.** Humans of all ages have a more difficult time regulating emotions and behavior when tired or overstimulated. Having downtime or a nap, going to bed earlier, or taking steps to promote more restful sleep can all help fulfill the need for rest.
- **Attention.** Running into a wall to get a laugh, kicking the driver's seat to get Dad to say something, skipping class and drinking alcohol to impress peers, and so on are examples of behaviors kids can use to get others to notice them. Seeing these behaviors as a cry for attention instead of an attempt to anger us can completely transform how we respond.
- **Autonomy.** "I can do it myself!" is a common refrain from children and teens because they're developing a need for autonomy. But this need is regularly thwarted for kids of all ages as the adults in their lives regularly tell them what to do. We can navigate this by creating opportunities for our kids to flex their autonomy, such as letting them make their own snack, helping them engage in many of the tasks we explore in chapter 9, or, for an adolescent or teen, letting them walk or drive to school on their own.
- **Power.** An offshoot of the need for autonomy is a need for power. A young child almost constantly has decisions made for them, and likely few opportunities to make decisions that heavily influence others. Parents can fulfill a child's need for power by letting them make some decisions for the family, such as what to get on a pizza or what to listen to in the car. Art is another powerful tool, as it allows the child to have total control over the world they create. In their art they can choose to allow all citizens of Silly Town to throw out their toothbrushes and declare Saturdays as Booger Eating Day. They make the rules in their art.
- **Physical discomfort.** This discomfort, caused by issues such as fatigue, hunger, dehydration, tight clothes, illness, or being too hot or cold can result in kids acting out. Because it's sometimes difficult for young children to pinpoint why they're uncomfortable, it can be helpful for parents to go into detective mode,

investigating whether the child's waistband is too tight, diaper is wet, tummy is empty, and so on.

Physical discomfort, such as muscle and joint aches and menstrual cramps, can also be a factor when kids are going through puberty. Detective mode can also be helpful during this time, as kids might be embarrassed to share these discomforts with their parents.

We're Programmed to Notice Negative over Positive

Thanks to negativity bias, humans are hardwired to notice the negative more than the positive, and to feel negative events more intensely than the positive ones. When evolution inserted this chip into the human mind, it was a survival mechanism that called attention to problems we might need to deal with quickly. This results in most humans requiring at least three times as many positive emotions as bad to perceive their day as a "good" one. Negativity bias is also connected to loss aversion, which is a cognitive bias that can cause the pain of losing to be twice as psychologically intense as the pleasure of gaining. Thanks a lot, evolution.

A study published in *Personality and Social Psychology Review* defined four elements of negativity bias.

- **Negative potency.** While a negative and positive experience can have the same level of importance in a person's life, the negative experience will be felt more deeply.
- **Steeper negative gradients.** As an event a person perceives as negative approaches, the intensity of that negative perception sharply increases, while the intensity of the positive perception of an upcoming positive experience doesn't increase as much.
- **Negativity dominance.** Humans commonly perceive the whole of an event or moment as more negative than the sum of its parts.
- **Negative differentiation.** Because negative events are more complicated than positive events, they require more cognitive resources, resulting in them being more memorable, intense experiences. Negative differentiation has also resulted in humans

having more vivid, varied vocabulary when describing negative emotions and events than positive ones.

While this negativity bias used to be a helpful tool for survival, it's not as necessary in the modern world and can even be harmful, especially in relation to parenting. Negativity bias often causes parents to focus more on all the ways their children aren't meeting behavior expectations and gloss over all the times they are meeting expectations. This has been too true in my relationship with my kids, and it breaks my heart. Before I became aware of negativity bias, I often focused on my kids' irritating or inconvenient behavior and rarely acknowledged the numerous times they put in ample effort to meet expectations.

There are a few strategies I found helpful in minimizing the impact of negative bias in my relationship with my kids.

- **Begin the day with gratitude.** Get yourself in a positive-parental frame of mind each morning by thinking of five things you appreciate about each of your children before you begin interacting with them. Be as specific as you can, as this specificity can make the gratitude more visceral. For example, instead of thinking, *I appreciate how loving my son is*, I could think, *I love how my son lays his head on my shoulder and pats my back when we hug.* It's totally fine if you often repeat the same pieces of gratitude, as this repetition will carve new positive pathways in your mind related to your children. You can also help your children start the day in a positive headspace by sharing these thoughts of gratitude with them.
- **Tune in to your five senses during positive moments.** The amygdala is a key player in negativity bias and uses around two-thirds of its neurons to search for negativity. When the amygdala locates negativity, it quickly and automatically stores it in our memory, whereas a source of positivity must be intently focused on for at least twelve seconds before it can implant in our long-term memory. As a result, we tend to dwell on negative experiences longer than we do positive ones. You can enhance your mind's ability to hold on to the positive by really leaning into the times

when your child is engaging in positive behavior. You can do this by dropping into the present moment by noticing what you see, hear, smell, feel, and taste. Then envision that you're expanding the positive emotions your child's behavior is eliciting and really savor the experience. The goal is to make the day's positive experiences as, or even more, intense than the negative, so the brain begins noticing and saving more of that positivity.

- **Breathe into mindfulness.** A study published in *Social Psychological and Personality Science* found that enhancing mindfulness by focusing on deep breathing helped study participants increase positive judgments and reduce negativity bias. So, as much as possible, take deep breaths right before and during interactions with your children. And if you notice lingering negative thoughts of your child, envision that each time you exhale, you're blowing that negativity out of your mind and clearing the slate.
- **Disrupt negative thought patterns.** If certain stimuli regularly trigger negative thoughts and emotions in you, commit to disrupting that pattern with a positive distraction. For example, if you commonly pick apart your conversations with your child and find reasons to feel guilty, break up that pattern by engaging in mindful breathing and a quick yoga pose when you start overanalyzing your parenting. Once you discover an effective negative-thought-pattern-disrupter, pledge to utilize it each time the pattern is initiated.
- **Rewrite negative talk.** When your mind starts spitting out thoughts such as *I'm so impatient* or *My child can be so destructive*, challenge yourself to edit them into something productive. For example, *I'm so impatient* can become *Building my capacity for patience is going to prove to myself that I'm capable of positive change. My child can be so destructive* might become *My child takes everything apart because she is so interested in how things work. Maybe I can foster this interest by getting her a workbench and tool kit and some old clocks at thrift stores that she can dismantle.*
- **Cut yourself some slack.** While your mental health will benefit from tempering your negativity bias, you don't need to be afraid

of occasional negativity. Humans are complex and flow through a myriad of light and dark thoughts and emotions every day. When you're having a moment that's tinged in darkness, you can meet that darkness with grace by breathing, remembering that it's temporary, then intentionally letting in some light when you're ready.

- **Teach your children about negativity bias.** When your child is old enough to understand this concept, share it with them, as it could transform the way they perceive the world. Hudson and I have been discussing negativity bias a lot recently, as he's going through a phase where even subtle triggers send him spiraling into darkness. He then starts saying, "I never have good days. No one likes me. Everything is hard for me," even if he just had a day surrounded by friends and doing things he loves. Learning about negativity bias is helping Hudson view himself and experiences through a more accurate lens and realize that fatigue and hunger are two issues that exaggerate his negativity bias.

Resisting the Urge to Ramble

The adults in the *Peanuts* TV specials, the "*wa-wa-wa*-ers," resonate with most people because they've experienced adults droning on and on, or they do it themselves. I've had out-of-body experiences watching myself deliver a sanctimonious monologue where I share the same message ten different ways. Even if my son had absorbed the message in the beginning, my "wa-wa-wa-ing" likely muddled the message.

Another factor is a child's short attention span. Typically, children can concentrate on one thing for two to three minutes more for each year of life. So a two-year-old's attention span is four to six minutes, while a four-year-old's is eight to ten minutes. But when the activity is listening to a parent disciplining, the attention span is likely much shorter.

Needless to say, it behooves us to keep our messages short, sweet, and clear, which is harder than it sounds. Many of us are hardwired to believe that using a lot of words will hammer in our message more effectively, but it usually just hammers that message into one ear and out the other. When faced with a discipline opportunity, challenge yourself to use as few words as possible to communicate the consequence and why it is occurring. If your child melts down and pleads with you to change your mind, you don't have to keep repeating your initial message, you can just offer comfort and acknowledge their feelings.

Communicating Nourishment Instead of Toxicity

In his book *The Art of Communicating*, Zen master Thich Nhat Hanh describes how the way we communicate is either healthy and nourishing or toxic and destructive. This idea is especially relevant during tense interactions, as it's easy for parents to "feed" the child toxicity that can poison their self-esteem and relationship with their caregiver and infect their mind with negativity. If we instead use nourishing words when disciplining, we can "feed" the child kindness, support, and inspiration.

Because crafting nourishing communication can be challenging in tense conversations, you will likely need to pause and really consider what you want to say. I'm consistently throwing the verbal equivalent of corn dogs and candy at my family, but I'm striving to mix more organic kale and wild-caught Pacific salmon into the mix. For example, I'm really working on serving more nourishment by shifting from a tense to a calm tone of voice in challenging moments. And when I force myself to try to understand the needs of the other, instead of my need to prove how right I am, the verbal nourishment more easily flows. This can often be as difficult as ensuring I eat enough veggies every day, but it doesn't stop me from trying.

Sources of Nourishment and Toxicity Are Everywhere

This idea of nourishing versus toxic communication can ripple into everything you and your family consume. For example, the food you eat communicates nourishment or toxicity to your body, while what you look at throughout the day (Instagram, or maybe TikTok?) communicates nourishment or toxicity to the mind.

Regularly asking *Is this nourishing or toxic?* can help you make communication and lifestyle shifts that promote joy, health, and harmony in your family life. And here's one of the most important parts: what you consider nourishing or toxic is totally up to you! Some people find a *Real Housewives* binge toxic, while others equate it to a salad overflowing with a rainbow of fresh veggies. Some parents might find the idea of their children playing a sport like football indigestible, while others would eagerly await the deliciousness of seeing their child play under those Friday night lights. To each their own metaphoric nourishment.

Protecting Yourself from Toxicity

In some situations, like if your partner is railing about all the things they hate about their job, or your child is screaming that you're a life-ruiner who should be banished to the island of poo-poo heads, the toxins are flying at you and impossible to avoid. While no one would fault you for meeting their toxicity with your own, a more supportive option might be to put up an energetic shield and remind yourself that just because they're serving toxicity doesn't mean you have to eat it.

You can also envision a soothing, loving light flowing from your heart to the heart of the person you're interacting with. This exercise can give you the superpower of sneaking nourishment into the lives of others. And if the other person seems to have a hard time disconnecting from toxicity, ask them if you can give them a hug, as this action can disrupt the toxic flow and provide a bite of nourishment.

Disciplining with Questions

Disciplining can be much more effective when parents shift from the role of judge and jury to that of a curious observer and troubleshooting partner. When we get away from the pigeonholes of "wrong" and "right," we can enter a field of possibilities to explore with our child. In this field, we can often find creative, effective ideas for helping children adjust their behavior without triggering a battle of wills. One of the quickest routes to this field is questions. Asking nonrhetorical questions when trying to understand or adjust a child's behavior can lead to interesting, informative communication, which can help the child feel like a participant instead of a victim of disciplining.

The first time I tried discipline with questions was after I found my son in the center of a stuffed animal explosion. This explosion occurred after I had told him over and over to not dump out his colossal basket of stuffed animals, because he never wanted to clean them up. Before that day, this situation usually led to cleanup commands and my son crying and yelling. But this time, I asked some questions.

Me: "What's your plan with the stuffed animals?"
Hudson: "These guys over here are fighting for the dinosaurs who want to eat ice cream, and those guys are trying to keep all the ice cream to themselves. It's a mega ice cream battle."
Me: "Oh wow! I hope the dinosaurs are able to get some ice cream. When the battle is over, what do you think the plan will be?"
Hudson: "To clean up?"
Me: "Yes! Exactly. How does that feel?"
Hudson: "Fine. But there's a lot of stuffed animals. Can you help me clean?"
Me: "I can help this time. But because it seems like you get overwhelmed when there is so much to clean up, what do you think you could do next time to make clean up easier?"
Hudson: "Get less out?"
Me: "Totally."
Hudson: "OK. Bye!"

By asking these leading questions, Hudson was able to offer ideas on how to resolve the issue. He seemed to take pride in his ability to participate in the solution and was then more willing to clean up. It felt like magic. While this magic doesn't always show up when I discipline with questions, it sure has sprinkled chill vibes over many of our interactions that used to be explosive.

Formula for Tense Discussions

Disciplining often flows into a difficult conversation, especially if more than one family member is involved. Crafting a formula for how your family navigates these difficult conversations can increase the chance that compassion and open-mindedness are woven in.

For example, you could have a formula of hugging before and after the talk, using quiet voices, having a special hand signal if someone starts raising their voice, and making the focus of the talk understanding the other person instead of being right. While some aspects of your formula might be too complex for a young child, they can likely handle a simplified version of it, such as the hugging and hand signal. As they grow, you can teach the more complex elements.

To inspire ideas for your formula, here is a breakdown of my favorite elements of four communication philosophies. Try them out, put your twist on them, throw some stuff out, mix some stuff in—just keep tinkering until you create a plan that feels right for your family.

Nonviolent Communication

Probably one of the most popular methods for conflict resolution, nonviolent communication (NVC), created by psychologist Marshall Rosenberg, is based on the idea that all humans are compassionate and that all our actions, including what we say, are part of a strategy to meet one or more of our basic human needs. During a discussion utilizing NVC, both people engage in empathetic listening and honest expression by observing what's happening in a nonjudgmental way, sharing how they feel and what their needs are, and then making a specific request. The objective is also to remove blame, judgment, and name-calling from the conversation.

For example:

- **Observing.** If your child keeps moving their feet when you're trying to put on their shoes, you can observe what's happening by saying, "I'm noticing that you're moving your feet as I try to put on your shoes."
- **Expressing feelings.** You can then acknowledge your feelings by saying, "I feel frustrated when your foot moves away when I'm trying to put on your shoes."
- **Gathering intel.** You can also gather information about your child's feelings by asking, "Do you feel like you have energy you need to get out before I put your shoes on? Or is there another reason you think your feet are so wiggly?"

- **Sharing needs.** Now you express your need by saying, "I'm hungry and need to go to the grocery store to buy food for dinner. We have to wear shoes to walk to the car and go inside the store." (You can find a list of common needs at https://www.cnvc.org/store/feelings-and-needs-inventory.)
- **Requesting.** Last is the request, "Would you be willing to keep your foot still so I can put your shoe on?" If your child is then like, "Um, no thanks!" you can ask if they have an idea for how to get shoes on their feet. They might then choose to put the shoes on themselves or get different shoes. But if they still refuse, you can calmly let them know that with no shoes, the only available option is you carrying them into the store and them sitting in the cart.

The Imago Method

This communication philosophy includes both parties agreeing to talk one at a time—no cutting the other off mid-sentence. The person talking is referred to as the Sender, and the person listening is the Receiver. After the Sender has shared a full thought, the Receiver mirrors, validates, and provides empathy. (Sometimes, the Receiver needs to request a pause if the Sender starts flowing into the next thought.)

- **Mirroring.** In the mirroring phase the Sender might say, "I feel annoyed when you rush me in the morning." The Receiver would then mirror the Sender's message by saying, "I hear that you're feeling really rushed in the morning. Is there more you want to share about that?" The Sender and Receiver repeat this pattern until the Sender confirms they don't have anything else to share on the topic.
- **Validating.** In the validation phase the Receiver might say, "It makes sense that you feel rushed in the morning because I move really fast and give you a lot of instructions."
- **Empathizing.** In the empathizing phase the Receiver guesses how the Sender might be feeling about what they shared, or reflect on the feelings the Sender has already shared.

Now the roles shift, and the process starts all over again.

Grice's Maxims of Conversation

Created by linguist and philosopher Paul Grice, this philosophy includes four maxims of conversation: the quantity, quality, and relevance of what a person's says, and how that person says it.

- **Quantity.** Be informative, but only provide truly necessary information.
- **Quality.** Be honest, and don't share information you lack evidence on.
- **Relevance.** Omit off-topic information. Stay on topic!
- **Manner.** Avoid obscure expressions and ambiguity.

When Your Disciplining Beliefs Conflict with Your Partner's

It's surprising how disciplining can create more tension between parents than between parent and child. If you have a partner, you hopefully share common values and agree on the general parenting philosophy you want to utilize. But that agreement can wither when it comes to discipline, as the disciplining techniques a person resonates with are often heavily influenced by their childhood. As a result, a person might want to emulate many of the disciplining techniques they experienced as a child, or do the opposite.

Here are suggestions for peeling back the layers of this issue and hopefully coming to an agreement on your family disciplining plan.

- **Write down the behaviors that require disciplining.** Because different behaviors often require varying disciplining strategies, it can be helpful to list all of your child's behavior that requires shifting. For example, that list might include throwing food, putting boogers in ears, not cleaning up, biting, or taking off clothes in public places. For older kids, behaviors such as missing curfew, skipping class, or getting poor grades might make the list.
- **Brainstorm disciplining ideas for each behavior.** After creating the list of behaviors, brainstorm strategies you could use for

each behavior. During this brainstorming you can also discuss the origin of your disciplining ideas. For instance, if your partner wants to utilize time-out if your child bites, or ground your teen if they miss curfew, you can discuss why your partner thinks that's an effective strategy and if it's something that fits with your parenting philosophy and values. This process can help you both gain a deeper understanding of where the other is coming from and feel more like partners than adversaries.

- **List the final disciplining plans.** Now that you've explored disciplining ideas, you can ideally come to a compromise on strategies that honor both parties' beliefs.
- **Plan for what to do when one parents veers off course.** Parents with conflicting disciplining beliefs can confuse kids and undermine discipline attempts, as the child gets mixed messages. While the aforementioned practices will help you develop a more cohesive disciplining plan, there will still be times when one of you deviates from the plan. In these situations, it's important to course correct so the stability of the disciplining doesn't waver.

Let's say you and your partner agree that if your child refuses to help clean up toys, those toys are put away for twenty-four hours, but your partner doesn't always follow through on this plan. This lack of follow-through could make your child less inclined to help clean up and could create tension between you and your partner.

Communication is key to correcting course. You could touch base with your partner to see if there's a reason they're not following through with the plan and discuss if it needs alteration. Once you reach a consensus, your partner can remind your child of the clean-up plan, acknowledge that they haven't been following through with applying the consequence, and share that they're recommitting to the plan.

Using Family Values as Inspiration for Family Rules

As you work on defining behavior expectations for your family, refer to your list of values and brainstorm rules that would support each.

For example, "valuing the health of the environment" could result in family rules such as these:

- Reduce the number of new items we buy.
- Recycle.
- Put food in compost.

The value "having compassion for others" could result in family rules such as the following:

- Don't engage in name-calling
- Offer support to someone experiencing emotional or physical pain
- Share

Including your child in this brainstorming can enhance their sense of ownership over the rules, and you might be surprised by the creative ideas they contribute.

What Behavior Does Your Child Expect from You?

I had a parenting *aha*, or maybe *uh-oh*, moment when I realized that while I spend tons of time considering how I want my kids to behave, I don't often consider how they want me to behave. This felt unfair, so I asked my son what his behavior expectations were for me. After he got through the unreasonable expectations of "always say yes, buy me everything I want, and let me get HBO on my iPad," we got to the doable behavior. Here are a few of his top expectations:

- Speak in a calm voice because your angry voice hurts my feelings.
- Look at me when I'm talking to you.
- Help me get time to talk when we're with a lot of grown-ups.
- Spend time with me each day without your phone.
- Be silly more because you're funner when you're sillier.

When I asked him to make this list, he was nine and able to articulate what he needed from me. Because this is difficult for most young children, you can try viewing your interactions with them through their eyes, then list the parental behavior you feel would light up their life.

Encouraging Pretend Tantrums

If reading this heading makes you question my sanity, I get it. What parent would want to encourage more tantrums? The answer is parents who want to lessen the intensity of their child's real tantrums. This concept was introduced by Dr. Alan E. Kazdin, a research professor and Sterling Professor Emeritus of Psychology and Professor of Child Psychiatry at Yale. Dr. Kazdin proposes that parents can remove harmful elements of tantrums, such as hitting or screaming, by challenging a child to have a pretend tantrum, without the harmful element.

Hudson's harmful tantrum element was screaming. When I asked him to have a pretend tantrum without screaming, he stuck out his tongue, punched a pillow, growled, stomped his feet, and whispered that I'm the meanest parent ever. The more we practiced these scream-free tantrums, the less he screamed when he was having a real tantrum. Pretty cool.

A Daily Fresh Start

If you feel like you spend most of your time disciplining your child, you might experience discipline fatigue and could even start disliking your child a little-itty-bitty-bit. None of this feels good, which is why regularly cleaning off the lens you view your child through can be life-changing. To do so, when you get into bed every night, envision all your child's indiscretions from that day as raindrops distorting your lenses. Then, imagine windshield wipers clearing all those drops, leaving behind clean lenses that will help you see your child anew tomorrow.

You can enhance this daily fresh start by looking for new things in your child each day, such as a new interest, mannerism, or word they're using. This can support you in remembering that your child is more than the person who consistently litters crumbs on the floor, forgets where they put the hat that's on their head, and doesn't know why there are candy wrappers underneath their bed. And from a scientific standpoint, your child is literally a new person each day as they're rapidly losing and gaining cells, in addition to neural pathways.

Guided Meditation

Listen to the guided meditation at the following link to gain a clearer perspective on your family's disciplining needs and unlock a creative array of possibilities for meeting those needs: https://www.baileygaddis.com/disciplining.

Writing Prompts

- What does the concept of "discipline" mean to me? Why do I think it's important?
- What are our current family rules or behavior expectations?
- What primary needs is my child trying to meet when engaging in unwanted behavior? How could I help them meet those needs in undisruptive ways?
- What expectations does my child struggle to meet? What are the potential reasons for this? How can I encourage them to meet these expectations?
- What consequences am I currently using that aren't working for my child? What consequences are working? What are new consequences I want to try?
- What behavior expectations does my child regularly meet? Do I regularly acknowledge them for this?
- What's my plan for tantrum management? How will I manage my own emotions during tantrums?
- What tone of voice does my child best respond to when being disciplined? Which words or phrases and posture?
- Do I want to create a cozy space for my child to process emotions after being disciplined?
- Am I engaging in behavior I ask my child not to engage in? Am I doing other things that encourage disruptive behavior?
- What behavior expectations does my child have for me?
- What is our family's formula for resolving conflicts that arise from disciplining?

Parenting Plan

Rules and consequences for the kids:

Rules and consequences for the parents:

Tantrum management plan for child:

Tantrum management plan for parents:

Conflict resolution formula:

7

ELEMENT 5: DISCOVERING YOUR FAMILY VALUES

Values are like a compass that can lead you to a better life. They guide your family toward actions and attitudes that make you feel like good, happy humans and hold you all together with your shared beliefs. In addition to informing how your family does life, values make the doing of life easier because your family spends less time and brainpower hemming and hawing over decisions when your values clarify what the "right" choice is for your family. Let's say "helping others" is one of your family values, and you decide volunteer work is an action that supports that value. It would then be easy for your family to choose between a ski vacation or a vacation to a tropical locale that offers an opportunity to volunteer at a wildlife sanctuary.

Family values also help children develop a strong sense of identity, as they belong to a group that has clear ideas about how they navigate life. This strong identity is a solid foundation the child can build their personal identity on, and it can make it easier for them to resist peer pressure and the potentially harmful messages they're exposed to through technology. In addition, having a significant piece of their identity linked to family can help children experience a deep sense of belonging. With their need to belong largely fulfilled by family, a child will likely feel less desperate to meet this need elsewhere, which supports them in being more discerning when making friends and determining what other influences they'll explore.

It's important to expose your child to family values early because that's when their brains are ripe for the learning. Humans are born with an excess of neurons and shed unused ones by around age six. Before that neuron dump, it's easier for children to learn everything from language and music to positive values. But all is not lost for children older than six, as the brain doesn't stop developing and maturing until one's mid-twenties and maybe beyond that age.

While you've already teased out many of your *parenting* values, in this chapter we're going to pull back the lens and discover your ideal *family* values and how to promote them.

After you've pinpointed your family values, we'll get into the fun of exploring how to weave them into everyday life. And let me tell ya, when you start living a life guided by your values, your personal and familial life blossom. Let's start planting those seeds.

Value Categories and Examples

The first step in crafting a stellar set of values is assessing how you want your family to operate in life's various categories. This assessment breaks down the development of values into bite-size pieces, making it easier to craft specific values that can translate into action and positive, familial evolution.

Here are example values for each category to get you started. As you contemplate each, jot down ideas of values to present to the family, and feel free to add other categories relevant to your family.

Social Values

This category encompasses your relationships with your community, family, and self.

Example of social values include the following:

- Protecting the physical and emotional health of others
- Standing up for those who can't stand up for themselves
- Volunteering in the community

- Practicing generosity and fairness
- Telling the truth in a kind way
- Engaging in teamwork when possible
- Utilizing compassionate communication and conflict resolution
- Focusing on how we're similar to others, before considering our differences
- Practicing self-compassion
- Balancing our own needs with the needs of others
- Acknowledging the feelings of others
- Asking for emotional support
- Showing vulnerability with family members

Ideological Values

This category will likely be influenced by your political beliefs, your economic beliefs, and other ideas and ideals related to the functioning of your state, country, and world. Here are several ideological values:

- Supporting equality for all, regardless of ethnicity, race, religion, or sexual orientation
- Advocating for the health of the planet
- Taking pride in our homeland
- Respecting other cultures, especially when traveling
- Following the law
- Campaigning for political candidates we believe in

Spiritual or Religious Values

This category centers around your family's religious or spiritual beliefs and informs how you perceive your existence and purpose, in addition to how you honor those beliefs through actions such as rituals. Examples of spiritual or religious values include the following:

- Praying to a higher power
- Exploring and cherishing the natural world
- Attending church once a week
- Meditating once a day

- Discussing religious or spiritual beliefs once a month during family meetings
- Continually learning about spiritual ideas we resonate with
- Committing to spiritual growth
- Volunteering at our church

Educational Values

This category includes values related to formal education and to the ongoing learning gained through the tapestry of life experiences. Here are a few examples of educational values:

- Consistently looking for learning opportunities
- Searching for joy and fascination in all learning opportunities
- Listening more than we talk
- Asking thoughtful questions
- Practicing diligence when completing school assignments
- Completing schoolwork before play
- Attending a four-year university
- Being open to bypassing formal education in favor of attending the "school of life"

Work and Economic Values

This category weaves together your family philosophy about work in and out of the house, finances such as salary and allowance, and how you choose to spend money. Example work and economic values include the following:

- Doing our best in all work tasks, even when we feel unmotivated
- Completing duties, including chores, in the agreed-upon time frame
- Contemplating why we work and how it contributes to the self, family, and world
- Celebrating achievements
- Not making excuses
- Thoughtfully considering purchases

- Saving more than we spend
- Spending more on experiences than materials

Recreational Values

This category is all about fun and play, and how you spend your time when not at work or in school. It ties in to how your family bonds, creates memories, tries new things, and engages in the richness of life. Here are examples of recreational values:

- Spending every Sunday doing an outdoor family activity
- Having a show that we watch as a family
- Limiting screen time to one hour a day
- Eating dinner together every night, without screens
- Having lots of impromptu dance parties
- Laughing as often as we can
- Scheduling ample time for rest
- Reading together, and often
- Traveling to a new place at least once a year and immersing ourselves in the local culture
- Encouraging one another in creative pursuits

Health Values

This category focuses on your physical health and how you can continually enhance your overall vitality. Example health values include the following:

- Eating fresh, balanced meals as often as possible
- Limiting fast food to once a week
- Getting to know our bodies, specifically the type of foods they do and do not like
- Going to the farmer's market once a week
- Cooking healthy meals together
- Exploring foods and movement practices from other cultures
- Drinking water instead of juice and soda
- Moving our bodies at least thirty minutes every day
- Breathing deeply

- Sleeping at least seven to eight hours (adults) or at least ten hours (kids) every night.

Moral Values

This category consists of your family's broader ideals about how you want to operate in this world. Not surprisingly, these values connect to and influence many of the values in the other categories. Here are some examples of moral values:

- Exhibiting courage
- Doing what we feel is right even when no one is looking
- Selecting the choice we feel is right, not the easiest
- Showing perseverance when faced with resistance
- Seeking validation from ourselves instead of others
- Taking responsibility for missteps
- Exhibiting patience for ourselves and others
- Leaving a space better than we found it
- Striving for fairness
- Honoring our commitments
- Searching for the learning opportunities in failure

The Project P.A.T.H.S.

We can also cull inspiration for values from fifteen positive behaviors outlined in curriculum from the Project P.A.T.H.S., a youth development program. The following fifteen positive behaviors, found to be conducive to healthy adolescent development, inform the Project P.A.T.H.S. and can also inform the formulation of your family values.

- Bonding
- Resilience
- Cognitive competence
- Emotional competence
- Social competence
- Behavioral competence
- Moral competence

- Self-determination
- Self-efficacy
- Beliefs in the future
- Clear and positive identity
- Spirituality
- Prosocial norms
- Prosocial involvement
- Recognition for positive behavior

If your mind is now buzzing with potential family values, I encourage you to pause reading and allow all that inspiration to flow onto the page, or screen. Capture it while it's fresh.

Primary and Secondary Values

As you brainstorm potential family values, you'll find that some feel more essential than others. For example, "treating others with respect and kindness" might seem more vital than "limiting screen time." Evaluating the importance of each value will help you determine which are primary and which are secondary.

Primary values are sacred to your family, influence many of your actions and decisions, and color your perspectives. Secondary values are important but have more wiggle room. For example, some families might feel that "eating dinner together every night" is a worthy value but not one that's paramount to the family's vitality.

Organizing your family values into these two categories can make it easier to manage them and help ensure that you're prioritizing what's most important to your family.

The Unique Needs of Family Members Can Inspire Family Values

Not surprisingly, the personal values of individual family members influence family values. For example, if quality time with family members is of utmost importance to Mom, "spending every Sunday together as a family" might become a primary family value. One of the most effective ways to uncover the personal values of family members is to observe and then discuss.

For about a week, pay attention to what lights up, or triggers, each family member, including yourself, and even your pets! Someone wanting the family to watch a show or work on a puzzle together, another lighting up when receiving help with chores, and someone else often seeking cuddles and verbal reinforcement all provide insight into family members' needs and the attached values.

After you've developed a solid idea of what values resonate with each family member, hold a family meeting where you share what you observed and together brainstorm how these observations can shape family values. Although it will be difficult for very young children to participate in this meeting, you can still share with them what you observed, such as "It seems like you really love it when the whole family is together" or, "I've noticed that having some alone time every day is very important to you."

Here are some examples of values that might come from this process:

- Offering a hug when a family member seems sad
- Acknowledging when a loved one does something kind
- Regularly stating what we appreciate about one another.
- Having a family game night every Friday
- Lending a hand when a loved one is struggling with a task

Exploring the Values You Want to Instill in Your Family

While you've likely already started a list of potential family values, we'll now go deeper into the values you want to instill. Our map into the depths is lined with questions that will support you in taking an honest look at the current state of your family and the values that will help everyone dial up the thrive.

Not to get too existential, but the overarching question I want you to consider when working through all the questions is the big "Why." Why did you have kids? Why is your family here? Why are you here during this moment in time? This "Why" helps you pull back the lens and get to the heart of what you really want for yourself and family. It will help ensure that the values you end up with are authentic and meaningful to your family.

I recommend first going through the following questions alone and then posing them to your family. I also suggest practicing free-flow writing when answering the questions—resist the urge to edit, second-guess yourself, or spell-check. Your goal right now is not to create a clean, complete list of values but instead to open the gates for your stream of thoughts. You'll then scoop family-value gems out of that stream.

- What are our current family values? Where did these values come from?
- Which values do we want to keep? Which do we want to ditch or edit?
- What do we most love doing together?
- What are the most important solo activities for each family member?
- How do we want to feel when we're together?
- What are my ultimate goals for our family?
- What are our wishes for the world around us?
- What are our family mottos?
- How do we want to be remembered?

Tip: Host the initial family meeting about values in a special location free of typical distractions. For example, have the meeting during a beach day or while on a hike. Or maybe go big: treat the family to a vacation and set aside a day to explore family values.

Writing Down Your Family Values

Now that you've poured out your thoughts, you're going to pluck out the family values you jibe with. During this process it's crucial that you actually write down the values. Stanford psychologist Kelly McGonigal shares in her book *The Upside of Stress* that writing about your values is incredibly effective in making people feel more powerful, in control, proud, and strong, in addition to more loving, connected, and empathetic toward others. McGonigal also shares that studies show that writing about values can increase pain tolerance, enhance self-control, and reduce "unhelpful rumination after a stressful experience."

To create your list of values, review your answers to the previous questions and write down values that jump out at you. Then, categorize each as a primary value or secondary value. You can then take this list to a family meeting and see what the others do and do not agree with. Put your final list of values in an often-viewed space and refer to it often.

TIP: Delete all the values your family feels you "should" have but don't actually have. Stay true to what actually matters to you and your family.

Creating Your Family Mission Statement

You're now going to uncover the pith of all these values by working with your family to create your family mission statement. This statement will encapsulate your family's overall goal and serve as a guiding light. When a family member is at a crossroads, they can consider the mission statement and see if it helps them make the choice that will best serve them and the family. This will likely result in family members making more consistent decisions and feeling a deeper bond, as you're all being guided by the same mission. And it's totally fine if you don't feel your family is currently "living up to" the values and mission statement you create. They serve as a goal. Something to strive for. Something to guide your perspectives and actions from this point forward. There's no need to judge yourself on the past—instead, focus on a future glimmering with love, joy, and integrity, however *you* define it.

> **My family's mission statement:** We strive to pause before all that we do and say to ensure we're coming from a space of love and respect. We treat one another as if it's the last time we'll be together. We prioritize connecting with and supporting one another while also creating space for our individual needs. We keep our hearts and eyes open for creative ways to improve and appreciate ourselves, family, and world.

After you've crafted your own family's mission statement, I recommend displaying it above your list of family values and regularly bringing it up, especially during those aforementioned crossroads moments.

What to Do When Family Members Don't Agree on Certain Values

As you work on your family values, you'll probably face some disagreement. The world is such a fascinating place because humans are unique beings with differing values. But it can be super-triggering when anyone, especially a family member, doesn't agree with a value you find important. This can push all your buttons and make you feel determined to change their mind.

For example, my client "Maggie" has a teenage daughter who doesn't share Maggie's value of "spending more on experiences than materials." Maggie was incredibly frustrated by this and went on a mission to convince her daughter that experiences are more important than stuff. But the more Maggie pushed, the more her daughter resisted. Their tension was finally relieved when Maggie realized that the value her daughter placed on materials was her choice, part of her journey, and likely a very natural value for a teen. Maggie also reported that once she stopped trying to push her value onto her daughter, her daughter became more receptive to it. Go figure.

To get to that space of receptivity, here are strategies for navigating the struggle of value disagreement. These strategies don't really apply to young children, as they're still looking to you for guidance on what to value. But that will surely change in a few years!

Discuss the Reasoning for Certain Values

Confusion is often a major piece of family members not sharing a value. To dissolve this confusion, you can explain why you hold a certain value and how it has affected you. You can then ask your family members to explain why they don't find the value important or why they find another value to be more important.

This communication can deepen your understanding of one another and help you find peace with where the other is coming from. But because this conversation might lead to an argument, it's important to set ground rules before starting. You can get inspiration for those rules from the Formula for Tense Discussions section in the previous chapter.

Remember That Value Conflicts Aren't Personal

When someone doesn't share one of our values, it can feel like they're saying, "You're wrong." But often, the differing opinion of a certain value isn't personal, it's just a result of the person's unique perspective. By realizing that a family member not sharing one of your values isn't a judgment on you but instead part of their solo journey, you can often find more acceptance for your differing opinions.

Resist the Urge to Change Their Mind

When you have a value you feel has improved your life, it's natural to try to convince a family member to adopt it. But because we're all walking different paths, a value that works for you might not have the same impact on your partner or child. Accepting this can be uncomfortable because most of us have a strong desire to guide our children, but the more we tolerate that discomfort, the easier it will become. Tolerating that discomfort sends a powerful message to your family members that you accept them exactly as they are and have no agenda to change them.

Leave the Disputed Value off the List

After you've found some peace with the value dispute, you can head back to the family values drawing board and determine if there is a certain value that would be a compromise or choose to leave the disputed value off the list. While it can be hard for you to nix a value you hold dear, remember that it can still be one of your personal values.

Removing the disputed value from the list can also help ensure the values on the final list are actually honored, as family members will be loath to respect the list if they feel their opinions weren't respected when it was crafted.

Discuss Differing Morals

This process might become trickier to navigate if it reveals that you and a family member not only disagree on a certain value but also have differing morals. Discussing it further might not result in a clean resolution, leaving your family with a values gray area. Nevertheless, diving into this discussion can help you begin to better understand your family member and open the door to ongoing discussions that can help you respect one another's views, even if you don't fully agree with them.

Plan for Instilling the Values

The values are listed, the mission statement is complete, and now it's time for the hard part: putting everything into action. Integrating family values into actions is the most potent way to fully embody them and is essential to help children develop a thriving sense of integrity, self-worth, and purpose.

Here are ideas for activities that can help you swirl family values actions into your child's life.

Play

One of the juiciest and lowest-stakes opportunities to expose your children to family values is by creating make-believe scenarios involving a particular value. For example, for the value "standing up for others," you could improv a scene where a teddy bear is saying unkind things to a stuffed penguin, and your child can decide how to support the penguin in this situation. This can be a fun way for a child to absorb values and tinker with various ways to apply them without feeling like they're receiving a lesson.

Art

If your child enjoys exploring the world through art, you can propose different value-related scenarios they can interpret through this medium. For example, if you suggest they draw the value "respecting the Earth," they might sketch different ways they could protect the health of a river or forest. A child can also use their artistic talent to make a card for a loved one going through a hard time, which can promote the value of supporting those in need.

Stories

Reading children's books is an easy way to promote values. For instance, reading a book about Rosa Parks provides examples of values like compassion and courage, while a book like *The Wonderful Things You Will Be* by Emily Winfield Martin can teach values such as exploring creativity and dreaming big. You can also make up stories that weave in family values.

Special Outings

Getting out into the world is a fun way to expose your child to real-life applications of family values. For example, a trip to the grocery store can be a lesson in making healthy choices, being respectful, and waiting one's turn, and a park visit can offer an opportunity to practice patience, cooperation, and compassionate conflict resolution.

Volunteering is overflowing with value-learning potential. When I was a child, my mom and I would visit a woman named Geneva at her nursing home. I was really young but have vivid memories of how much it meant to Geneva when we stopped by. This experience sparked my passion for volunteer work, which I continued into adulthood.

There are age limitations for many volunteer opportunities, but alternatives for the really young ones include collecting toys and taking them to a donation center, planting trees, or helping you make a meal and deliver it to a family in need.

Regularly Discussing the Values

While I don't think talk alone is an effective way to instill values, coupling action with talk can help your family values better resonate with your child. Family-value chats can occur any time, any place, but I find dinner and car time to be opportune moments, as you have a captive audience. During these chats I encourage you to point out examples of how your child and other family members are exhibiting various values instead of focusing on how certain values aren't being honored, as feeling like the values are a chore or a source of shame can cause a child to resist them. You can encourage your child to engage in this discussion by asking how they feel about specific values, for example, "How does it make you feel when you share your toys with friends?"

These chats can also include an annual reevaluation of the values, where the family decides whether some values should be tossed or added.

Kids Do What We Do More Than What We Say

A frustrating truth about parenting is that kids do what we do way more than what we say. Darn. When this truth sunk in for me, I had gotten so good at telling Hudson all the right stuff. "Just do as I say, kid, and you'll have the integrity of Abe Lincoln." But alas, Hudson mainly took note of my actions that would have put Honest Abe to shame. Kids are savvy to our hypocrisy and would call BS if they didn't think we'd reprimand them for using bad f-in' language.

While kids parroting their parents' actions is frustrating on the surface, there's gold beneath, as this dynamic can push you to really start embodying your family values. It can inspire you to reflect on your past actions and become more present during your future actions so you can assess how you're measuring up to the values you spearheaded.

As you work through this self-analysis, note which values you habitually disregard so you can figure out how to break that habit. You might realize that certain values that sound good to your family aren't important enough for you to put into action. And there's nothing wrong with that! It just means you might want to cross that value off your list. There are few things as detrimental to your self-esteem as trying to live up to values that don't actually matter to you.

You can also thrill your child by asking them to tell you when you are, or are not, exhibiting family values. Because children are often the ones being called out for ignoring values and rules, it can give them a sweet taste of power to have permission to also call you out.

When Your Child Strays from the Values

Not surprisingly, children won't always live up to family values. When they don't, some parents experience a mental fear fiesta. The main event at this fiesta is a film showing all the horrible ways a value-defying incident could affect the child's future. For example, "Oh my god, my kid stole a fiver from my purse, which means he's totally going to be a bank robber, or like a crypto thief or whatever the thieves are thieving these days." And so on and so forth. This panic can cause us to have an out-of-proportion reaction to the child's behavior and potentially lead to us shaming them or even injecting them with our fears about their future.

If your mind ever receives an invite to a fear fiesta, try the following.

1. Pause and remember the FEAR acronym: false evidence appearing real. A kid tinkering with something like stealing or lying does not a future criminal make. That behavior is false evidence of a future fraught with trouble.
2. Next, focus on what's happening in that moment. When you isolate the incident and don't connect it to the future, you'll probably realize it's not that big of a deal and probably a sign of normal development. This doesn't mean you'll ignore the issue; it just means you'll be able to handle it in a calmer manner.
3. Reflect on the incident and determine what might have triggered it. For example, if your child said a hurtful phrase you've never heard them say before, you might realize they learned it from a new show they started watching. This detective work can help you determine if there are shifts you want to make in your child's life to make it easier for them to honor family values.

The Power of Why

To understand your child's potential misunderstanding of certain family values, and their motivation for connected behaviors, give them a taste of their own medicine by filling your interactions with "whys." These "whys" can activate your curiosity when spending time with your child and might lead to revelations.

Here's an example of a "why convo" a client shared with me.

> PARENT: "Wow, you screamed really loud when your brother took your doll. Why?"
>
> KID: "I wanted you to notice that he took the doll, and I wanted him to know I'm mad."

PARENT: "Why?"
KID: "Because when I ask him to give doll back, he doesn't. I need help getting her back."
PARENT: "Why?"
KID: "Because she's my best friend and makes me feel safe."
PARENT: "Why?"
KID: "Because she always plays the games I want to play and doesn't tell me I'm wrong."
PARENT: "Why?"
KID: "Because she knows I have good ideas and am perfect just as me."

This interaction helped my client realize that her daughter wanted more help advocating for her needs when playing with her brother. She also suspected her daughter needed more self-esteem boosting.

You can obviously use more than the word *why* in these conversations, but the idea is you're only asking questions. You're not judging or telling your child what they should think, you're simply digging deeper and deeper into their thoughts. This kind of convo can be an incredible experience for a child, as they'll likely be able to sense that they have your full attention and you're genuinely interested in what they have to say.

The "why convo" can also help us realize that when children plaster us with "whys," they're not trying to irritate us but really want to know more about the topic at hand. The world is a mystery to children, and they're thirsty for information. "Why" is the quickest way to get a sip of that knowledge.

Guided Meditation

The meditation at the following link helps you achieve a bird's-eye view of your ideal vision of yourself, family, and the world so you can pinpoint the family values you want to suggest: https://www.baileygaddis.com/family-values.

Writing Prompts

- What are my heartfelt wishes for myself, my children, my partner, my extended family, and the world?
- What are the most important facets of my family's life?
- What are the personal values of each family member?
- Which current familial habits need to be reevaluated, augmented, or even eliminated?
- Which current familial habits do we want to continue?
- What are our primary and secondary family values?
- Am I doing anything to undermine certain family values?
- What activities will help us put our family values into action?
- What's our plan for when family values aren't honored?
- How often will we reevaluate family values?

Parenting Plan

Primary family values:

Secondary family values:

Family mission statement:

Activities to promote family values:

8

ELEMENT 6: TRAVERSING THE JUNGLE OF THE PARENT-CHILD SOCIAL SCENE

THE PROVERBIAL "THEY" DON'T WARN US that parenthood returns us to the social vulnerabilities reminiscent of middle school. Only this time it's worse, because now you're not just navigating your own social vulnerabilities but your kid's as well. And they'll likely be put in situations where they're left out, pushed down, embarrassed, and more. They'll probably also be the perpetrator in some of those situations. But it's all normal, especially when they're little and still learning social graces such as asking nicely for a toy instead of pushing another child into the sandpit and swooping in on their loot while the child is wiping sand out of their eyes.

And then our kids enter adolescence, and all the social issues clear up. Ha! I wish. As children navigate the social landscape of these later years, it can feel like we're watching them participate in the Hunger Games and can't do anything to help. It's like the more they seek independence, the more life throws at them gnarly social dynamics, such as bullying. Needless to say, this phase of parenthood can be heartbreaking, perplexing, and oh so frustrating. But while we might have less direct influence on our child's social life during this stage, there are still ways we can offer guidance and support.

As we do our best to guide our children through socializing, we're also on our own awkward journey of trying to make friends with other parents. For me, there are few things as nerve-racking as walking up to a circle of chatting moms at places like school pickup or the park. Sure, these mom circles are often much nicer than the circles of girls I encountered in middle school, but feelings of exclusion, insecurity, and jealousy still crop up.

To make this essential part of life a little less painful, and maybe even uplifting, we're going to explore ideas to help you craft the Social Life portion of your Parenting Plan in a way that honors the social preferences of both you and your child. We'll work on customizing plans for things like social situations that meet the timing and location needs of you and your child, boundaries during social interactions, bullying, breaking up with friends, working through social insecurities you or your child might experience, and more. And because life includes a ton of other responsibilities, we'll also tackle how to craft a social calendar that fits into your family and work schedule.

My hope is that by the end of this chapter you feel confident in your ability to build a thriving social life for you and your child and to guide them through the unpredictability, beauty, and potential pain of interacting with their peers. And if you have a "caterpillar tummy" of nerves, as my son calls it, about all this socializing, you will be equipped with strategies for replacing those nerves with excitement for the possibility of fresh friendships and emotional growth.

The Importance of Play

One of the primary reasons we want to get young kids into the social scene is because it's essential for their emotional intelligence (EQ), or their ability to regulate emotions and connect with others. Playing with other kids not only provides the most potent opportunities for a child's EQ to blossom but also builds cognitive learning connections in their brain and can help them form lasting bonds through shared exploration and amusement.

Play can also foster brain development and intellectual resources such as creativity and theory of mind, which is the ability to recognize that other people can have mental states different from yours and to understand those varying mental states. In addition, a study published in the *American Journal of Public Health* found that young children who exhibit social competencies such as sharing, cooperating, or helping other kids might be more likely to seek higher education and receive well-paying jobs. Last, and not surprising, play can spark positive emotions like interest, contentment, pride, and love.

As a child ages, the positive impact of play continues, supporting them in exploring and understanding complex social dynamics, building resilience and creativity, reducing stress, and providing other benefits that make life way more interesting and enjoyable. Sadly, many of us have been programmed to believe that as we age, play should take a back seat to more serious pursuits, and we lose the benefits. Sure, we acquire more responsibilities as we age, but allowing ourselves to still prioritize play can have a profound influence on almost all aspects of our human experience.

So in the case of play, the juice box is worth the squeeze—for all ages.

Stages of Play

The sociologist Mildred Parten made the valuable observation that play in young children can be categorized into six stages: unoccupied play, onlooker play, solitary play, parallel play, associative play, and cooperative play. Understanding these stages can help you form realistic expectations for the type of play your young child can engage in. For example, a parent expecting a two-year-old to engage in ample cooperative play might freak when their child refuses to allow their cousin to play dollhouse with her. But that freak out is unnecessary, because that play behavior in a two-year-old is normal. Even when the child is older, it's natural for her to occasionally revert back to an earlier stage of play.

Knowledge of the stages of play also helps parents support their child in navigating the stage they're currently in. For example, if Grandma is pushing a three-year-old to play a board game, Dad can step in and remind Grandma that kind of play isn't part of the stage the child is in.

Dad can then help Grandma find an activity that is appropriate for their child's age and stage.

Here's a breakdown of each stage.

- **Unoccupied play.** From birth to three months, children typically watch anything they find interesting but do not engage with it. If nothing catches their interest, the child's eyes might scan their surroundings or focus on their hands or feet.
- **Onlooker play.** From birth to age two, children can exhibit onlooker play, meaning they observe the play of others but don't engage. Sometimes the child moves closer to the play or occasionally asks a question.
- **Solitary play.** Those zero- to two-year-olds might also engage in solitary play. If the child's play intersects with another child's play during this stage, typically the only interaction that occurs is one child taking the other's toy.
- **Parallel play.** Between a child's second and third year, they'll start tinkering with parallel play. This play involves the child doing their own thing alongside another child.
- **Associative play.** Somewhere between age three and four, and sometimes earlier, children start throwing associative play into the mix. This is when children become more interested in what other children are saying or doing and start engaging with them. They might even willingly share toys.
- **Cooperative play.** By age four to six, children are ready to work together. This is when make-believe play starts taking shape and children assign themselves roles such as firefighter and kitten stuck in a tree. During this stage, children cooperate when crafting the rules, such as coming up with a storyline and casting roles. This stage is much more complex than previous stages and often indicates the child has reached a higher level of social and intellectual maturity.

How to Find Friends

One of the trickiest parts of socializing is figuring out where to find people you and your child want to befriend. If your child has siblings, cousins, or other loved ones they often see, that's great and will certainly support their social development, but it's also important for them to spend time engaging with children of their same age and stage of play, and you with their caregivers.

Here are ideas for where to meet other parent-child pairs:

- **Education-based classes, such as Resources for Infant Educarers.** These classes offer a mix of playing and learning that can provide ample fodder for conversation after the class.
- **Play groups.** These informal groups usually meet on a regular day and time at the park or someone's home and consist of kids playing and parents chatting. Play groups can be found through social media groups or word of mouth. You can also start your own and expand your social circle by asking the people you invite to invite others with children of a similar age.
- **Libraries.** Libraries often host story time and workshops for young children and are a great place to strike up a quiet convo with another parent.
- **Parks.** Offering to push your child on the swing when you spot another parent-child duo at the swings, commiserating with a mom trying to figure out how to collapse the stroller, or offering apple slices to the parent holding a kid who's screaming, "Hungry now!" are just a few of the numerous friend-meeting opportunities the park provides. And when you're ready to shake things up, you can do something crazy and visit a new park.
- **Swimming, tumbling, music, or other classes.** Socialize your child while also tiring them out by signing them up for one of the many classes offered by organizations such as the YMCA or local recreational centers. Many of these are classes that require parents to stick around, which often leads to those parents becoming friends.
- **Parent groups.** Organizations like MOMS Club and MomCo have chapters across the United States that host parent meetups,

which typically include food and a speaker or activity. This is an efficient way to make parent friends, as there are lots of local parents in one place and the kids aren't there to distract you.

- **School.** This is one of my favorite ways to meet new parent-kid friends because the kids do most of the work for us. For example, if Maddie forges a bond with Maxwell, it'll feel totally normal to text Maxwell's parents asking if they want to have a playdate. While initially nerve-racking, school drop-off and pickup are also great times to strike up connections with other parents.
- **Apps like Peanut.** Meeting new parent-child duos can feel a lot like dating, which is why there are now apps that can help you platonically match with parents you might be a good fit for. Popular apps include Peanut, Hello Mamas, Mama Leave, Fatherli, and DadApp. There are even apps to help you find platonic coparents, which I think is amazing and might just transform our society.
- **Sports, theater, or other organized groups.** When your child gets older, signing up for extracurriculars such as sports, theater, or additional activities that bring together kids with a common goal can be an excellent way for them to forge quality bonds. You can piggyback on this bonding by volunteering for the group when you're able, as it will likely involve you getting to know other parents.

Engaging in any of these options can feel like stepping into a parenting labyrinth that contains ample opportunity for not only exciting discoveries but also social threats. Although the potential threats might seem scary to both you and your child, pushing yourselves through the fear can support the blossoming of your child's emotional intelligence and social life while also creating opportunities for you to make new friends and prove to yourself that you're a courageous badass.

With that said, it can be helpful to assess how far you feel comfortable pushing your child, depending on their disposition, interests, and so on. While pushing through the initial discomfort can often result in a breakthrough and an amazing experience for all, you might push through only to realize that the group might not be the best fit. This doesn't mean you or your child is at fault, it just means we all have different environments where we thrive.

To assess if a new group is meeting your child's unique needs, you can develop criteria that help you assess if the group is worth continuing. For example, does it include kids your child is bonding with? Does it stretch your child's creativity? Does it challenge them in helpful ways? If your kid is older, you can create these criteria with them.

When I was growing up, the prevailing belief was that quitting anything, especially a sports team, was "weak." Thankfully, it seems many people now understand that finding where we fit can take some trial and error, and that quitting something that isn't right for you or your child, to find something that is, might be one of the bravest things you can do.

How Long Can You and Kiddo Hang?

A young child's ability to keep their chill usually expires after a certain amount of time. And once it expires, stuff can get crazy: punches and hair pulls, shrieks, and straight-up anarchy might ensue. Because of this, it's important to thoughtfully time your kid's social interactions. I didn't do this when Hudson was little, and it bit me in my stretchy-pants-covered tush frequently, as he also did on one such occasion (ouch). I so desperately wanted us to make friends that I'd say yes to play groups that coincided with nap time, outings that got us home way after bedtime, and other events that meant I wouldn't have time to work that day. I was sacrificing our needs in favor of being social, and it wasn't sustainable.

Once I started honoring our timing needs, social interactions felt more relaxed and balanced. I wasn't harboring unfair resentment toward our new buddies for unknowingly throwing off the rhythm of our day, and Hudson wasn't melting down halfway through swim time at Little Buddy's house.

I was able to achieve this balance after considering the following.

- When does my child nap? Do as I rarely did and view your child's nap schedule as a sacred period of time that will cause the bowels of Earth to tremble if it isn't honored. No friendship is worth losing a nap!

- When does my child eat? While a social engagement during lunch or snack time is totally doable, it's wise to bring some of the foods your child eats during that meal.
- How long can we stay interested in one location and set of people? If socializing drags on and on, it's possible that your child, and maybe you too, will get bored. Figuring out the timing sweet spot for you and your child can help you set a time frame for get-togethers or only choose classes that meet for a certain amount of time. For example, you might say, "We'd love to come over at 10, and we'll be able to stay until 11:30."
- What else do I need to do that day? As a human with many responsibilities, it's fair to sometimes turn down social offers or reschedule if you have a lot to do. Your parent-child social life will survive you putting your personal and professional schedule first when needed.

Here are a few more timing tips and tricks for socializing that I picked up in the parenthood trenches:

- **Have a go-to excuse for leaving if things go sideways.** While you can certainly be honest about your reason for cutting out on a social engagement, discomfort over that honest-talk can make some people (like me) stick around, even when everything is unraveling. If the thought of saying something like "Your child is being way too rough, so we're going to leave" makes you squirm, come up with go-to excuses for exiting. For example, "I totally spaced on a call I have to do in thirty minutes," or "My partner texted, and they need me to drop something off at their office ASAP." Or "My neighbor just called and said they saw a UFO abduct my cat and I think I left the oven on and I think my kid is on the verge of diarrhea. Later!"

  Tip: If they're old enough to understand, you can give your children a code word to use if they're ready to leave the hangout but don't feel comfortable announcing it.
- **Plan for things to run late.** On the flip side of trying to get away from a social engagement, you might find yourself staying longer

than expected because everyone is having so much fun. Because of this possibility, I like to schedule an hour buffer after social engagements.

- **Don't be afraid to reschedule.** Rescheduling texts are one of the most common messages parents of young children send and receive. Sometimes a playdate actually happening feels like a miracle. So don't feel guilty if an hour before a meetup, your child is freaking out and you decide that her being around others is not wise. When you're on the receiving end of a rescheduling text, remind yourself that it's absolutely not personal and all about what's happening for that family.
- **Wait until the day of to tell your child about a playdate.** If your child is old enough to get excited about an upcoming playdate, it's often best to hold off on sharing the news until the day of, because of all that aforementioned rescheduling.

Older Kids

When kids are old enough to have drop-off playdates, you probably won't be as engaged in their interactions as you were when they were younger, but if you're hosting the "date" you'll still have to be "on" and attend to the needs and safety of an additional child. While this play time with peers is important, you can shoot for quality over quantity and protect your energy by setting a clear pickup time with the other parent. It's also helpful to request a specific pickup time when you're the one doing the drop-off.

In the past, I'd often say to another parent, "The kids are doing fine. Your very loud, sweet, and always hungry child is welcome to stay until whenever!" Or at least a version of that. I thought this "whenever" pickup time would build goodwill and be fun for the kids, but instead it frequently resulted in the kids getting bored, everyone getting cranky, and me requiring a long nap.

Location Considerations for Social Interactions

Much like timing, location has a major impact on how a social situation unfolds. For example, if your child is terrified of animals, a playdate at the zoo might not be ideal. Or if your child is at a stage where they yell all their words, the library might be stressful. Here are some geographic factors that can help you craft social engagements that set up you and your child for quality interactions:

- Where does my child thrive? At the park? On a nature walk? In a cozy playroom?
- What locations are tricky for my child? Are there ways to make these locations less tricky? For example, if your child has a hard time sharing toys, you can make their room off-limits during a playdate and instead host everyone in your backyard. Don't be afraid to make decisions that make life a little easier for you and your child.
- Who will be at the location? Often, who is at a certain location is more important than the location itself. For example, if your child consistently has conflict with a certain child, you might opt out of a music class the other child attends. Or if your child struggles with big groups, you might turn down an invite to a large playgroup. You get to be picky about people.

Big Emotion Management in Social Settings

After creating the Big Emotions section of your Parenting Plan, you hopefully have a clear idea of how to support your child through big emotions. But because being around other people, especially those we don't know very well, can sometimes throw a wrench into our best-laid plans, we're going to consider ways you can adapt your plans in social settings.

- **Keep an eye out for cues.** Most kids display certain signs before they totally lose their marbles. For example, my daughter makes frequent high-pitched squeaks when she's feeling agitated. If I act when these squeaks begin, I can often soothe her before she gets to tantrum territory. You're probably well aware of your child's pre-meltdown signs, but if not, you can start taking note of what they often do before unraveling.
- **Focus on your child more than on saving face.** I regularly have the urge to throw my parenting instincts and plans into the wind

in favor of appearing a certain way to others. The main people affected by this decision are my kids. They deserve a mama who pushes past her desire to save face and instead supports them in their big emotions in the manner they're used to. I'm working on it.

- **Remember that we've all been there.** I can almost guarantee every parent has been in a public meltdown situation with their kid. So when it's happening to you, the other parents are likely silently commiserating with you instead of judging (unless they're real jerks). You are not being tested on your parenting skills and do not need to be embarrassed by your child having an emotional display.
- **Say less when you want to say more.** It can be incredibly triggering if another parent says or does something insensitive in relation to your child. While no one would fault you for clapping back in such a situation, it often stirs up more trouble than it's worth. When I've been in situations where choice words for another parent filled my mouth, I've never regretted swallowing them until I processed the situation. When I feel like it's important to address something the other parent said or did, I typically write an e-mail at least twenty-four hours after the incident so I can thoughtfully explain my feelings.

Social Boundaries

You can create more harmony during parent-child social time by setting boundaries. To create these boundaries, consider your child's personality and needs, and what you are and are not OK with happening during that social time.

Here are some examples of social-interaction boundaries for children:

- Keep hands to yourself unless both parties agree to a gentle hug or holding hands.
- Leave beloved toys at home.
- Only use kind language.
- Come to a parent for support when you feel upset.

Examples of social-interaction boundaries for parents:

- Leave after an hour.
- Do not allow other adults to touch my child unless they are keeping my child from harm.
- Remove my child if they or another child are consistently rough.

Older Kids

While you won't be present for all your older child's social interactions, you can still discuss the social boundaries you and they feel are important. This not only can help you reiterate rules you've set for them, but also allows you to share hopes for how your child is treated by peers, and vice versa, and boundaries that could make those hopes a reality. In addition to social boundaries, this can be a good time to discuss physical boundaries and consent, depending on your child's age.

When I first determined my social boundaries as a teen, after my mom forced me to attend a weekend workshop I secretly ended up loving, I felt like my social life went from quicksand to solid ground. While I didn't always honor these boundaries, they helped me feel more secure and understand that my comfort, safety, and needs weren't less important than those of others.

Helping Your Child Effectively Communicate with Peers

Fostering the development of your children's communication skills can smooth the edges of their time with other children, helping to ensure all involved have a more positive experience. Here are some ideas to start with:

Provide Consistent Messages About Physical Force

You can minimize the chance that your child will communicate through physical force by dissuading them from using that force with you or other family members, at any age. I wasn't great at this because I wasn't too bothered by my son tugging on my leg, pulling my face toward his when he wanted to say something, or squeezing me as tight as he could around the neck when hugging. The problem was, if he did these things to another child, he could hurt them. I gave very mixed messages by letting him use that force with me, but not with others. Things got better when I finally became consistent.

This consistency was especially important when my son wanted to tussle with a friend, which was always. Other parents would often say, "It's fine. Let them be. They're having fun," until someone got hurt and chaos ensued. This scenario led to so many tense moments and injuries that I put a complete kibosh on physical force with others, even if it was "just for fun." When such a situation would eventually arise, I'd tell the other parent that I no longer allowed Hudson to engage in this type of play because it had resulted in too much injury. Most parents would understand this and support me in reminding the kids that physical force with one another wasn't an option. This same boundary can be set with siblings.

With that said, I could tell my son still had the urge to kick and punch, so we enrolled him in Tae Kwon Do classes. It was a game changer. He suddenly had a safe outlet for his combat proclivity, and was taught how to control it and when it was and was not appropriate to engage in. If your child seems to have the need to express their power through their body, it can be interesting to explore safe and stimulating outlets that allow them to fully explore whatever needs to come out.

Don't Interject When Kids Are Having a Nonphysical Disagreement

I'm always tempted to jump in when my kids are having a disagreement with other kids. But often, they're able to resolve issues on their own. Giving children the space to work out their issues, while we subtly supervise, can do wonders in teaching them how to navigate tricky social dynamics and boosting their self-esteem.

Promote Empathy

Jane Goodall said, "Empathy is really important . . . Only when our clever brain and our human heart work together in harmony can we achieve our full potential." Helping your child learn to connect their brain and heart can significantly affect their friendships. Being able to see a situation from another's point of view and connect to that person's joy, curiosity, or pain will help the people they interact with feel seen and heard.

While young children typically aren't able to fully understand the concept of empathy, they are naturally developing it. We can support them in this development by pointing out others' emotions and encouraging them to notice if there's anything they can do to support those people. For example, if your child sees a little boy crying at the beach, you could ask your child why they think the boy is sad. Your child might then notice that the boy's sandcastle was ruined by a wave. You can ask if your child has ideas about how to support the child, and they might decide to approach the boy and ask if they can help them build a new sandcastle. The idea is not to force the child into empathy but instead help them notice opportunities for expressing it. Guidance toward empathy can be life-changing when kids enter middle and high school, where it sometimes seems empathy goes to die. We'll get deeper into this shortly.

Dispute Resolution Plan

When children are unable to resolve a conflict, parents have to step in. But when you're navigating this with the parent of the other child, the journey to resolution can feel fraught with land mines, specifically if your resolution strategies conflict.

Set yourself up for a smooth-ish conflict resolution session by trying the following.

- **Ask the other parent for ideas.** Unless a situation requires immediate action, you can ask the other parent how they would typically navigate such a conflict. This question encourages them to pause and really consider how to move forward, instead of simply acting on instinct. It also gives you a heads-up about what to expect from them.
- **Offer your ideas for conflict resolution.** After learning how the other parent would like to resolve the conflict, you can share your ideas and suggest a compromise. For example, if Callie says that the kids both need a time-out because they keep fighting over a

toy, Jessie might suggest that they instead take the kids into the backyard where there is a playscape, and no toys to fight over.

- **Avoid blaming.** A natural instinct for many is to figure out who is at fault when an interaction goes awry. This fault-finding can lead to intense feelings of shame and injustice, as most conflicts live in the gray area. Children are often more receptive to an adult's attempts to resolve a conflict if no one is blamed and the primary goal is to regain harmony instead of reviewing all the "wrongs" of each child. This can also help you avoid making the other parent bristle.

Tweens and Teens

Looking back on my middle school experience, I'm shocked by my and my friends' lack of conflict resolution skills. If we were upset with someone, we of course wouldn't discuss it with them but instead talk behind their back. There are few things as gut-wrenching as having your friends go silent when they see you walking toward their cafeteria table.

In one of my more empathetic middle school moments, I wrote a letter to a friend who was being left out of a sleepover, expressing my regret that she wouldn't be there. She forgot the note in the computer lab, where another girl in our friend group found it. This girl shared my note with the rest of the group, ridiculed it, and convinced them that I was now the enemy. They confronted me as a pack when I walked up to them at the Friday night football game. It was immediately clear that they had no desire to resolve anything, but instead to let me know that I was now persona non grata. The girl I'd written the letter to was with them, and now taking my place at the sleepover.

Sadly, this type of story is common in middle school and can of course roll in to high school. While there are many factors at play, I believe one is the lack of conflict resolution skills among adolescents. Thankfully, some schools are starting to weave this into their curriculum, but you can also do your kid a solid by sharing the conflict resolution methods you develop in your Parenting Plan. They probably won't use them perfectly, but at least you're planting seeds that might reap more compassionate, effective resolution skills.

Supporting Your Child Through Social Anxiety

As you introduce your child to the wild world of forging friendships, they might reveal social anxiety. Young children experiencing social anxiety tend to retreat during social interactions, hiding behind a parent, avoiding eye contact and talking, and generally having a difficult time connecting to others. In extreme cases, children can have uncomfortable physical symptoms such as nausea or shaking. Often, the brain of a child with social anxiety is more sensitive to perceived danger, such as the danger of rejection, which can cause an intense fight-or-flight response in social situations. In addition, a study published by Cambridge University Press found that genetics could make some children predisposed to anxiety.

If your child is exhibiting signs of social anxiety, the following are ideas to help them work through this potentially debilitating issue. Many of these ideas can also be adapted for older kids.

Explore Whether Their Anxiety Is Actually Yours

We love our children so deeply that it often feels like they're an extension of us. This can result in us transferring our anxiety to our children, or perceiving anxiety in them when we're the only anxious one.

If you tend to feel social anxiety, pay attention to whether your child mimics your habits in social situations, such as posting up in the corner, focusing on your phone (which is equivalent to a child homing in on a solo activity), and generally avoiding interaction. If you notice them mirroring you, you could try changing your habits, a tricky but doable process we'll soon explore. When you break through some of your own anxious habits, it will likely be easier to determine if your child has their own social anxiety or is actually a social butterfly looking to emerge from a cocoon of anxious conditioning.

Share Your Social Insecurities

Being transparent about your social insecurities can be one of the greatest gifts you give your child. They likely view you as the most amazing person in the galaxy and might find it comforting that even you find socializing difficult. To do this, you could explain how your body feels before and during a social engagement and discuss nervousness over the potential of saying the wrong thing or being left out. Then, as you begin finding strategies to ditch the anxiety, you can share those tools with your child.

Find Examples of a Beloved Character Dealing with Social Insecurities

You can help normalize social anxiety by finding books or television episodes that depict one of your child's favorite characters navigating these insecurities. A resource like CommomSenseMedia.org can help you find shows that convey productive methods for navigating social anxiety and difficult social dynamics.

Talk Through an Upcoming Social Situation

Reduce fear of the unknown by breaking down what your child can expect from an upcoming engagement. For example, you could say, "We're going to the birthday party after naptime. When we get there, we'll say happy birthday to Charlie and then choose an activity. They'll have face painting, cupcake decorating, and games. After that we'll eat pizza and cake, then continue playing until you're ready to leave."

Set a Goal for Each Social Interaction

Make social interactions feel more manageable by helping your child set a goal for each. For example, before going to a playgroup, you and your child might decide that the goal is to ask one child if they want to play with blocks or participate when the kids play hide-and-seek. After they accomplish their goal, you can give them the choice of staying or quietly leaving.

Practice Relaxation Techniques

Teaching kids techniques such as taking ten deep breaths before getting out of the car to go to a gathering can help them lessen their anxiety before and during social situations.

Help Spark a Connection

While you don't want to be your child's voice, or hover when they're socializing, it's sometimes helpful to foster the initial connection between them and another child. For example, if a girl at a birthday party has a dinosaur shirt on, you could say, "I noticed the dinosaur on your shirt. My son Miles really likes dinosaurs. What's your favorite dino?" Hopefully, the children can then carry on the dino discussion. The idea is to help the kids find common ground, then back away.

Avoid Pushing or Shaming

Because we so badly want our children to connect with others, it can be tempting to coerce them into socializing or brush away their concerns. For example, a parent saying, "You have nothing to worry about! The park is fun. Just go play," could make a child feel unheard and even shameful about their anxiety. Even if the anxiety doesn't make sense to the parent, it might feel like life or death to the child. Acknowledging their fears and utilizing gentle encouragement can go a long way toward chipping away the anxiety.

Acknowledge Progress

Inspire your child to continue tiptoeing into a social life by noticing and honoring when they do something as small as saying hello to another child or offering them a toy. Helping them notice these social wins can support them in realizing that they are capable of connecting with and having fun with others.

Seek Support

If your child is four or older and has exhibited signs of social anxiety for six months or more, they might have social anxiety disorder. In this case, the child could benefit from cognitive behavior therapy with a child psychologist.

Releasing Expectations

When engaging in the daunting task of making new friends, expectations can wreck the self-esteem. For example, if you start fantasizing about you and your child having a friendship with the mom and child you met at the park, you might be bummed if they don't reciprocate your desire to meet up again. Typically, adults (at least the emotionally mature ones) don't opt out of a friendship to be cruel, or because they think you're unworthy of their friendship. Often, a friendship not starting or not continuing is the result of busyness. That mom who ghosts you might have such a hectic schedule she barely has time to visit her sister . . . who lives next door to her.

So whenever possible, live in the moment and trust that the friendships you and your child are meant to have will organically evolve.

Resisting the Urge to Judge

It's human nature to judge others. Our brain wants to compare and find reasons to feel good about ourselves. For example, if you see a child biting their sister at the park, you might think, *I can't believe that child is biting. My child would never do that.* This is like a mental pat on the back. A win for the ego. But the bummer with these judgments is that they can then make humble pie so much harder to swallow when it is inevitably served.

Another curse of judging other parents and children is that we might get paranoid that they are doing it to us. And it might not just be paranoia, because when we put that judgmental energy out there, we attract it. It's also all too easy to inadvertently pass our judgey habits on to our kids. They're listening to everything we say and learning from us how to assess differences between themselves and others.

Here are ideas that can help you and your child avoid the bad juju and yucky feels of judging:

- **Replace judgment with empathy.** As soon as I become aware of a judgment, I challenge myself to replace it with kindness. For example, *That sweet little dude is having such a hard time, he thinks his only option is to bite. My child also struggles with how to manage big emotions. Sending love to that boy and mama!*

You can do the same if you hear your child make a judgment such as, "That girl has such a weird outfit on." You might respond by saying something like, "She doesn't seem to mind being different. I think she looks like an exotic flower, and I really like the snakeskin pattern on her leggings." This statement doesn't shame your kid for making a judgment but gently offers a different, more open-minded point of view.

- **Understand that change can be uncomfortable.** It was difficult for me to reign in my tendency to judge as I'd become addicted to it. When I began this shift, I was navigating numerous insecurities and judging gave me little, toxic ego boosts. It's like I was trying to steal pieces of healthy self-esteem from others. So phasing out judgments put my ego in withdrawal. It was no longer getting its boosts, and it ached—it was desperate for reassurance that we were OK. This forced me to seek other, healthier ways of nurturing my self-esteem, like spending time with the friends who really get me, writing about what I love about myself, and going deep into nature to gain perspective.
- **Remember how judgments isolate.** After the high of judging someone fades, we might feel alone because the judgment sticks us on an emotional island. Instead of embodying the belief that we're all one, we dig into the belief that we're different and somehow better than that other person. When we get off that emotional island, kind, interesting people and perspectives often find their way into our life.

Supporting Your Adolescent Through Social Challenges

Some of the most courageous among us are the preteens who wake up every day and brave the confusion of puberty, the struggle of desperately wanting to be an adult while still a child, and the anxiety of entering a social gauntlet that can grind them up and then spit them out a changed person. A double-blind study of over thirteen hundred students beginning middle school reported that entering said social gauntlet can frequently cause a decreased sense of social belonging, a decline in academic performance, and an increase in disciplinary infractions and truancies if they do not receive enough emotional support. This suggests that social support should not be an afterthought, only to be focused on after academics, but at the forefront of the guidance adults provide during this incredibly vulnerable time in life.

Because parents aren't able to be with their child during many of the social challenges they encounter, one of the only tools we have, beyond sometimes being able to select the school our child attends, is our words and how we use them to affect our child's perspective of themselves and their peers. The aforementioned study found that offering the following perspective shifts supported many students in experiencing improved social and psychological well-being, reduced instances of misbehavior, increased attendance, and increased grade point averages.

Social struggles and insecurities are really common at this age. You can help your child feel less alone by reminding them that most of their peers, even those who seem super confident and popular, aren't immune to social struggles. This perspective shift can destigmatize your child's issues and maybe even encourage them to talk with other students about it, potentially creating a bonding opportunity. It could also be helpful to model vulnerability by sharing some of your past and current social struggles and how you traversed them.

The worst of the issues will probably be short lived. When a child enters a new grade, or even more intense, starts at a new school, social struggles and insecurities might feel all-consuming and without end. While it's normal for a kid to think that a red-hot problem will be burning them for eternity, the reminder that "this too shall pass" can provide perspective and create an environment of hope.

Social struggles, such as having no one to sit with at lunch, someone making fun of your outfit, or a friend suddenly ignoring you, are due to external issues, not personal inadequacies. Humans of all ages, but especially adolescents, tend to blame themselves when others treat them poorly. They think that if they were just more interesting, or fashionable, or whatever, kids would be nicer. You can help at least some of your child's self-esteem stay intact when navigating unkindness by reminding them that the behavior of another kid has much more to do with the kid's issues than your child's.

What About Bullying?

According to a study published in the *International Journal of Environmental Research and Public Health*, bullying is "intentional and repeated aggressive behavior toward another person in which there is a real or perceived power imbalance, and the victim of bullying feels vulnerable and powerless to protect themselves." This study also found that for the over 167,000 kids aged twelve to seventeen who participated in this study, verbal bullying was the most prevalent type of aggression, and it had the greatest negative effect on mental health.

Bullying goes beyond the standard social struggles most adolescents experience and enters the realm of trauma where a child's physical, psychological, and social functioning are affected and anxiety, depression, suicidal ideation, or self-harm can become serious threats. Bullying is not something kids should have to "tough out." It can have devastating consequences and requires intervention from parents and teachers.

Parents can help thwart bullying by reporting the behavior to teachers and school administrators, seeking support from school or private practice counselors, and in extreme cases changing schools or alerting the authorities. Beyond those options, research has shown that one of the most effective ways parents can help children who are victims of bullying is to put ample attention and intention into four different areas of parenting.

- **Parental supervision.** Parents might be able to become aware of and mitigate some of the negative effects of bullying by being involved in homework completion, staying up-to-date on academic performance, keeping track of their child's whereabouts when not at home or school, maintaining open communication with teachers and with parents of the child's friends, and actively engaging in other supervisory activities. These activities might seem like no-brainers, but it's easy to let them slide as life gets busy and trust in our maturing kids to "handle it on their own" increases.
- **Familial connectedness.** A very painful aspect of bullying is the victim feeling separated from the group and "other than." Parents

can help kids know they matter and belong by promoting family connectedness through family dinners, shared activities, and reminders to family members to provide the bullied child with extra emotional boosts during this tough time. While adolescents have an intense need to belong to their peer group, reassurances that they belong and are accepted by their family can offer a solid, comforting foundation to build on.

- **Intentional bonding.** Parents can increase the chance that their child will open up about the specifics of the bullying, and maybe even absorb some of the guidance they provide, by prioritizing one-on-one bonding opportunities like making a pizza pit stop after school, playing a favorite game together, or finding other activities that offer opportunities for both fun and conversation.
- **Peer support.** Another heartbreaking result of bullying is that children can start believing they're unworthy of friendship and thus isolate themselves. Parents can help temper this by creating opportunities for their child to hang out with a kind, supportive friend. For example, consider having a double date with a friend who has a child around the same age as yours, offering to take your child and a friend of their choice to the movies, finding ways your child can explore a hobby with like-minded peers, or anything else you think would link your child with compassionate peers who could help them start the healing process.

  When I was the victim of bullying in middle school, my parents started driving me across Austin to a kid's musical theater group. I was able to connect with kids who shared a common interest and were more focused on being creative than socially powerful. It was a lifeline my parents made many sacrifices to provide me.

NOTE: If you don't think your child will willingly tell you if they're being bullied, you can look out for common signs, such as the sudden development of anxiety; issues with sleeping, eating, or engaging in hobbies; becoming easily upset; or just seeming "off."

Making an Anti-Bullying Plan

An essential aspect of supporting kids through bullying is helping them make a clear plan for what they'll do when the attack occurs. Even if they don't always follow through with their plan, having it can serve as an anchor of support and minimize their anxiety when in proximity to the bully. Building this plan can also teach them valuable skills, such as how to advocate for themselves and others, examine the potential underlying causes of someone's words and actions, maintain a healthy sense of self-worth despite negative external forces, and display other layers of competence that build strong character.

Not surprisingly, this plan will be most effective if it emerges from your child's beliefs. While you will, of course, offer insight, you can make this a more valuable process by encouraging your child to take the lead, and then champion their ideas.

The following questions can help your child shine light into the dark crevices of bullying, hopefully making it less haunting and a space they feel empowered to conqueror.

- How do you define bullying? What are some of the different ways someone can bully?
- How do you feel when you're bullied?
- What are reasons someone might bully others?
- Do you understand that being the victim of bullying is not your fault?
- What do you think would be the best thing to do if someone bullies you verbally? What about physically?
- Who are safe people you can go to when you're bullied?
- What are actions that could help you stay calm when you're being bullied? What about after you're bullied?
- Can you think of any instances where you might have been the bully? If so, why do you think you did that? Is an apology needed?
- How can you prevent yourself from engaging in bullying behavior?
- What could you do if you see someone else being bullied?

As you discuss these questions, I encourage you and your child to take notes, specifically jotting down ideas that could be incorporated into the plan. You can then review the notes together and brainstorm action steps your child can take when being bullied.

Tip: If your child is hesitant to discuss this topic, you can find an age-appropriate book, podcast, or TV show that addresses bullying and use the content as organic prompts for your discussion.

Here is the anti-bullying plan my son made:

- Press my pointer finger and thumb together and pretend that all my anger is being smashed between the fingers.
- Keep my face totally chill and don't say anything unless I know I can say it calmly. I don't want to give them the satisfaction of seeing me upset or making me say or do something I'll regret.
- Drink some water and go to the bathroom if I feel like I can't control my anger.
- Walk away from conversations that are heading to a mean place.
- If someone is physically attacking me, I'll protect myself while calling out for an adult. If I'm physically able, I'll separate myself from the other kid.
- Avoid being around someone that's acting like a bully.
- Spend more time with my really nice friends who like the things I do.
- Say something nice about the kid that someone is saying mean things about.
- Do lots of nice things for people. That always makes me feel better.
- Not share rumors and ask people to not tell me any gossip.
- If I really need to vent about someone, I'll tell my mom instead of my friends.
- Ask a teacher for help, and keep to myself, on days when I feel really upset and like I might say something mean to someone.

After creating this list, you can print, and even laminate, it so your child can keep it in their backpack to review whenever needed. You can also print a list that includes traits they and you love about them. Seeing this can be a powerful reminder that they're special, loved, and never alone, and a much needed salve on days when the bully strikes.

Navigating Your Relationship with Other Parents

While different, friendships between parents can be just as nerve-racking as friendships between young children. These connections have many unpredictable elements that can push the relationship off course, such as one child smacking another or having to cancel a playdate because Kona missed his nap. It often feels like there's a lot riding on these friendships, as it's common to convince ourselves that if we don't get an "in" with a certain group of parents, we and our child will be left out. This can lead to false beliefs that we're not worthy, or cool, or whatever it is that inner critic is cooking up.

So why do we put up with this emotional chaos? Because quality friendships with other parents are golden. They provide empathic ears into which you can pour your parenting struggles and triumphs, stories that help you remember you're not the only one, and trusted people you can call on if you need support. Building this community can make parenthood feel less lonely, and even fun, but it usually takes time.

A study by associate professor of communication studies Jeffrey Hall at the University of Kansas found that it takes about fifty hours of time with someone to go from acquaintance to casual friend, ninety hours to go from casual friend to friend, and two hundred hours to move from friend to good friend. That sounds like a lot, but the commitment is worth it. Once you gather a few tried-and-true parent friends—those who come over with a pizza and start folding the pile of laundry on your couch without asking—you'll realize that all that time socializing was well spent.

Let's go deeper into the nuances of friendship and belonging, and explore the parallels with the social dynamics adolescents and teens experience, so you're further equipped to guide your child through this passionate, powerful phase of life.

Exploring the Consuming Need for Popularity

I felt like I had emotionally regressed twenty years when I dropped off my son at his first day of preschool. After high school my need for popularity had mostly dissolved as I forged a tight group of friends that had no hierarchy, but my friendship-bliss-bubble popped that morning. I was awkwardly standing behind a group of moms chatting and laughing on the playground. They were in an airtight circle, and it was clear they knew each other well. As I watched, a nauseating combination of exclusion, unworthiness, and self-consciousness gurgled up. These moms had done nothing wrong, but they still triggered all my adolescent insecurities that stemmed from a need for belonging. This need had reigned supreme in my early years and caused me to dress, talk, and think like the kids I thought were cool. I sacrificed my authenticity for inclusion.

With the need for popularity reignited, I felt anxious and needy during every preschool pickup and drop-off. I was terrified I'd be brushed off after trying to start a conversation, or I'd say something embarrassing, or I'd be the only one standing alone when the kids filtered out of the classroom. I felt high on the days when I had what I considered social success. And then the next day I would crash after oversharing about constipation with a mom I'd just met.

Because I was only immersed in this environment for a short period each day, and I was equipped with a variety of coping skills I'd learned over my thirty-five plus years, my emotional regression faded about six months into the school year. By this time I'd gathered enough quality parent-friends to bring me back to the truth of why friends really matter. Their purpose is not to make us feel popular but to help us feel safe to be ourselves, to laugh often (and not at others), and to feel supported in the valleys and peaks of life. The more I reconnected to that truth and nurtured my quality friendships, the more the Pandora's box of popularity obsession closed, at least temporarily.

Understanding the Two Sides of Popularity

Popularity is two-faced. On one side you have "likability popularity" and on the other "status popularity." When children are young and do not yet understand how to use manipulation, comparison, and so on to gain social capital, they become popular by being nice and helpful. Typically, the most "likable popular" young children are those who are cooperative, help others, and serve as fair and subtle leaders. If this were the type of popularity we all strove for, the world would be a better place.

But enter status popularity. The desire for this type of popularity snakes its way into the brain around puberty when hormones start reshaping circuits in the brain. This type of popularity leads to a desire to be seen, have influence, and, for some, exhibit dominance and power, which can result in making fun of others, gossiping, and, essentially, playing social chess. This is the type of popularity that can create lifelong issues.

Research published by University of Virginia professor Joseph Allen reported that those who place high value on their social status in youth have more challenges with interpersonal relationships as they age. These people may forfeit quality friendships in favor of focusing on increasing their status and minimizing the social status of others. This fixation on status can then lead to anxiety, depression, and substance abuse.

Understanding these two types of popularity can not only help us return to our early childhood roots and once again strive for likability instead of status but also support us in offering our children gentle guidance and the powerful example of striving for kindness, helpfulness, and cooperation, instead of power. To learn more about the science of popularity, I recommend reading the book *Popular: The Power of Likability in a Status-Obsessed World* by Mitch Prinstein.

Dealing with Social Insecurities

Now that we've established social insecurities à la middle school might bubble up as you and your child enter the parent-kid social scene, let's brainstorm ways you can deal with those insecurities.

Before we get to my ideas, let's explore the most important thing—your thoughts on this topic.

- What makes you nervous about socializing with new people?
- Where do you think your social insecurities come from? How do they feel in your body?
- What are things you do to soothe those nerves? What are additional strategies you might try?
- How might your child benefit from you working through insecurities and creating friendships with other parent-child duos?
- What are your favorite elements of the friendships you currently have?

- What are some fulfilling social interactions you've recently had?
- What are affirmations you could use when social insecurities appear?
- What do you love about yourself?

Following are ideas you can shape to your liking to dissolve the social insecurities you just explored so you can forge friendships in peace.

Remember That a Friendship Not Panning Out Is a Blessing

While it might feel like a painful rejection when an acquaintance doesn't transition into a friendship, it's one of the best things that could happen to you. It can mean the dynamic was a little off, or that conversations felt forced. Or maybe the other person was simply too busy at this time in their life. Regardless of the reason, you were saved from a friendship that might have caused long-term frustration. In addition, not becoming friends with the people who aren't your people leaves space for the friendships that are meant to be. So relax into the knowingness that you don't need to force things and can let relationships organically evolve.

Seek Out People Who Inspire You to Be Yourself

The age-old advice to "just be yourself" is something I've always struggled with. My desire to be liked has caused me to become a master chameleon. Before I checked myself, what I talked about, the language I used, and even the patter of my voice was strongly influenced by what I thought would make the person I was talking to most comfortable. And sure, a small degree of this can help when first meeting someone, but after a while it should be replaced by your true self. But that didn't happen to me. I just kept chameleon-ing in an effort to please.

When I noticed this character trait, I tinkered with being myself with acquaintances I'd historically changed for. One of two things happened: either that person got uncomfortable and the acquaintance-ship died a natural death, or I finally formed a real connection and a friendship formed. Realizing how good it felt to be myself, I also started exerting less effort with people I found it hard to be "real" around. I shifted my attention to those whom I could have an easy laugh with, drop a few curse words without them cringing, and skip the small talk and go straight to the topics that really mattered, like complaining about our spouses.

Know How to Psych Yourself Up

Before socializing, it can be helpful to apply techniques that help you confidently approach the experience. These techniques can be anything you like, but my favorites are the classic deep breathing, car dancing with my kids to a favorite song, and mentally reciting affirmations such as *It's just as important that I like them as that they like me*, *If the friendship is meant to be, it will be*, and *This interaction is not a sign of my self-worth.*

Plan Interactions with More Than Two People

As you're acclimating to the parent-child social scene, consider alleviating the pressure by putting yourself in situations that involve more than one other parent. This ensures there won't be as much pressure on you to keep a conversation going, and you can test out multiple potential friendships at once.

Regularly Meet Up with Your Non-Parent Friends

Stoke your friend-making confidence and remind yourself of your awesomeness by also investing time in your non-parent friendships, especially the friendships that have existed longer than your kids and involve people who knew you when you could throw down shocking amounts of tequila and hold your own at karaoke. Prioritizing these friends not only ensures the friendships last but also takes pressure off the new friendships you're forming as you're reminded that you already have an amazing base of friends.

Equip Yourself with Conversation Starters

One of the hardest parts of socializing is striking up an engaging conversation, especially with people who answer questions with one word. Ugh. Here are some of my go-to conversation starters:

- Give a compliment.
- Commiserate about something the other person seems to be struggling with. Or, better yet, offer to help.
- When approaching a stranger, ask a general question, such as the time, or what nearby kid-friendly restaurant they'd recommend.

When meeting up with people I know, I make a list of interesting things that have recently happened in my life, questions about the lives of the people I'll be seeing, or general topics that might be a shared interest. These prompts help the convo quickly move past small talk and into the type of conversation that forges deeper friendship.

When my son is experiencing social insecurity, before starting a summer camp for example, I sprinkle ideas such as interesting conversation starters, reminders about focusing on friendships with people who really light him up, and strategies for developing a positive attitude into our casual conversation. If I sat him down and said, "We are now going to work on ways to make you socially secure," his eyes would glaze over. Instead, I slip in my ideas when he's telling me the happenings of his class, sharing thoughts on the actions of characters in books or movies we're watching, and in the rare times when he openly shares a social insecurity with me.

Breaking Up with Parent-Child Friends

Despite your efforts to create amazing friendships, some will feel inauthentic, unsatisfying, or even toxic. This can result from dynamics such as the other child acting in ways that make your child uncomfortable, the other parent speaking to your child in a way you dislike, the other parent subtly putting you down, or a number of other things that sour a friendship. If you decide a friendship no longer works for you, it can be tricky to break up, especially when the other parent is actively trying to continue the friendship.

Here are ideas for exiting a friendship without ruffling too many feathers.

- **Write a letter.** Letters are a thoughtful, thorough way to compassionately express your feelings and potentially bypass a tense conversation. A letter also allows the other person to review your thoughts in their own time. But be careful with what you write, as the letter might be shown to others or kept indefinitely. Keep it as kind and clear as possible.

- **Phase out meetups.** If you don't need to exit the friendship ASAP and you feel uncomfortable telling the other parent your concerns, you can phase out the friendship. For example, if you typically meet up every two weeks, you might beg out of every other meetup, then continue to decline invitations until the relationship peters out.
- **Break up in person.** If you are a much braver person than me and prefer discussing delicate issues in person, you can break up during a one-on-one meeting. If you do, I recommend planning out what you're going to say, and brainstorming ways to make your messages gentle and nonjudgmental so an argument doesn't ensue.

  Tip: Whatever you do, don't bad-mouth the parent to other parents or your children. Even if they got super unpleasant when you broke up, speaking poorly of them will just stir up drama and cause hurt.
- **Maintain the kids' connection.** If you're in a situation where you want to exit your friendship with the parent but continue the kids' relationship, it's possible, but delicate. While being honest about your feelings with the other parent is an honorable option, let's be real. Unless the other parent has the tolerance and grace of Buddha, they'll probably be offended that you don't want to hang with them as much and thus limit the time their child spends with yours.

  A more tactful option might be to ask one of your child's other caregivers to accompany them when on a playdate with the parent-child duo in question. You could also find ways the kids can be together that don't involve a lot of parent interaction, such as extracurricular activities that just require parent drop-off and pickup. While it might initially be a tricky line to walk, it is possible to engage in this partial breakup, especially as the kids age and require less parent involvement in their friendship.

Older Kids

There will likely come a time when your child has a friend, we'll call them X, that you hope your child breaks up with. Maybe you suspect X is unkind to your child or engages in illicit behavior, or maybe you just get an overall bad vibe. But unfortunately, gone are the days when you can sever the tie by simply not planning more playdates. While you can deny your child's request to take them to X's home or allow X to come to yours, your child will likely still find ways to maintain the friendship, especially if the kids go to school together, or have smartphones.

If you want to encourage a breakup of the friendship in question, you probably need to go about it really gently, as kids sometimes have a desire to spend *more* time with a friend their parent isn't cool with. In addition to the aforementioned limits, like not allowing X to come to your home, your best chance of triggering the breakup is to consider and discuss the following points with your child and hope they eventually see the light.

- Discuss specific behavior you've witnessed in X, not personal judgments of them.
- Ask your child how they feel when they're with X. Is X nice to them? What do they get out of the friendship?
- Ask your child to make a list of traits their ideal friend would have. Doing this could help your child realize X doesn't check enough of their boxes.
- Discuss other ways your child could spend their time if they no longer hung out with X.
- Determine what, if any, unwanted behavior your child was exhibiting before they met X, and what behaviors began after. (In some cases, we might discover that X is just mirroring our child's behavior and isn't the core issue.)
- You might want to limit defensiveness by noting the many ways you trust your child and their judgment.

These are just some of the many angles you can come at this situation from. Although this is a complicated phase of parenting where you no longer have total control of your child's social life, you also can't leave it completely up to them. Keep tinkering around with potential limits and points of view you could share to help your child connect with the friends who lift them up and drop the ones pulling them down. Because life is messy and ever-changing, your child's friendships will never be perfect, and that's OK. It's what keeps life interesting.

Creating an Ideal Formula for Your Child's Social Life

Now that you've considered the type of parent-child socializing you want in your life, it's time to weave it into your schedule. To start, research opportunities for socializing in your area, make a list of the ones you feel would be a good fit, and then determine how much socializing the two of you can handle.

To start mixing the socializing formula you just created into your life, peruse your schedule to see if there are times available when you and your child will be in a good place to interact with other humans. Then, slot those social opportunities into the schedule and commit to going, even if you're nervous.

If it feels near impossible to fit additional social opportunities into your schedule, try the following:

- **Nix lower-priority activities.** Pinpoint the nonessential engagements on the schedule that you're always hoping will be canceled. For example, maybe your older child is in a soccer league that they hate but your partner really wants them to play. Talking with your partner and child about cutting this activity could bring immense relief and extra time you can use to help your little one make some friends.
- **Ask for help.** Sadly, many of us have the mistaken belief that asking for help is a sign of laziness or weakness. This often leads to martyring ourselves to keep the family afloat. But I propose that asking for help is the ultimate sign of courage. So if you're open to it, consider delegating certain tasks on your weekly schedule. For example, maybe you can move cleaning day to Saturday so

your partner can help. Or you can ask your mother-in-law to pick up your older child from school every Wednesday so you can take the little one to music class.

- **Combine socializing with other activities.** If you still feel like there's no breathing room in your schedule, get creative and brainstorm ways to mix your parent-child social life into certain engagements. For example, if you go to the farmer's market every Sunday, you might invite that mom and child pair you just met at the park to join you.

Guided Meditation

The meditation at the following link will support you in releasing social insecurities, envisioning your child having a thriving social life, and reveling in the truth that you and your child are amazing people worthy of deep, meaningful friendships: https://www.baileygaddis.com/friendships.

Writing Prompts

- What locations or groups can you frequent to meet new parent-child friends? Or connect your older child with new friends?
- Do you want to use apps to meet friends?
- What would an ideal friendship look like for you? And for your child?
- What are your nonnegotiables for your friends? And for your child's friends?
- Which current friendships do you want to nurture? Which of your child's friendships do you want to nurture?
- Are there any friends you or your child need to break up with?
- Does your child have any friends you're uncomfortable with? What's your plan for navigating your influence over these relationships?
- Do you have social insecurities? If so, where do you think those insecurities stem from?
- Does your child have social insecurities? If so, where do you think those insecurities stem from?

- What would it feel like to release social insecurities? How do you think you can start that process for yourself? How can you start that process for your child?
- What resolution techniques have worked for you in past conflicts between your child and another? What about conflicts between you and another parent? What are strategies that didn't work for you?

Parenting Plan

Favorite parent-child socializing activities:

Desired frequency of socializing:

Favorite old friends to keep in touch with:

New friendships to nurture for me:

New friendships to nurture for my child:

Qualities of an ideal friend for me:

Qualities of an ideal friend for my child:

Resolution plan for conflicts between children:

Resolution plan for conflicts between parents:

Pre-socializing preparation plan:

What makes my child an amazing friend:

What makes me an amazing friend:

9

ELEMENT 7: CREATING A FAMILY SCHEDULE AND ROUTINES

As a former home organizer and current neat freak, routines, organization, and cleanliness are three of my primary lifelines. Maybe you can relate? If not, I'll bet having at least a semblance of order is important to you. I'll also bet that this order can support you and your family in becoming a more relaxed, symbiotic ecosystem.

Through my years working with parents to organize both their home and overall life, I saw how finding the level of "order" and resulting routines that were right for them allowed them to thrive. This makes sense, as scheduling these routines helps families know what to expect from their day. Schedules and routines offer a framework for what needs to happen when, so the mind can be free to focus on more enjoyable pursuits instead of scrambling to figure out how to get *x*, *y*, and *z* done.

While some believe creating and scheduling routines makes life rigid, many are surprised to find that this planning and order result in more space for fun and spontaneity, and enhanced pride and comfort in oneself and one's home. Families might also experience less conflict as everyone becomes more attuned to the rhythms, needs, and mental and physical capacities of other family members.

So let's change your life by creating a time map of your day, transforming you into a routine-making master, discovering the natural rhythms and needs of your family members, and keeping your house and kid clean, while also getting all their poop and pee in the toilet.

Wielding the Magic of Routines

A complaint I've often heard is that sticking to routines is boring and makes every day feel like the last. I totally understand this, because I used to be the one making that complaint.

In my early twenties I lived by the tenet, "I'll do that when I feel like it." But the problem was I rarely "felt like it," especially when "it" was a task like exercising, doing laundry, or getting an oil change. What I did feel like was baking, binging reality TV shows, and partying with friends. When this lifestyle eventually led to depression and anxiety, I turned to routines. I started waking up at 7:00 AM, making the bed, exercising, and then showering, followed by a short meditation. I would then eat a healthy breakfast and work for three hours. I'd take a thirty-minute break and get back to work. After 6:00 PM I had free time for fun stuff like laundry, dishes, and talking myself out of cleaning the toilet, and I would be in bed by 10:30. I also broke up work tasks by category. For example, on Monday I'd focus on writing projects, Tuesday I'd take care of clerical work, and so on.

The first month of this regimented life was hard. When I didn't feel like doing "it," I had to push through major resistance to stick to my plan. And sometimes I didn't stick to it. But by the end of the month, the routines created drastic shifts in my life, leaving me happier, healthier, and more productive.

When I had my son, my routines had to change, but that wasn't too difficult because my dedication to routines was embedded. I had been living the benefits of a routine, organized life, and it felt organic to weave it into motherhood. I'm still regularly tempted to shrug off my routines with the support of the remote, a cozy blanket, and a pint of Ben and Jerry's, but if I stick to my plan at least 80 percent of the time, I stay relatively sane and happy.

With all that said, it's difficult to continue routines if you find many of the tasks mundane. To dissolve the blah, try the following:

- **Make every act an act of love.** When you're doing things like washing dishes or changing a diaper, acknowledge that what you're doing is a profound act of love. You're acting in service to your family; you're offering time and care to help it thrive. You can also consider how blessed you are to have people who need you, and whom you can support in both simple and complex ways.
- **Liven up tedious tasks.** Most boring activities have space for fun and creativity. For example, turning on dance music while doing the dishes can groove the monotony out of that dirty job. Or, telling your child how much you love them, and what your hopes are for their future, while changing their diaper can turn that stinky job into a moment of connection. One of my favorite ways to entertain or enrich myself during solo activities is by listening to an audiobook or podcast.
- **Summon the Zen force.** If meditation and mindfulness are on your wellness to-do list, nurture two birds with one mind by being as present as possible when doing monotonous tasks. For example, when vacuuming, quiet the mind by fully focusing on the vibration of the machine, the patterns it makes in the carpet, and the white noise it creates. Who knows, the days that are filled with chores and errands just might become your most relaxing.
- **Delegate.** If you feel you have an unreasonable number of obligations, or you feel certain tasks could be done more efficiently by someone else, delegate. This might mean asking your partner to take over the job of mopping every Sunday, hiring a gardener, or doing whatever else is needed to have others complete the tasks that make you say "ugh."
- **Teach your children these ideas.** Do your kids a major solid by incorporating these ideas into their routines, helping them become more efficient, content humans.

The Dilemma of Leaving Things Half Done

One of my biggest issues with schedules is moving from task one to task two at the scheduled time when task one isn't complete. With the exception of massive tasks like writing a book, I have a hard time stopping something before it's done. And when I do leave something undone in an effort to honor the schedule, my mind feels cluttered, because it wasn't able to check off the task. If you can relate, here are some ways to navigate this dilemma:

- **Time common tasks.** A major scheduling issue, and one of the primary reasons many of us are chronically late, is that we don't know how long it takes to accomplish various tasks. You might allot forty-five minutes to shower and get ready for a date with a friend, when it actually takes you sixty minutes. Figure out how much time you need for various bites of life by timing yourself and children doing the tasks and then recording the times.
- **Add in time buffers and fun.** Because you'll likely be tackling tasks while tackling children, timing might vary depending on the day. You can create space for this by adding buffers of, say, fifteen minutes before and after tasks on your schedule.

  Because life is more than checking off to-dos, be sure to sprinkle time for fun and doing nothing into your schedule. While it might seem rigid to schedule fun, doing so will ensure you actually have it. Before I started doing this, I would go days, sometimes weeks, without doing something like jumping on the trampoline with my kids, working on a crossword, or reading for pleasure.
- **Break big projects into reasonable chunks.** If "organize the house" is on my schedule, I won't sleep until every room is organized. Because that's not sustainable, I now force myself to break up large tasks. For example, "This Sunday I'll organize the linen closet, next Sunday I'll organize my closet, and so on." This strategy provides a sensible stopping point and allows my obsessive brain to press pause on a project until the day and time it's scheduled to commence.

Simple Chores Provide Children a Sense of Responsibility and Belonging

Chores get a bad rap because, well, they can be dull. It's more fun to make a mess. But anyone who has completed a chore knows that it often results in as much satisfaction as filling the floor with Legos—or at least almost as much. Simple chores also give children a sense of purpose and belonging and help them take ownership over the state of the home. As children grow, the chores might even inspire them to mitigate messes because they understand what it takes to clean them up.

Here are some ways to help ensure your children tap into the benefits of contributing to home care:

- **Explain the purpose of the chore.** Offering simple insight into why a chore is important can help children commit to the task. For example, when asking kids to put dirty clothes in the hamper, you could say, "We put clothes in the hamper to keep your bedroom from smelling stinky and help the floor stay clean so you can find the toys you want to play with." Now, instead of being told to do a boring chore that doesn't make sense, kids connect the chore to avoiding stink and playing with toys.
- **Sprinkle wonder into acts of service.** Infuse some mysticism in the historically not mystical act of chores by encouraging your child to imagine magic flowing from their hands into the home as they help with things like wiping up a spill, rinsing a dish, or hanging up a wet towel. The more they help, the more the magic spreads.
- **Ask what they think needs to be done.** Children gain a sense of ownership over chores when they're the ones to discover them. For example, you could say, "We're going to play a game where we walk through each room in the house and try to discover what needs to be done." Then, when you're in the kitchen your child might spot a dirty dish they can put in the dishwasher, in the living room they might find a stack of books they can put back on the shelf, and in the bathroom a glob of toothpaste they can clean up.

Parenting Around the World: Japanese children are often expected to help with tasks like sweeping and wiping down surfaces when at school and at home. Many schools around the world also incorporate simple cleaning tasks into young children's daily routines.

Routines Allow the Release of Energy

I was equally impressed and horrified when I read a UK study that found children can use the same amount of energy in a day as high-endurance athletes. How can you help your kids expend all this energy without allowing them to play "the floor is lava" all day? The answer is simple: assign them energy-sucking chores like raking leaves, dancing while changing the sheets, and doing a lap around the house before getting the iPad out.

Outlining the Daily Needs and Rhythms of Each Family Member

As you carve routines into your family schedule, you might find it challenging to ensure the needs and rhythms of each family member are honored. When these factors aren't considered, the routines could unravel when the person whose needs are not met unintentionally (or maybe intentionally) sabotages the plans. This can be especially true of a child whose eat-play-sleep cycle is interrupted.

To navigate this issue, observe and record the needs and daily rhythms of each family member for at least a week or so, then sculpt a schedule of routines designed to leave each family member feeling respected, satisfied, and willing to work the schedule.

Helpful Routines and Child-Friendly Tasks

I was shocked when I realized how willing my children were to help with at least some aspects of our family routine. A request to wipe her face saw my daughter vigorously rubbing a napkin all over her face (with varying degrees of success). A request to clean a dish saw my son scrubbing that dish until it was spotless. A request to vacuum saw my robot vacuum repeatedly bumping against a chair and getting stuck under the couch . . .

A whole new world appeared when I registered that young children did not yet associate daily routines (especially chores) with drudgery. They still viewed these activities as novel skills to master.

Here are some tasks many children are able to help with, with varying degrees of supervision:

- Making the bed
- Putting dirty clothes in the hamper
- Bringing clothes to the laundry room
- Picking up toys
- Feeding an animal
- Rinsing off a dish
- Scrubbing their body in the bath or shower
- Hanging up towels
- Laying out clothes for tomorrow
- Getting a snack (which can be made easier by keeping healthy snacks in a drawer or cabinet they can access)
- Watering plants
- Gathering fallen leaves
- Putting a dirty diaper in the pail

TIP: Assess how you can make these tasks easier for your child. For example, you could pull your child's bed away from the corner so they can easily access both sides when making the bed, put a step stool in the kitchen and bathroom, and organize their clothes in drawers they can access.

PARENTING AROUND THE WORLD: Starting around age three, many Japanese children are sent on errands that might require using public transportation, crossing a busy street, or exchanging money for goods. And at age four, many take the train to school on their own. Japanese parents believe it's important for their children to develop the independence and worldly knowledge these solo outings foster from an early age.

Adding Fun Twists to the Tasks

While daily activities such as making the bed might feel novel and exciting in the beginning, they can quickly lose their sparkle. To maintain that pizazz, consider the following.

- **Bed-making dance party.** You can help your children start their day on a high note by playing a favorite, lively song and encouraging dancing as you help them make their bed.
- **Dirty socks "three pointers."** Make the containment of dirty clothes a game by having your child pretend the clothes are a basketball and the hamper the hoop. And when they make the shot, make sure the crowd goes wild.
- **Peekaboo dressing.** Make the phenomenon of a shirt going over the face, or a hat going on the head, less traumatizing by working peekaboo into the process.
- **Dust treasure hunt.** Encourage your child to help you dust by hiding small surprises, such as stickers or notes, under objects they'll need to pick up to dust.
- **Cleanup race.** Help your child focus on cleaning by timing how fast the two of you can put away toys. If you have an organization system for the toys, make sure the receptacles are accessible and labeled so everything doesn't end up in a pile in the closet.
- **Cleaning tool belt or bucket.** Make your child feel like an official helper by allowing them to decorate a small tool belt or bucket that contains safe cleaning supplies such as a spray bottle of water, small duster, paper towels, and so on.

Play Breaks Between Tasks

While most adults have been conditioned to power through one task after another, a child's attention is regularly pulled to all the newness and wonder around them. When we ignore this aspect of a child's nature and push them to go from one task to another, such as taking a bath right after picking up toys, it might be difficult to get them to cooperate. If we can instead offer even just a few minutes of free time after each task, children have the opportunity to move their body, lean into their curiosities, and reset their brain so it can then focus on the next task.

PARENTING AROUND THE WORLD: In Finland, elementary-aged kids take a fifteen-minute break every forty-five minutes. These breaks allow them to release some energy, making them more focused when engaging in school tasks.

How Clean Is Clean Enough?

As you shepherd your child into routines that involve cleaning, you'll need to determine your cleaning criteria. These criteria are different for each family, as some are totally fine with a bit of mess while others require a pristine home. To create these criteria, consider the following categories and outline your needs for each.

- **Bedroom.** Do you want beds to be made every morning? Is there no eating in bedrooms? Do all items need a home? Should everything return to that home before bedtime?
- **Bathroom.** Do males need to lift up the seat and clean urine spills? Should everyone check to ensure everything flushed? Should hair be cleared from the drain after each shower? Do toothpaste spots need to be wiped off the mirror daily?
- **Kitchen.** Does everyone need to wash their own dishes before leaving the kitchen? Do crumbs and spills on counters, the floor, and in the fridge need to be wiped up promptly? Should lids always be used with skillets to prevent splatter?
- **Living room.** Is there no consuming of food or drinks that can stain? Must crumbs be vacuumed up before leaving the room? Should throw blankets be folded and pillows fluffed up after use? Should family members take all personal belongings with them when leaving?
- **Laundry.** How often should bedding and clothing be washed? Should whites and colors be separated?

As you consider the level of cleanliness you desire for each space, remember that your child probably doesn't share your exact cleanliness needs and might have a hard time meeting your criteria on their own. This often means that an additional set of criteria is made for your child. For example, while you might find it important to wipe up wet spots on the bathroom counter after handwashing, you might decide it's unreasonable to put this expectation on your child until they're older. But you might decide that taking off shoes before coming into the house is a reasonable request for your child. Or you might determine that while you don't think they need to bathe every day, you do want them to brush their hair every morning and teeth twice a day.

As your child ages you'll likely develop higher expectations for them. To ensure these shifting expectations don't cause too much conflict, clearly communicate them and provide a grace period as your child acclimates to a new expectation.

Tips and Tricks for Maintaining a Clean Enough Home

While getting kids invested in cleaning up after themselves is helpful, it can still be difficult to maintain a house that doesn't make you want to run away to a hotel where glorious cleaners tidy your space every day. Every! Day! But because that's not a reality for most of us, we have to get scrappy when it comes to having a house that meets our personal standards.

There's a fabulous array of methods for keeping it clean, but these are some of my tried-and-true picks.

- **Make some toys less accessible.** One of my biggest tidy-home-hurdles used to be the constantly spreading layer of toys on the floor. Some days I felt like I spent half my time cleaning up toys that would be dumped out again ten minutes later. I captured some sanity by rotating toys into bins inaccessible to my children and only getting them out when all the other toys were cleaned up. This has resulted in it being almost impossible for my kids to create a toy-splosion. The kids also glean more excitement from their toys because they don't have constant access to all of them all the time.
- **Give everything a home.** Random stuff piles up when we haven't decided where the stuff should live. When every item has a

home, even if that home is the bottomless-pit toy chest, it's much easier to clean up, as you don't have to think about where to put that thing. And when new stuff enters the home, give it a home ASAP.

- **Have a nightly family "stuff sweep."** At the end of every day, give each family member a bag or basket and have them go through the house collecting all their stuff that's spread during the day. Then have everyone return the stuff to its home.
- **Keep cleaning supplies easily accessible.** The easier it is to access cleaning supplies, the more you and the family will use them. For example, before I bought a hand vacuum to store in the kitchen, the floor under my daughter's highchair was always littered with crumbs. I would cringe every time I stepped on this wasteland of discarded food with bare feet, but I rarely cleaned it because the vacuum was on the other side of the house.

Transitioning from One Activity to Another

A major struggle for my family is transitions. When our minds get in the groove of a certain activity, it's jarring to start something new. We have to pause, then gently work ourselves out of one groove so we can nestle into another. It's a process, and when we don't honor this process, crankiness and agitation ensue.

Think about how each member of your family handles transitions. Does your partner get testy, your kids confused, and you overwhelmed? Or is your partner a pro at transitions and doesn't understand why you and the kids seem discombobulated during this process? Flash back to recent transitions and assess what that process was like for each of you.

You might realize that certain transitions were easier than others. For example, you and the kids might flow naturally from the car ride home from school to snack time, while the transition from dinner to bedtime causes major tension. Clarifying how various transitions affect your family can help you create customized methods for smoothing them and ensuring realistic expectations for yourself and your family.

Here are some ideas that work for my family.

- **Set a timer for five minutes before the transition.** Preschools often alert children a few minutes before an activity will end because it gives them time to wrap things up and start mentally preparing for the next activity.
- **Envision yourself completing the first steps of the next activity.** When that five-minute timer goes off, start visualizing yourself and children seamlessly, and even joyfully, entering the next activity. You can also share this visualization with your children, saying something like, "After we clean up the toys, we're going to start making dinner. When we get to the kitchen, we can turn on some fun music and work together to get out ingredients. We're making soup tonight. Won't it be fun to mix all the ingredients together like we're making a magic potion?" Visualizing and verbalizing this upcoming activity can help you clarify and prepare for it, while also recognizing the joy you can all glean from the experience.
- **Give the current activity closure.** Another important aspect of transitions is closing one activity before starting the next. For example, in the previous example, you and the kids would want to straighten up the room you were playing in to "close" playtime so you can calmly enter dinner prep. This closure helps the mind fully focus on the next activity because it's not lingering on all the aspects of the previous activity that still need doing.
- **Commit to starting.** It's natural to resist moving to the next activity when you're feeling comfortable in the current one. While life often has room for flexibility, allowing you to occasionally skip an activity in favor of lingering on your current one, it's often necessary to force ourselves to keep the train moving.
- **Discover additional transition-softeners**. Using the previous ideas as a jumping-off point, explore transition-softeners that might work for your clan. Ask yourself which transitions are the hardest and why, and which are easy and why. Then brainstorm how to make the tricky transitions more tranquil.

Promoting Personal Hygiene

Crafting a plan for how to get your child invested in personal hygiene habits like handwashing, bathing, teeth and hair brushing, and effective sniffle and sneeze etiquette can set them up for a safer, more hygienic life. It can also prepare them, and you, for the journey of potty learning, if they haven't already conquered that feat. While there are many ways to teach children about hygiene, following are tips my clients and I have found helpful. Use them as is or, better yet, be inspired to make them your own.

Handwashing

A few minutes before typing this, I pulled my daughter's hand out of the toilet. As I was pulling it out, she stuck her other hand in the trash. Yeah. Little hands go everywhere, especially places where germs gather.

According to the Centers for Disease Control and Prevention, the ideal handwashing procedure is wetting hands, turning off water, lathering hands with soap for at least twenty seconds, then thoroughly rinsing. Because most young children can't count to twenty, you can teach them a silly handwashing song that lasts for at least that long. You can also place a stool beneath all the sinks they might use and have an easy-to-use soap dispenser, and towel, within arm's reach.

To inspire children to wash their hands after using the bathroom or touching an unsanitary surface, you can share simple information about germs without creating fear. For example, you can explain that if certain germs get into the body, they can make us sick and prevent us from doing fun things like playing or eating yummy meals.

However, it's important to find a balance between handwashing and exposure to helpful bacteria found in the natural world. Let your kids get a little dirty sometimes. There are many benefits children can receive from getting a little dirty.

- Exposure to the soil-based bacterium *Mycobacterium vaccae* can elevate a child's mood by activating a group of neurons that produce serotonin. Research also suggests that exposure to this bacterium can lower a child's anxiety and promote learning.

- Not having enough exposure to parasites, bacteria, and viruses in early life can increase a child's risk of developing allergies, asthma, and autoimmune diseases like diabetes.
- Playing in dirt can support a child's cardiovascular health.

Bathing

Although young children are not yet conjuring the bodily odors of puberty, regular bathing minimizes issues such as itchiness from leftover poop particles in private parts, relaxes a child before bed, and provides a great opportunity for water play. While young children need constant supervision when bathing, you can help them build autonomy by encouraging them to gently scrub all their parts, practice washing their hair, turn off the shower or bath water, drain the tub, and retrieve their own towel.

In addition, most kids don't require daily hair washing—once a week is usually fine.

You can potentially prevent pre-bathing meltdowns by letting your child select water toys they only get to play with when bathing. You can also play fun music, blow bubbles, and put a few drops of an essential oil like lavender or orange in the tub or shower to make it more of a sensory experience.

If these tricks don't reduce your child's reluctance, investigate what about bath time bothers them and how to remedy the issue. For example, when one of my clients realized her son was scared of water going in his eyes, she had him wear goggles when bathing. Another client whose child didn't like being chilly before and after a bath now uses a portable heater to warm the bathroom.

Parenting Around the World: A common practice among Mayans in Central America is bathing children in super cold water to soothe heat rash, regulate a heightened emotional state, and support deeper sleep. Wim "the Iceman" Hof would be proud.

Hair Brushing

While it might seem like hair brushing doesn't affect health, it's helpful in stimulating blood flow, hair growth, and the distribution of oil across the scalp. But however important hair brushing might be, this activity can be a fast pass to yelling and tears, sometimes for both child and parent. One of the most obvious ways to limit the struggle of hair brushing is to give your child a short hair style, but if they or you aren't into that, here are tricks for minimizing messes in the tresses.

- Select gentle products that work for your child's hair texture.
- Get a child-specific hairbrush.
- Start brushing at the end of hair and move up.
- Offer fun hair accessories that can be used after brushing.

Teeth Brushing

For obvious reasons, children should brush their teeth for at least two minutes twice a day. But just because they should, doesn't mean they easily will. Luckily, there are ways to get your child invested in, or even excited by, the prospect of brushing teeth.

- Let them pick their own toothbrush.
- Choose toothpaste in a flavor they like.
- Play a fun two-minute song when they brush.
- Tell them that teeth feel left out if they don't get brushed.
- Brush your teeth at the same time.
- Read a book about tooth health. Books like *The Tooth Book* by Mark Bacera and *Brush, Brush, Brush!* by Alicia Padron are great options.

Sniffle, Sneeze, and Cough Etiquette

Kids are notorious for smearing boogies and spewing sneezes. However, you can help your child limit their germ spreading by cleverly convincing them to put the boogies in a tissue and the cough or sneeze into their arm.

- **Make their "cough pocket" smell good.** Encourage your child to stick their coughs and sneezes in their "cough pocket" (the crook of a bent elbow) by spritzing their "pocket" with an essential oil spray (if they're wearing a long-sleeved shirt). To make, mix about twenty drops of your child's essential oil of choice with four ounces of water in a glass spray bottle. Before spiritizing your child's cough pocket, do one spritz in the air to ensure they don't have any negative reactions to the oil. Tip: Chamomile, eucalyptus, and lemon oil are all helpful for relieving cold symptoms.

- **Offer fun tissues.** Nowadays you can get tissues printed with a variety of kid-favorite characters and tissue dispensers in the shape of a shaggy dog, mermaid, unicorn, robot, and much more.
- **Read germy books.** Help your child understand why it's important to keep germs to themselves by reading books such as *What Are Germs?* by Katie Daynes and *Germs Are Not for Sharing* by Elizabeth Verdick and Marieka Heinlen.

Motivating Older Kids to Manage Hygiene, Home Care, and Other Routines

When kids hit puberty, they can get stinky. Really stinky. An amalgamation of changes, such as increased sweat production and the activation of sweat glands in the pits and groin that cause smellier perspiration, results in a child who should probably shower almost daily, depending on their activity level. A heap of other factors like the mouth growing increased odor-causing bacteria, the scalp releasing more oil, pores becoming likelier to clog, and other super fun changes require that older kids step up their hygiene game.

This can be a tricky transition as kids aren't used to the level of hygiene maintenance now required and many aren't bothered by, or even aware of, things like stinky pits and oily hair. I've had friends report that their kids can be so lackadaisical about washing their hair it appears wet even when it's not, or balk at things like flossing only to develop rank breath. My son is currently going through puberty, and while he seems immune to the smell of his underarms and breath, I sadly am not. Luckily, he's in the habit of getting in the shower every day but is not yet consistent with soaping up the smelly bits and getting shampoo in his hair. We're working on it.

Puberty doesn't just require better hygiene but also comes at a time when kids receive more responsibilities at home and school. While they might already have good habits such as hanging up their wet towel, putting their laundry in the hamper, or washing their dishes, many aren't quite there yet. The same can go for school-related responsibilities like studying independently and keeping assignments and materials organized.

Although many kids have been gradually developing the habits and routines this phase of life requires and don't need many shifts or additions, some might need ample support and motivation to level up.

Following are ideas for figuring out the new or updated routines you think are important for your child, then getting them on board.

Review Your Child's Current Routines

You can gain a clearer picture of the new or adapted routines you want your child to adopt by noting which tasks, such as showering, room cleaning, or caring for clothes, they still rely on you to complete. This review makes it easier to then determine the tasks you think they can now do autonomously.

Include Your Child in the Development of New Routines

It can be much easier to get your child on board with new routines by asking for their input when drafting a plan. For example, you might together determine that while they are now responsible for selecting their own outfits and putting dirty clothes in the hamper, you will still do their laundry for the time being. Or they will now pack their own lunch but can have more say in the food they eat by going to the grocery store with you once a week. I've also found that letting a kid choose their own deodorant, shampoo, conditioner, and other hygiene products, within reason, can inspire them to actually use these items. Overall, this inclusion and potential compromise can help kids subscribe to the routines and reduce resistance.

Consider Special Privileges Your Child Might Be Mature Enough to Handle

You can soften the blow of all the new responsibilities by offering your child perks such as a later bedtime, a "dumb phone," or permission to ride their bike to a friend's house on their own. The chosen privileges will vary based on family circumstances and values, but offering a few might lessen the emotional growing pains of this time of significant transition.

Honor Consent and Privacy Requests

Puberty is a time when kids who used to be fine with their parent seeing them naked, or being in the same room when they're pooping, can develop the need for more privacy. This provides potent opportunity for parents to help their kids understand that no one is allowed to touch their body, or disregard other safety and privacy requests, without their consent. So while it might feel odd asking your child if they consent to a hug, or you being in the bathroom when they're showering, for example, this is setting up your child to expect and advocate for the safety, privacy, and overall respect they deserve and, of course, to provide the same to others.

Make Routines as Easy as Possible to Remember

One of the hardest parts of sticking to routines can be remembering them, especially when you're a kid with your head filled with thoughts of that anime show your parents said you can't watch or how you're going to become a famous YouTuber.

My sweet boy is very forgetful, so we put a checklist in the bathroom to help him remember steps such as deodorant application, washing his face with soap, and so on. We also have a checklist in the car that includes all the items he needs to bring to school. He has the same list in his backpack to ensure all the items make it home and his lunch doesn't turn into a moldy science project as it sits forgotten in his desk. Last, he has a checklist at home to remind him of what he needs to do before he gets sucked in to his daily allotment of screen time. While he sometimes loses the lists, or forgets to look at them, they do minimize the amount of nagging I have to do, thus improving our relationship and making him feel more independent.

There are many ways you can help your child remember their routine tasks, including using one of those big chore calendars, stickers on the bathroom items they need to use, or a daily planner (extra points for the Hello Kitty or Lisa Frank variety), so consider what makes your kid tick and toy with strategies you think might resonate.

Sprinkle in Fun

As most kids have not yet developed the adult skill of forcing oneself to forgo fun in favor of monotonous activities (pats self on back), they're not going to want to do things like laundry, flossing, or bed making unless it has a zing of amusement. Earlier in the chapter I provided ideas for adding that zing to routine tasks, so I encourage you to review those and see if you want to adapt a few for your kid. My son now loves showering because he gets to listen to the Greek mythology podcast he's obsessed with. This inspired me to do the same with true crime podcasts, and I now spend an embarrassing amount of time in the bathroom.

Potty Learning

After years of strapping a flailing child into a diaper, it can feel like the possibility of getting all their poo and pee into the toilet is about as likely as fairies cleaning your home as you sleep. But lo and behold, most humans eventually learn to use the toilet—they just need some guidance to get there.

Because this topic has been explored extensively and a slew of advice, which you probably already know, is available, I'm just going to review some interesting research and a few considerations and resources to support you in building a unique potty plan.

Potty Learning Research

While I'm a firm believer that you're the leading expert in the potty learning techniques that will work for your child, here is some quality research that could inform your plan.

- **Age matters.** A study published in the journal *Pediatrics* found that the younger a child is when they begin potty learning, the longer it will likely take them to be fully "toilet trained." The study reported that children starting the potty-learning process at between eighteen and twenty-four months of age took about thirteen to fourteen months to become toilet trained, while children starting after twenty-seven months of age took ten months or less.

- **Child-oriented potty learning has had positive results.** The child-oriented toilet training method encourages a very gradual entry into potty learning, and only when the child exhibits signs that they're ready to begin. A study published in *Pediatrics* that reviewed the potty-training records of 1,170 children found that the child-oriented toilet training method resulted in 79.5 percent of the children becoming skilled in both bowel and urinary control.
- **Positivity promotes progress.** Research published in *Archives of Pediatrics & Adolescent Medicine* indicated that by utilizing positivity during potty learning, and not using potentially shaming words such as *stinky* or *gross*, parents could shorten the time a child needs to complete potty training.
- **A medical issue could be thwarting potty-training.** A Belgium study revealed that lower urinary tract symptoms, which can be caused by issues like urinary tract infections, can delay a child's potty-training success. Another study, published in *Pediatrics*, reported that constipation can cause stool toileting refusal (STR), or a refusal to poop in the toilet. STR can arise from the painful passing of a hard stool that causes the child to associate pooping on the toilet with discomfort. You can help your child avoid this by ensuring they drink plenty of water and eat fiber-full foods like beans, blueberries, avocados, and apples. You can also sneak in fiber by mixing ground flaxseed into a pancake or muffin mix, or smoothies.
- **Bedwetting is expected.** Children wearing diapers to bed when potty learning is completely reasonable, as a study in *Pediatrics* found that most children aren't developmentally able to not wet the bed until they're four or five years old. Bedwetting beyond those ages can also be normal. A British cohort study reported that about 30 percent of children experience bedwetting at 4.5 years and about 9.5 percent still wet the bed at 9.5 years. For many children, bedwetting tapers off about ten months after they can regularly go all day without soiling their pants.

Using Incentives (aka Bribes)

Although some people are against using incentives during potty learning, others swear by it. I feel either option is great if it feels good to you.

If you're on the fence about whether to bring external motivators into your child's potty learning, examine your family values to see if this option is in alignment or conflicts. I found that incentives weren't a breach of my family's values, and offering them was a game changer. However, incentives work so well with my kids that I'm currently evaluating if I lean on this tactic too much.

Helpful Potty-Learning Books

If you want to go deep into the topic of potty learning, here are some books I found helpful and some that inspired my kids to poop on the toilet instead of under tables.

For parents

- *Stress-Free Potty Training* by Sara Au and Peter Stavinoha
- *Success with Potty Training* by Beth Allen
- *Ready, Set, Go!* by Sarah Ockwell-Smith

For kids

- *Once Upon a Potty* by Alona Frankel
- *Let's Go to the Potty!* by Allison Jandu
- *Potty* by Leslie Patricelli

Creating Your Customized Potty Plan

Review the following to begin outlining the plan you feel would best suit your child.

- How do I feel about changing diapers? Does it drive me crazy? Or is it now second nature? While I believe a child should largely inform when potty learning begins, your needs obviously matter as well. For example, if diaper changes are always a battle, you might be motivated to start potty education sooner than later. (As

I write this, I'm holding a bag of frozen blueberries on my jaw because my daughter kicked me in the face when I was changing her diaper.)

- Is my child soon starting a school that requires toilet use?
- Is my child interested in the toilet? Can they talk to me about pee, poop, and the potty?
- How much time do I have to devote to potty learning?
- How old is my child?
- What time of year is it? Some parents find it's easier to start potty learning in warmer months when their child can be diaper-free outside. Some parents might want to avoid beginning this process around the holidays.
- What is my child's typical routine?
- Does my child show clear cues when they need to use the bathroom?
- When does my child typically soil their diaper during the day?
- Does my child have fears or concerns about potty learning?
- How long do I want my child to sit on the toilet? Do I want to do things like sing or read to them when they're there? When potty training my son, I found that two or three minutes on the toilet was sufficient.

  NOTE: It's recommended that children not sit on the toilet for longer than five minutes.

Guided Meditation

The meditation at the following link helps you to envision your ideal day with your family. You'll imagine your family flowing through the routines you create, noticing which expectations you are letting go of and how you easily move through transitions and situations that used to create struggle. You'll then be guided through many of the self-soothing techniques from this chapter so they become easier for you to pass on to your child. Visit https://www.baileygaddis.com/routines.

Writing Prompts

- What are my daily must-do activities? How long does it take me to complete these activities?
- What are my child's must-do activities? How long does it take them to complete these activities?
- What are daily, or weekly, tasks or experiences that would bring more joy to my personal and family life?
- What are reasonable chores for my children?
- How can I make boring tasks more fun? How can I help my child understand how these tasks benefit them?
- What tasks do I want to delegate?
- What is my child's current bedtime routine? What is and is not working?
- What is my current bedtime routine? What is and is not working?
- Where does my child sleep, and how do I feel about the arrangement? Do I want to make a change?
- Is it challenging for my child to fall asleep? If so, how can I help them move past these challenges?
- What self-soothing techniques do I want to teach my child?
- Do I suspect my child has sleep issues that require the assistance of a specialist?

Parenting Plan

Family Schedule Outline

Morning schedule:

Afternoon schedule:

Evening schedule:

Weekend schedule:

Plan for transitions:

Chores for child/children:

Plan for getting child/Children invested in schedule and chores:

Tasks to delegate:

Hygiene Plan

Handwashing:

Bathing:

Hair:

Teeth:

Sniffle, sneeze, and cough etiquette:

Potty-Learning Plan

Age at which we will start:

Materials we will use:

Initial techniques we'll utilize:

Plan for accidents:

Adults who need to know our plan:

10

ELEMENT 8: PROMOTING HEALTHY FOOD, SLEEP, AND SAFETY CHOICES

WHETHER WE LIKE IT OR NOT, food is a major part of life, especially after having kids. Some find joy in food buying and prep while others view the process as Groundhog Day. Although it's fairly easy to feed ourselves before having kids, parenthood often reshapes food habits to meet the needs of children. Sometimes this reshaping is a simple process, but often it requires that we brush up on the basics, such as what kind and how many nutrients humans need at various ages, where toxins lurk, how to get healthy food into potentially picky eaters, and how to deal with food allergies.

If you're like my husband all things food feels second nature. If you're like me, you spent a good portion of your adult life living off only a few food groups, and not the colorful ones. Regardless of where you fall on this spectrum, having a Food section in your Parenting Plan allows you (and your partner, if applicable) to clarify how you want to feed your family in a way that aligns with the nutritional needs, schedule, and preferences of each family member. Understandably, this can be a daunting task, especially when faced with kids who laugh in the face of any food that isn't beige and covered in cheese, butter, or syrup.

I'm not a foodie, so when it comes to developing a food plan for my family, I need all the help I can get. If you're already a pro on this topic, feel free to skip the parts of this chapter that make you say "duh."

Why Childhood Nutrition Is So Important

Eating quality food enhances the rapid physical and mental development children undergo. Studies have shown that early childhood nutrition affects things like reading comprehension, cognitive ability, likelihood of completing secondary and college-level education, and early adult employment and wages. Food also plays a big role in emotion regulation, immune system health, energy levels, concentration, and many other key components of life. Parents laying the foundation for healthy eating in a child's early years increases the chance that the child will continue this healthy eating into their adult years, when parents aren't always there to ensure that more than pizza is being consumed.

Assessing Your Family Food Culture

Every person has a different relationship with food. For example, my husband thinks a lot about food and is the main shopper and cook in our family. He also has a greater need for elaborate meals than I do. I enjoy good food but would also be content eating the same meals almost every day. Our varying ideas have occasionally caused tension in our relationship but have also forced us to create a family food culture that blends our approaches. This culture consists of easy, healthy breakfasts; often on-the-go lunches sometimes just composed of snacks like veggies, crackers, and cheese; and simple home-cooked dinners, occasional takeout, and an elaborate meal for a special occasion. Our kids are given the same food my husband and I are eating, and we try to eat together as often as possible but are also content if that doesn't always happen. While there are definitely things we'd like to tweak, our food culture works for us and ensures all family members have their nutritional needs met.

To figure out if you'd like to adjust aspects of your family's current food culture, first take a moment to review it. Then, answer the following questions to unlock ideas on how you might improve that culture.

- Do you or another family member enjoy cooking? If not, do you want to figure out how to make meals easier? Maybe throw some extra veggies on a frozen pizza and call it a night?
- What types of dishes work well for your family?
- Are their certain nutrients you feel are lacking in your family's typical meals?
- Do you want to offer a set or à la carte menu for family meals?
- What is the most enjoyable type of breakfast experience for your family? What is the most enjoyable type of lunch experience for your family? What is the most enjoyable type of dinner experience for your family?
- How can you adjust your family schedule to create more enjoyable meals?

Basic Dietary Needs

When I started researching this topic, I realized how little I knew about the specifics of a child's dietary needs. While I give my kids fairly healthy food, I hadn't been too aware of whether they were getting enough of the essential nutrients until now. Those essential nutrients include vitamins, minerals, carbohydrates, protein, and fat, but that's not the whole picture. For example, the many types of vitamins and minerals we require are found in various foods, there are simple and complex carbohydrates, protein is found in many more foods than just meat, and not all fat is created equal.

NOTE: Because certain health conditions and other circumstances can influence a child's dietary needs, it's always best to discuss your child's food plan with their care provider or a registered dietitian.

To break it down, here are the basic nutrients kids need and why they're important.

- **Protein.** Protein provides essential amino acids that help children grow and develop properly. Protein is part of every cell in the body and helps build and repair muscle, tissue, skin, nails, and hair. Protein also helps build hormones, enzymes, and a healthy immune system. Many sources of protein (in addition to certain veggies and legumes) also provide iron, which is needed to produce red blood cells and build muscle. Good sources of protein include seafood, lean meat and poultry, eggs, beans, peas, soy products, and unsalted nuts and seeds.

- **Fruit.** Fresh fruit is a great source of fiber, vitamins, and minerals, which support healthy bowel movements and kidney function, reduce the risk of certain types of cancer, and enhance cognitive function.
- **Vegetables.** Eating a variety of veggies provides essential vitamins, antioxidants, fiber, and other nutrients. Veggies are especially helpful for lowering a child's risk of developing chronic diseases like heart disease, stroke, and some cancers as they age.
- **Grains.** Foods containing healthy varieties of grains provide fiber, carbohydrates (the body's primary source of energy), protein, and various vitamins and minerals. All these goodies fuel a child's mind and body for all that learning and development they're engaged in. Getting ample grains is important at all times but can be especially helpful when a child starts potty learning, as the fiber in grains can make stools easier to pass. Good sources of grains are whole-grain bread, cereal, pasta, oatmeal, popcorn, brown rice, and quinoa.
- **Dairy.** The high amounts of protein, calcium, and vitamin D many dairy products provide are essential for the development of a child's bones and reduce the risk of certain chronic diseases. However, because of dairy allergies and lactose intolerance, some children need to strengthen their bones through alternative sources. Good non-dairy sources of calcium include chia seeds, almonds, dried figs, white beans, kale, broccoli, sweet potatoes, butternut squash, and calcium-fortified orange juice.

Following are general portion recommendations for children from ages two to eight. The exact portions your child needs will depend on their activity level and dietary or health circumstances.

Daily guidelines for children ages 2 to 4

- Calories: 1,000 to 1,600
- Protein: 2 to 5 ounces (The palm of your hand is about the size of a 3-ounce serving of meat.)

- Fruit: 1 to 1.5 cups
- Vegetables: 1 to 2 cups
- Grains: 3 to 5 ounces (There's typically about 1 ounce of grains in a slice of whole-grain bread, 1 cup of cereal or oatmeal, or ½ cup of cooked rice or pasta.)
- Dairy: 2 to 2.5 cups

Daily guidelines for children ages 5 to 8

- Calories: 1,200 to 2,000
- Protein: 3 to 5.5 ounces
- Fruit: 1 to 2 cups
- Vegetables: 1.5 to 2.5 cups
- Grains: 4 to 6 ounces
- Dairy: 2.5 cups

Daily guidelines for children ages 9 to 12

- Calories: 1,400 to 2,200
- Protein: 4 to 6 ounces
- Fruit: 2 to 2.5 cups
- Vegetables: 2 to 3.5 cups
- Grains: 5 to 7 ounces
- Dairy: 3 cups

Daily guidelines for children ages 13 to 18

- Calories: 2,200 to 3,200
- Protein: 4 to 7 ounces
- Fruit: 2 to 2.5 cups
- Vegetables: 2.5 to 4 cups
- Grains: 6 to 10 ounces
- Dairy: 3 cups

How Much Water Do Kids Need?

In addition to food, it's obviously essential to get water into our kids. One- to three-year-olds need at least 4 cups of water per day, four- to eight-year-olds need 5 cups, seven to twelve-year-olds need 7 to 8 cups, and thirteen-year-olds and up need 8 to 11 cups. The amount of water children require also depends on their activity level and the climate they live in.

While beverages like fruit juice do contain water, plain, filtered water is one of the best options to keep kids hydrated as it doesn't contain sugar; supports the health of joints, bones, and teeth; promotes blood circulation; regulates mood; and improves concentration. It's pretty much a miracle liquid. Alas, getting a child to drink enough water can feel like an exercise in futility. Here are some ideas for making water more appealing and tracking how much water your child drinks.

- Make the process of hydration more fun by helping your child freeze herbs like mint or small pieces of fruit in ice cubes and add them to water.
- Give water a splash of taste by squeezing some fresh orange into it, or a dash of something like organic cherry juice.
- Encourage your child to drink water every time you do.
- Tell your child that water is like a magic elixir that gives us special powers, like the ability to move our body, have lots of energy for fun, think up creative ideas, and easily poop!
- Let your child pick out a fifteen-ounce reusable kid cup or water bottle and determine how many times they'd need to empty it to reach the recommended daily amount. For example, if a three-year-old drinks all the water in the cup three times a day, they'll get more than the recommended 4 cups.
- Offer kids foods with high water content like watermelon, cucumbers, strawberries, celery, tomatoes, and blueberries.

Children are likely dehydrated if they're urinating less frequently than usual and the urine is dark yellow; their skin is flush; their lips are dry and mouth is sticky; and they're fatigued or agitated. If you suspect severe dehydration, it's best to alert your child's pediatrician.

Navigating Allergies

Now that there's more awareness around food allergies and access to testing, it's more common for children to be diagnosed with at least one type of food allergy. Food allergies can change the landscape of the family food plan and potentially create frustration among family members.

When my son's lactose intolerance was discovered, it created a lot of friction in our family. While my husband doesn't eat much dairy because of a mild allergy, I live for it. I could eat a pint of ice cream every night if it didn't thwart my health. So when my son was cut off from dairy, he would have big feelings if he spotted me eating any form of dairy. This led to the dilemma of whether to remove all dairy products from our family food plan.

We compromised by cutting dairy from shared family meals but still keeping dairy-based snacks in the house that my daughter and I could enjoy. If my son gets triggered when witnessing us eat dairy, I let him express his feelings but also remind him that while his lactose intolerance is frustrating, it doesn't mean others can't enjoy this type of food. We're all on individual journeys to find the foods that help our bodies thrive. The deeper we got into this issue, the more alternatives we found, such as lactose-free ice cream and dairy-free pizzas that softened his sorrow of having to bid adieu to beloved Lady Lactose.

If you know or suspect your child has a food allergy, here are ideas to help you maneuver this challenge.

- Request an allergy test from your child's pediatrician.
- Offer tasty alternatives, especially at special social events like birthday parties. For example, if your child has celiac disease, you can bring a gluten-free cupcake for them when attending a birthday party.
- Use an app like Fig to find foods in grocery stores and restaurants that your child can eat.
- Explain how the food your child is allergic to affects their body. While some allergies create an obvious reaction, such as a stomachache or rash, other reactions might be trickier for a child to connect with the allergy, like fatigue, headaches, or "brain fog."

Helping your child understand what the food does to their body could help them adjust to their dietary restrictions.

- If your child seems upset or embarrassed about the allergy, you can normalize it by sharing that over five million children in the United States have a food allergy and that many children grow out of egg, dairy, and soy allergies.

How Diet Influences Behavior and Mood

A study published in the journal *Nutrients* reports that a healthy diet supports children in coping with stress and regulating emotions, and research in *Nutrition Reviews* finds that good nutrition improves a child's cognitive development, concentration, irritability level, and ability to learn. A healthy diet can also lessen symptoms of ADHD.

To enhance your child's emotional health through food, here are some good sources of nutrients that are especially helpful for mood regulation.

- Vitamin B6: Eggs, bananas, avocados, spinach, chickpeas, sweet potatoes
- Folate: Legumes, asparagus, eggs, citrus fruit, broccoli, papaya, bananas, avocados
- Choline: Eggs, fish, shitake mushrooms, cruciferous veggies, almonds, red potatoes
- Omega-3: Salmon, eggs, walnuts, chia seeds, flaxseed, spinach, seaweed

To pinpoint how various foods affect your child, keep a food journal for a week, recording each meal and what your child's behavior is like following it. While factors like sleep, interactions with others, and so on can also obviously affect your child's behaviors and 'tude, this journal might help you uncover food behavior patterns.

TIP: To determine if your child is actually hungry or just trying to resolve an emotion such as boredom or sadness (often with fat-, salt-, or sugar-laden foods), offer them a healthy snack like carrot sticks or avocado on toast.

Parenting Around the World: Many parents in South Korea teach children that food is better when shared with others. They also do not fulfill a child's food craving the moment it arises but instead require that they wait for the scheduled mealtime.

Common Dietary Challenges

Food is a common topic of discussion for parents because it can feel like an insurmountable challenge to get enough healthy food into the kids. Factors like busy lifestyles, the allure of fast food, and kids who won't eat anything that isn't beige can make feeding children feel equivalent to a job at NASA.

Here are some of the most common food challenges parents experience, and ideas for working through them.

- **Not having enough time.** You can work through this challenge by prepping healthy snacks once a week and purchasing nutritious, nonperishable snacks to stash in the car for on-the-go mini-meals. Ordering groceries online can also be a lifesaver and prevent impulse buys.
- **Having a picky eater.** All this talk of a well-balanced diet can feel worthless if you have a child who refuses everything but bread and butter. However, through trial and error many parents of fussy eaters find at least some items from each food group their picky eater will consume. For example, you can make a list of all the fruits and vegetables you think your child might enjoy and then expose them to each.
- **Putting excessive pressure on yourself.** While the dream is our children consuming the recommended serving from each food group each day, this isn't always possible. So I urge you to take it easy on yourself, commit to doing the best you can, and know that your best will look different each day. My best today is giving my kids cinnamon toast for breakfast and lunch. But it's on whole-grain bread, so there you go.

Navigating Food and Body Image Issues

Like most complexes, one's food and body image complex often starts at home. The relationship the people closest to a child have with diet, weight, and overall appearance can heavily shape a child's relationship with these aspects of self. In extreme cases, these issues can result in the development of anorexia, bulimia, avoidant/restrictive food intake disorder, or binge eating disorder. While these disorders are more prevalent in children twelve and older, they're becoming increasingly common in children under twelve.

If you ever suspect your child is dealing with any of these disorders, it's crucial to ask their doctor for a referral to a mental health professional specializing in eating disorders ASAP. But what I want to explore now is how we might prevent those eating disorders from developing, as well as body dysmorphic disorder, which causes a person to intensely worry about flaws in their appearance.

While talking with our children about these issues as they age is of course helpful, the most potent way we can support our children in developing a healthy relationship with food and their body is by modeling it ourselves. What our children hear us say about food, our weight, and our appearance largely shapes their perspective on those topics. We can do them a great service by developing a healthy relationship with food and our bodies, while also being careful about what we say and how we act in front of our children in regard to this topic.

The following questions can help you explore your perspective on food, weight, and appearance and if there's anything you want to change, or emphasize, with your child. As you answer, know that these questions aren't intended to make you feel shame. They're just an opening to help you explore how this topic relates to your family.

- Am I overly restrictive with my food intake?
- Am I frequently on a diet?
- Do I frequently use food as a reward for myself or my child?
- Do I feel like it is important for my child to finish their entire plate of food? Or do I only want them to eat until they are full? Do I feel like I serve them portions that are too large?

- Does my child listen to signals from their body when they're hungry or full? Or do they put off eating even if they know they're hungry? Or continue eating well after they're full?
- Does my child have an extreme aversion to certain tastes and textures?
- Does my child frequently make excuses about why they don't want to eat?
- Does my child hide or hoard food?
- Do I have certain eating habits I would like my child to adopt? Or do I feel I need to allow them to develop their own type of eating plan, within reason? (For example, if you are a vegan, do you feel it is important for your child to also be a vegan? Or are you open to exposing them to meat?)
- Ideally, how would I like my child to view food in relation to their health, appearance, and culture?
- How do I feel about my body? How do I speak about my body and overall appearance?
- What kind of comments do I make about my child's appearance? About the appearance of others?
- What does my child say about their body or appearance?
- What types of body image messages do I feel my child is receiving from the shows, books, and toys they play with?
- What type of perspective about their body and overall appearance would I like my child to develop?

Practicing Intuitive, Mindful Eating

Because crafty food manufacturers have perfected the creation of foods with just the right amount of salt, sugar, and fat to leave us wanting more, it's common for food to be consumed mindlessly. We can change this by tuning in to how our body feels and the circumstances we're navigating when considering when and what to eat. For example, if you drive past a fast-food restaurant when stressed, you might have a sudden craving for fries and a milkshake. When you have this craving you can ask, *Am I actually hungry? Or do I want this food because I want a distraction from my stress? Or am I just tired and processing that as hunger?* While you might still pull into the drive-through, you're at least aware of where the motivation for the food is coming from. And then, when you're eating the food, you can receive ample enjoyment by really focusing on each bite, smelling the aroma, paying attention to the textures, and noticing the various flavors. Eating food slowly also gives your body time to communicate fullness, helping you avoid overeating.

When you feel hungry but don't have a particular craving, you can ask your intuition for guidance on what to eat. Your intuition might express a need for more greens or protein, or maybe a hearty meal that can help sustain you through an active day. Bringing your intuition into dietary decisions can allow you to make more thoughtful choices about food that can enhance your overall health and relationship with food. Your child can also get in on all this intuitive goodness.

Here are some ways to pass on the art of intuitive eating to your child.

- Share your thoughts when determining what you want to eat, or how you feel about your meal, as this offers a real-time example of intuitive eating.
- Do your best to make the eating environment calm and quiet.
- Whenever possible, offer your child two healthy options at each meal so they can practice listening to what their body wants.
- When your child asks for food but you suspect the desire is coming from a non-hunger-related source such as boredom, investigate and help them fulfill their need without food, unless of course you determine they really are hungry.
- Before your child starts eating, ask them to notice all the colors, shapes, and aromas of their food.
- Ask them to close their eyes when taking the first few bites so they can really savor their meal.
- Encourage your child to eat slowly, take small bites, and fully chew the food before swallowing.
- Have your child take occasional pauses during the meal to check in with their body and determine if they're full.
- After they eat, ask them how they feel. This can help them understand how some foods energize them, while others can make them feel sluggish or even cause stomachaches or headaches.

Teaching the skill of intuitive eating can set up your child for a lifelong, healthy relationship with food and support you in transforming your nutritional practices and perspectives.

Parenting Around the World: French parents teach their children from an early age that it's important to slow down and savor meals.

Sneaky Ways to Infuse Nutrients into Treats

While some kids are all about veggies and other healthy stuff, a majority of kids live for pizza, grilled cheese, or chicken fingers. So, how are we supposed to prevent our kids from getting scurvy? Enter trickery! Here are some ideas that can get healthy foods into your kid without them knowing.

- Make smoothies that incorporate fresh or frozen fruits and vegetables.
- Cook green eggs (blend eggs with spinach, then scramble).
- Bake spinach or beet brownies.
- Mix applesauce or bananas into pancake or muffin batter.
- When baking cookies, use whole-grain flour and slip in a bit of flaxseed or chia seeds.
- Sprinkle hemp, flax, or chia seeds into oatmeal.
- Swap regular pasta for chickpea pasta.
- Use an ice cream maker to make "ice cream" out of items like bananas, almond milk, peanut butter, and fresh fruit.
- Add shredded vegetables to pasta sauce.
- Air-fry sweet potato chips.
- Swap mayonnaise for smashed-up avocado.
- Swap sour cream for Greek yogurt.
- Mix mashed-up sweet potatoes into macaroni and cheese.
- Mix any vegetable with a mild taste into foods like meatloaf, meatballs, shepherd's pie, chicken pot pie, lasagna, and pretty much any type of casserole.

As there are seemingly endless incognito ways to make dishes healthier, create a list of your child's favorite foods and brainstorm how to infuse them with hidden nutrients.

Tips for Getting Kids Invested in Healthy Eating

While there is ample satisfaction in sneaking nutrients into your children's favorite dishes, it's helpful to support them in developing an innate desire to adopt a healthy diet, as you won't always be the one making food choices for them.

Here are a few ideas that might help you in this worthwhile endeavor.

- Explain how certain foods help their body. For example, you can share how carrots help the eyes, salmon makes the brain happy and smart, beans and figs help us poop, berries help us not get sick, and so on. You can also explain how healthy food turns into the energy they use to play, and that food is like building blocks that help them grow.
- Make up silly songs about how different foods help the body.
- Help them create a place mat that displays the food groups they need to eat at each meal and how each food group helps them. For example, by protein you could draw your child running and playing, by the grains section you can draw them sitting on the toilet (a major crowd pleaser), and so on.
- Let them choose new fruits and veggies to try.
- Purchase kids' cooking utensils, nylon knives, and an apron of your child's choosing.
- Have them help you make a meal. Experiencing the joy of cooking can heighten a child's interest in eating good food and appreciating what goes into preparing it. You can also let them choose some of the dishes you make from a kids' cookbook.
- Mix art into food prep by having your child arrange the food in fun shapes. For example, you can show them how to make flowers out of strawberry slices, a silly face with fried eggs and sliced black olives, or a Christmas tree sandwich with cookie cutters.

PARENTING AROUND THE WORLD: In Chile, if anyone, even a stranger, offers a child candy, it's seen as a sign of affection. It's also impolite if the parent or child refuses the candy.

Fostering Quality, or at Least Good-Enough, Sleep

Sleep might be one of the most hotly debated parenting topics. Parents and experts alike have big feelings on the "right" way to get kids to sleep, which can make parents feel like failures when getting their kids to sleep seems more difficult than surviving Mordor.

Luckily, there is ample research on sleep. In this section, I'll share the most relevant evidence-based information and support you in determining the sleep strategies that will best suit your child. In addition to building your customized sleep plan, we'll examine how to deal with the judgment you might receive about your plan and how to stand tall in your choices.

Why Everyone Is So Obsessed with Sleep

Sleep has a massive impact on mental and physical health. And while adults (or at least some adults) can hide the toll a lack of sleep has on them, children cannot. Kids are prone to wail, act manic, and just overall lose their ship if they're not getting enough quality sleep.

But when kids do get quality sleep, it's like a magic elixir that supports the following:

- Memory
- Brain development
- Learning
- Impulse control
- Social skills
- Focus and attention
- Mood regulation
- Weight management
- Physical development
- Immune system

What Happens During Each Stage of Sleep

While it might seem like we just fall asleep at night and wake up the next morning, a lot happens in our mind and body in the interim. This interim is composed of sleep stages that affect how we dream, how the sleep is supporting our health, and how mentally restorative the slumber is. If two people get the same amount of sleep one night, but person one has disrupted sleep stages because of things like stress, discomfort, recent changes in their sleep cycles, or other factors, they're not going to receive as many benefits as person two, who smoothly moved through the sleep cycles multiple times.

Another factor influencing how humans move through the sleep cycle is age, which we'll explore in a moment.

Sleep Development in the First Twelve Years

The human body does not come out of the womb automatically following the typical sleep stages. It takes many years for it to figure out the nuances of sleep. Understanding this, and what sleep patterns often look like in the early years, helps parents assess if their children are getting enough quality sleep.

Here's a review of general sleep development for each phase of childhood.

- **0 to 1 year old.** Babies typically sleep sixteen to twenty hours a day, with much of that sleep happening during the day, much to the chagrin of exhausted parents. Throughout their first year, babies adjust to sleeping more at night and often shift to requiring twelve to sixteen hours of sleep a day. Until they're about six months old, babies spend half their slumber in active sleep and the other half in quiet sleep. Active sleep involves rapid eye movement (REM) and all those weird sounds and erratic breathing patterns that freak out many new parents. Quiet sleep is what it sounds like. Babies don't enter the non-REM (NREM) and REM stages until they're a bit older.
- **1 to 5 years old.** During this phase children often require eleven to fourteen hours of sleep a day, and preschoolers need ten to thirteen hours. Children get a portion of this sleep during their daily nap or, if the parent is lucky, naps. By the age of two, most kids only take one nap a day, and by age five, sadly, the nap is

often a fading memory. This age range is also when kids start wailing, "But I no tired!" as they yawn and rub their eyes.

- **6 to 12 years old.** By this age, kids need about nine to twelve hours of sleep a day and are experiencing the typical sleep cycle. Hopefully, by this age good sleep hygiene has been established and children aren't frequently waking up at night.

Potential Reasons Kids Resist Sleep, and What to Do About It

As you might have noticed, it can be challenging to get kids to go to sleep. And then they wake up and crawl in your bed, and you're too tired to move them, so you end up sleeping on a sliver of bed with no blanket and a tiny foot periodically kicking your ribs. It's divine.

So why oh why do children resist something that feels so lovely and makes life better? There are many reasons, and although some might seem silly to grown-ups, they are perfectly legitimate to kids. These reasons can sometimes result in such intense resistance that bedtime can feel like Battle Royale. But take heart my fellow grown-ups: there are ways through.

In addition to the following sleep barriers, I've offered remedies you can put your own spin on if you think they could work for your child.

- **Loneliness.** Being alone can feel intolerable or incredibly scary for some children, causing them to resist sleep.
  Potential remedies: Brainstorm how to help your child feel close to you, even when you're not in the room. For example, you can set a family photo by their bed, play a recording of you singing their favorite lullaby, or give them a stuffed animal to cuddle that you say you're filling with love as you hug it.
- **Not wanting to miss out.** If your child loves to be part of the action, they will likely resist sleep if they think fun will be missed.
  Potential remedies: Tell your child all the boring stuff that will happen after they go to bed, such as dishes, laundry, and watching the news. You could also put a sound machine in their room to block noise that might pique their interest.

- **Excess energy.** Not surprisingly, if your child isn't tired, they're not going to want to sleep.
  Potential remedies: Add activities to your daily schedule, like a trip to the park or family dance party, that can help your child expend excess energy. You can also create a prolonged sleep ritual, such as a bath with a few drops of lavender oil, some chamomile tea, sleepy time books, a head scratch, and a few lullabies. You can also ask your child's pediatrician about melatonin chews.
- **Busy brain.** If it's hard for your child to quiet their mind, it can be difficult to give in to sleep.
  Potential remedies: Utilize relaxation recordings (like the ones at https://www.baileygaddis.com/hypnosis-for-children) that can help your child soothe their mind and fall asleep. You can also minimize stimulating activities at least an hour before bedtime and engage your child in a conversation to allow them to get out all their thoughts from the day.
- **Nerves about tomorrow.** If a child has a big event happening the next day, nerves and a racing mind could make sleep elusive.
  Potential remedies: Talk through the ideal unfolding of the event, envisioning everything going smoothly and even being fun. For example, if you're going on a flight and your child is afraid of planes, you can minimize the fear of the unknown by providing a detailed description of what they can expect, emphasizing the fun elements of the experience.
- **Fear of the dark.** Overcoming a fear of the dark can be a lifelong process, as we have to train our brain to not conjure scary thoughts of what lurks in the unseen.
  Potential remedies: Shift your child's perception of the dark from scary to fun by making shadow puppets, enjoying a constellation projector, or playing with glow-in-the-dark objects. You can also ask your child to brainstorm how they can feel safe in the dark. For example, my son decided that he feels safest when wearing earplugs and an eye mask to shut everything out.

Physiological Sleep Challenges

In addition to mental and emotional sleep issues, kids might struggle to fall, or stay, asleep because of the following issues that affect their physiology.

- **REM sleep rebound.** If a child chronically gets low-quality sleep or has high levels of stress, they can experience REM sleep rebound, which means they spend an excessive amount of their sleep cycle in REM sleep. Because there's ample brain activity in REM sleep, this rebound can result in an irritable and overtired child.
  Potential remedy: Do whatever you can to lower your child's stress levels and improve their sleep hygiene. As they start having higher quality sleep their sleep cycle should balance out.
- **Hunger.** If your child's body doesn't have enough stored-up energy to support metabolism and brain function during sleep, they might experience low-quality sleep.
  Potential remedy: Have your child eat a nutritious meal about two hours before bedtime.
- **Hormone irregularities.** The interdependence of hormones and the body's circadian rhythms means that low-quality sleep can screw up a person's hormone levels and vice versa. Hormones that are especially entwined with sleep include melatonin, estrogen, progesterone, and testosterone.
  Potential remedies: If you're concerned that your child might have hormone imbalances, ask your child's pediatrician for a referral to a pediatric endocrinologist.
- **Pediatric obstructive sleep apnea.** A child could experience breathing irregularities throughout the night if they have a narrow upper airway, or a blockage in this area. This condition is commonly caused by abnormally large tonsils and adenoids, which are lymph tissues in the upper airway between the nose and back of the throat.
  Potential remedies: A pediatrician might recommend certain medications, or removal of the tonsils or adenoids.
- **Periodic limb movement disorder (PLMD).** The verdict is still out on what causes PLMD, a sleep disorder characterized by a

person making involuntary limb movements that can interrupt sleep, but it's believed that it has something to do with the regulation of nerves connecting the brain and limbs.
Potential remedy: Pediatricians typically prescribe medication for PLMD if it's significantly affecting a child's sleep.

- **Sleepwalking.** About one in three kids, especially those four to eight years old, sleepwalk. This phenomenon occurs when a child moves from a deep to light stage of sleep and gets stuck there. They can then get up and wander the house, urinate in the closet, or even leave the house. If a child regularly sleepwalks, it might lead to chronic fatigue.
Potential remedies: If you find your child sleepwalking, it's best not to wake them but instead lead them back to bed. You can also ensure that all doors and windows are locked at night so they can't leave the house, and put a baby monitor in your child's room or a bell on their door, so you're alerted when they're on the move. If the sleepwalking affects your child's energy level or causes them or you distress, speak with their pediatrician and take heart that most children grow out of this.

What to Do About Extreme Sleep Challenges

If you suspect your child has sleep issues serious enough to require the support of a specialist, your first stop should be the pediatrician. These doctors can provide a preliminary evaluation and a referral to a specialist who can hopefully help you resolve the sleep challenges.

This specialized care may include several elements.

- **Cognitive behavioral therapy (CBT).** A counselor trained in CBT can help you discover the potential thoughts and behaviors causing your child's sleep issues. The counselor then uses various techniques to swap the negative thoughts and behaviors with positive alternatives that can hopefully result in better sleep.
- **Sleep log.** Often, one of the first steps a CBT specialist recommends is keeping a log of the child's bedtime routines, when they wake in the night, and when they get up in the morning.

- **Actigraphy watch.** Specialists can evaluate a child's sleep by having them wear an actigraphy watch for a week or so. This watch records your child's movement, how long it takes them to fall asleep, how often they wake up in the night, how much light is in the room, and the duration of sleep.
- **Overnight sleep study.** If it's suspected that breathing issues or excessive movement is disrupting your child's sleep, a specialist might suggest an overnight sleep study that tracks breathing, movement, and in some cases, brain activity.
- **Bloodwork.** If the pediatrician suspects thyroid problems or acid reflux is causing sleep disruptions, they may order a blood test.

Deciding Where Your Child Will Slumber

While some will read this heading and think, *Um, duh, the kids sleep in their own beds, in their own rooms*, it's not that simple for many families, my own included. There are various configurations for familial sleep, and none are right or wrong. It's all about what works best for each family.

I've often heard, "If you let your kid sleep in your bed, they'll never leave," but I don't find that to be true. As children age, factors such as peer pressure and physical comfort cause children to desire their own bed. But before that happens, children and parents may find that they get the best sleep when utilizing an unorthodox sleep arrangement.

Here are examples of sleeping arrangements my clients have used.

- The kid, or kids, sleeping in the parents' bed.
- Kids sleeping on a mat on the parents' bedroom floor.
- Parents taking turns sleeping with the child in the child's bed.
- One parent sleeping in their bed with the kids and the other parent sleeping in another room.
- Parents creating a room of beds that the entire family sleeps in.

If you're struggling with this issue, here are questions to consider that can hopefully lead to your ideal solution.

- Does your family's current sleep arrangement foster quality sleep for all family members? If not, what specific issues disrupt sleep? What are potential solutions?
- If you have a partner, do the two of you differ in where you think your child should sleep? If so, what are potential compromises?
- What conditions do you think would provide the highest quality sleep for all family members?
- Are you resisting a sleep arrangement you're drawn to because you're worried you'll be judged?
- What are all the potential sleeping arrangements in your home?

After answering these questions, list the sleep arrangements that bubble to the top. Then, give each option a try for a week or two to see what provides the highest quality sleep for all involved.

How to Get the Kid Out of Your Bed

If the last section made you realize that you really don't want your child sleeping in your bed anymore, let's make that happen. Whether your child in your bed is disrupting your sleep, sex life, or late-night reality TV and ice cream binges, you get to lovingly kick them out without guilt.

Let's explore ideas for making your bed a child-free zone.

- **Develop a timeline for the bed shift.** If you want to make the eviction a gentle process, create a timeline. For example, you might decide that for a week, you'll put your child down in their own bed but then let them come into yours if they wake up in the middle of the night. For the second week, if they wake up in the middle of the night, they can sleep on a pad on your bedroom floor. The third week, if they come into your room, you bring them back to their bed and lie down with them until they fall asleep.
- **Question your kid.** Ask your child questions about why they don't want to sleep alone in an effort to discover how you can remedy these issues. While we often think we're clocked into the reasons our kids feel a certain way, we sometimes get surprising answers when we ask for their thoughts.

- **Read them books about other children making the shift to their own bed.** Because one of the biggest motivations for children to make certain changes is other children, they might be inspired by books about favorite characters learning to sleep in their own bed or talking to friends who recently started sleeping in their own bed.
- **Make their bed appealing.** Increase your child's excitement, or at least begrudging acceptance, of sleeping in their own bed by letting them pick out bedding that features their favorite characters; a bed frame in the shape of a car, castle, or whatever they're into; a night-light or star projector; and a special stuffed animal. You can also get an essential oil diffuser and use your child's favorite sleepy time scent, such as lavender or chamomile, at bedtime.
- **Utilize incentives.** If bribes don't offend your sensibilities, consider using them when coaxing your child into their own bed. For example, offer a trip to the ice cream shop or a new toy if they sleep in their bed for a week.
- **Release guilt.** If your child desperately wants to sleep in your bed, you might think, *Am I being selfish by putting my sleep needs ahead of my child's sleep wants?* The answer is no. To function as a human and be a present parent, you need quality sleep.

  TIP: Ignore people who say, "If you hadn't let them sleep in your bed in the first place, this wouldn't be an issue." Or better yet, just don't tell them about your sleep tribulations.

Additional Tips for Healthy Sleep Hygiene

Following are ideas to tinker with as you craft the sleep section of your now almost complete (yay!) Parenting Plan.

- ***My Goodnight Garden.*** Here's a link to a story I wrote for my children that works like a charm at bedtime: https://www.baileygaddis.com/my-goodnight-garden.
- **Self-hypnosis.** Have your child close their eyes, take three deep breaths, then imagine they're walking down ten stairs into a sleepy room in their mind. You can help them envision the room by

describing beds made of fluffy clouds, their favorite baby animals cuddled up, and anything else they find relaxing.

- **Tapping.** As discussed in chapter 4, Emotional Freedom Technique is a method of tapping at various points on the body to reset our energy on issues such as fear of the dark, restlessness, or anything else that's causing distress. Visit https://youtu.be/k3TTGzSi1DY to learn the basics of tapping and pass on the teaching to your child if they're old enough.
- **Remaining passively awake.** Have you ever experienced the frustration of worrying so much about not falling asleep that it actually keeps you awake? A popular method for overcoming this issue is to remain passively awake, meaning that once you're in bed you try not to think about falling asleep. Letting go of this worry can help you and your child relax enough to finally fall asleep.

Creating Safe Environments

A muscle relaxant, a serrated knife that had slipped under the dining room rug, a looped cord hanging from a window, and a poisonous houseplant are just some of the hazards I found when reviewing my home's safety status when my son was young. These hazards would have been the first things he reached for had I not found them first.

Children are curious risk-takers who learn about the world through exploration. So of course they're going to head for hazards, as they're usually the most interesting things in the room. But in an effort to minimize ER trips, we can strip the home of as many hazards as possible, especially in the spaces children most inhabit.

Here are some ideas for creating habits that make your home full of safety nests, in addition to ideas for keeping older children safe:

- **Pinpoint where your child spends the most time.** While you want to make your entire home as safe as possible, it's especially important to ensure safety in the spaces where your child spends the most time. For older children, you can do your best to assess the safety of locations they frequent outside the home and consider if there are any you want to make off-limits.

- **Turn frequented areas into no-free havens.** Removing all potential hazards from a space can allow your child to freely play there without you needing to regularly intercede with a "no" or "be careful!"
- **Fill the safety nests with fun.** Increase the time your child wants to spend in their safety nests by providing stimulating toys that foster solo play. Ideal items include open-ended creative materials like blocks and other building materials, colorful scarves, cardboard boxes and tubes, pipe cleaners, and popsicle sticks. Materials that stimulate at least one of the child's five senses, like essential-oil-scented Play-Doh, crayons, and fabric swatches of varying textures, are also great.

  If you have an older child, it can be fun to stock a common area in the home with items they might enjoy, such as favorite books, puzzles, or even a video game system you can play together. The idea is to entice older children out of their room with a space that honors their interests and promotes time with family.

Creating an On-the-Go Safety Kit

Because there are often more hazards outside the home than inside, it's wise to leave supplies in the car that can help keep your little one safe. Here are some examples:

- Stroller to use when walking near busy streets
- Bright top or light-up shoes to put on your child at the park to increase visibility
- Badge for your child's shirt that lists your phone number in case they get lost
- First aid kit

Crafting Safety Rules

Fortify your child's safety by making a list of rules for them and the adults caring for them. To create these rules, envision your child in each of the following locations or situations, pinpoint various hazards that could occur, then brainstorm guidelines that could increase safety.

Safety plan categories:

- Kitchen:
- Eating:
- Bathing:
- Play:
- Sleep:
- Stairs:
- Car:
- Park:
- Parking lots:
- Interactions with strangers:
- Pools and other bodies of water:
- Etc.:

After creating your rules, it can be helpful to use the teach, act, model, and shape (TAMS) routine from the book *Raising Kids Who Choose Safety* by David Schwebel. You talk to your kids about the rules, act out and model them through your behavior, and then, hopefully, their behavior is shaped.

Screen Games and Online Searches

One of the biggest dangers older kids face is the influence of media. The things my son has seen on YouTube and in games that I didn't properly screen still haunt us. These experiences led me to get obsessive about parental controls available on the devices he uses. Luckily, most devices now offer fairly comprehensive parental controls that allow us to control the amount of time our kids spend on a device and curate the type of content they can access.

But because parental controls do not guarantee kids won't find harmful content, it can be helpful to regularly talk with them about media use and make an evolving plan for what type of content they can access. I've found that my son is much more receptive to the parameters my husband and I set when we include him in the planning and allow for a few compromises. However, there are still times when he flips his lid when I say no to a creepy game or gory anime show, for example, so we're definitely a work in progress.

Tip: Visit https://www.commonsensemedia.org/ to research the appropriateness of the media your child wants to consume.

Guided Meditation

This meditation helps you summon the motivation and creativity to help your child make healthy choices, while also fortifying your patience for those moments when they refuse your guidance: https://www.baileygaddis.com/healthy-choices.

Writing Prompts

- How often does your child need to eat?
- How often do you need to eat?

- What are your child's favorite dishes? How can you sneak nutrients into those dishes?
- What does your child typically eat in a day? Are there aspects of their daily menu you want to tweak?
- Is there a food group your child won't eat? How can you make options from that group more appealing?
- Is there anything about your own diet you want to adjust?
- Does your child have any allergies? If so, how can you adapt their diet so they still receive all required nutrients?
- Do you want to have a set menu for each day of the week?
- Does it work with your schedule and personality to do meal prep on the weekend?
- How can you make healthy eating easier for your family?
- Do you want to create a go-to grocery list that includes your family's favorite healthy foods?
- How do you want to inspire your child to invest in healthy eating? What meals could you prepare together?
- What bedtime routine seems to be the most effective for your child?
- What bedtime routine seems to be the most effective for you?
- Are your family's current sleeping arrangements fostering quality sleep? If not, what are shifts you can make to improve this?
- Does your child have any sleep challenges, such as fear of the dark or sleepwalking? If so, is it something you think requires professional support, or an issue you can help your child resolve on your own? What are your ideas for helping them overcome their sleep challenges?
- Do you have any challenges? If so, what are your ideas for overcoming them?
- Are there any elements in your child's room or your room, such as light from a device or an uncomfortable mattress, that could be lowering sleep quality? If so, what are things you can do to make the room more optimal for quality rest?
- What self-soothing techniques does my child use, if any, and are there new ones I can teach them?
- If your child's bedtime routine is interrupting yours, how can you weave them together so everyone can get optimal sleep?

- What is your safety plan for the situations and locations that pose a safety risk for your child? (See Safety Plan categories on page 264.)
- How can you get your child onboard with the safety plans?
- What parental controls are available on the devices your child uses?
- What type of content do you feel is appropriate for your child to consume? How do you want to discuss this with them?
- Are there any changes you want to make regarding your child's media use? How do you want to discuss this with them?

Parenting Plan

Nutrition

Our family food philosophy:

Plan for managing my child's eating challenges:

Plan for managing my eating challenges:

Morning eating plan:

Afternoon eating plan:

Evening eating plan:

Go-to shopping list:

Sleep

My child's bedtime routine:

My bedtime routine:

Plan for creating an ideal sleeping arrangement:

Plan for moving my child through sleep challenges:

Favorite self-soothing techniques:

Safety

Media plan:

On-the-go safety kit materials:

You can find the additional Safety Plan categories on page 264.

11

ELEMENT 9: PARENTING WITH YOUR PEOPLE

LUCKILY, PARENTING DOESN'T UNFOLD IN A VACUUM. Even if you have a single-parent household, it's likely that a rainbow of other adults will affect your child through the years. And while this rainbow is full of wonder and adventure, it also contains challenges, as each adult has a unique way of relating to children. This uniqueness has the potential to foster growth in you and your child, but it can come with pains as you navigate differences in communication styles and disciplining practices, and scheduling. But these pains are worth it, as building a village will give you more time to care for yourself and give your child a solid sense of safety and connection in addition to a range of enriching experiences.

Building Your Parenting Village

Thoughtfully crafting a village that deeply enriches your family's life could be one of the greatest gifts you give yourself and your child. The village exposes your child to a range of personalities and styles of being that help them become a more resilient, well-rounded person. You can make the relational ecosystem of the village even more vibrant by making the values and plans from your Parenting Plan the cornerstones of how the village functions.

Here's a breakdown of how to recruit your parenting people.

- **List what you want.** Write down the elements you want in your child's life, such as humor, adventure, stimulating conversation, a clean environment, healthy food, and so on. You can also list elements you want in your own life, such as a person to vent to, someone to veg out with, a dance partner, and so on.
- **Explore who can meet these needs.** Brainstorm which adults in your life, or even which offerings at a local community center, for example, could help you weave those elements into your family's life.
- **Meet people who can fulfill these needs.** If you don't know many people in your area, you can consider ways to meet potential "villagers." Chapter 8 provides a variety of ideas on where to meet other parents, but you can also meet like-minded adults by joining a gym, taking a dance class, or doing anything else that puts you in the presence of strangers who might just end up becoming beloved villagers.
- **Ask for specific support.** As you pinpoint adults who can fulfill specific roles in your family life, write down how you'd like to invite them to participate. For example, if your brother and your child share an interest in rock climbing, you might ask him if he'd be willing to take your child to a climbing gym every other week. Or if your list includes "laughing more" and "making more healthy food," you might ask your funny friend, who also happens to be a great cook, to come over twice a month to show you how to make healthy meals while also engaging you in laugh-till-you-cry conversation. Forming these specific asks makes it easier for your people to know how they can support you and when to show up.

While it can feel overwhelming to spend time thinking about and then crafting this village, and nerve-racking to be vulnerable enough to ask for help, the results of this community building will likely be life-changing for you and your family.

Communicating About Child Care Without Eye Rolls and Gritted Teeth

If two people disagree on the "right" way to navigate a certain aspect of a child's life, the resulting convos can be incendiary. However, it is possible to walk the line between honoring your parenting beliefs and plan and staying open to the other person's point of view. Being intentional about how you communicate with the other adults who care for your child can infuse harmony into the parenting village. This harmony can then make future communication easier and provide your child with beautiful examples of effective collaboration.

Here are ideas to help ensure your communication with fellow villagers is productive.

Review Your Parenting Plan

Periodically reading your Parenting Plan can keep your customized ideas front-of-mind when communicating about a certain child care topic. It's also helpful to share your Parenting Plan with your villagers to provide an in-depth view of how you're hoping to raise your child.

Request Suggestions for Parenting Plan Revisions

If you find that an aspect of your Parenting Plan is no longer working, it could be interesting to ask certain members of your village for their thoughts. Collecting these thoughts from the adults who know your child best could help you address the topic in question with a fresh, innovative outlook.

Something else you might experience is one of your villagers having an issue with an aspect of your Parenting Plan. While an understandable reaction is defensiveness, you might open a door to a bevy of compelling ideas if you at least hear out the other adult. As you listen, remind yourself that being open to a discussion about your differing views doesn't mean you agree with them or are going to change that aspect of your plan, it just means you're open.

Outlining Your Expectations

Clearly communicating your expectations for the interactions between your villagers and your child will make everyone's life easier. For example, if your sister has your daughter at her house every Wednesday afternoon, you can brainstorm how you'd like that to look. You might decide that you're only OK with your child watching thirty minutes of TV if your sister helps them find an appropriate show. You might also give your sister a breakdown of how you typically communicate with and discipline your daughter and which of those tactics you want her to utilize. After listing these expectations, share them with the adult in question, making it clear that what you're sharing aren't laws, but instead ideas that you'd like to discuss to ensure their time with your child feels good for all.

For many, this sharing of expectations can feel uncomfortable, as the mind might scream, *Are you crazy? This person is already doing us a massive favor. Won't it just piss them off to share all these expectations with them?* The thing is, when you share these expectations in a manner that makes it clear you want to collaborate in the creation of an amazing relationship between that adult and your child, the adult will likely be relieved. It's like you're handing them a cheat sheet for how to connect with your child and giving them permission to share ideas they might have for putting a twist on certain expectations.

Discussing the Formula for Tense Discussions

When you're parenting with other peeps, you will have some tense conversations. Help ensure these conversations don't go sideways by reviewing the Formula for Tense Discussions in your Parenting Plan.

Staying on Topic

Conversations can quickly go into dangerous waters when they veer from the original topic. To avoid this, commit to staying on topic while also helping your conversation partner do the same.

For example, when my client Siobhan was talking to her mother-in-law, Jean, about not giving her child so many cheap plastic toys, Siobhan felt tempted to say, "And I also feel like you give Harlow way too much sugar." However, sugar wasn't the topic at hand, so she put a pin in the sugar and stuck to the plastic.

When Jean said, "Well I don't feel like toys are the problem, I think the issue is all the screen time you let Harlow have," it seriously triggered Siobhan, but she didn't take the bait. She said, "We can discuss screens another time, but right now I want to focus on the toys." Siobhan and Jean, through sticking to the primary topic, were able to reach a compromise.

Not Taking Conflict Personally

Researchers have found that people who typically take conflict personally value interdependence more than independence and care deeply about what others think of them. This can be a strength in some ways, as someone who values interdependence can be incredibly thoughtful and put in ample work to create harmony in relationships. But this desire to maintain harmony can lead to the avoidance of conflict.

What should conflict avoiders do? Lean into the discomfort. Have that difficult conversation, even when everything in you is begging you to keep the peace. Speak your mind, trusting that you'll survive the conflict and might even create a deeper bond and enhanced harmony with the other person.

TIP: When engaged in a parenting conflict, view criticism or advice as drops of possibility. This reframe helps you process what the other person is saying more objectively and determine if their opinions and suggestions are worth further exploration.

Asking for a Babysitting Sesh Recap

Having a quick powwow with the adult who just cared for your child gives them a chance to review their time with your child and share, for example, that your child didn't want to hold hands when crossing the street or refused to eat anything but French fries. You can also ask how the caregiver managed these situations, so you know if you need to discuss these topics with your child. This check-in, however brief, can create a more collaborative relationship and fortify your sense of community.

Coordinating Schedules

A primary topic of discussion in my household is scheduling. It feels like we're always trying to figure out who needs to be where when, who is getting that person there, and who is taking care of the smallest child when it's all happening. So, this is a topic I think a lot about, and I actively try to find ideas that will make it easier to coordinate schedules. Following are the most successful strategies we've used so far.

- **Create a shared digital calendar.** A shared calendar through a service like Google is a game changer. You can give all the main caregivers in your child's life access to this calendar and ask them to add anything that's relevant to your village schedule. For example, the two people on my shared calendar are my mom and husband, as they're the primary people supporting me with the kids. If someone wants to schedule a meeting with me at 2:00 PM on a Tuesday, for example, I can look at the digital calendar to see if my mom or Eric will be available to watch Grace during this time.
- **Give everyone their own color.** Make the shared calendar easier to decipher by assigning everyone their own color. For my family, I'm purple, my daughter is pink, my mom is yellow, my husband is green, my son is blue, and orange is an all-family event. If I'm trying to remember when my daughter has her next check-up, for example, I'll scan the calendar for pink events. On the kids' calendar entries, we note who will take them to the activity.
- **Include addresses or other instructions in the calendar notes.** Avoid panicked, last-minute texts or calls from a fellow villager by entering addresses and any other relevant instructions to the notes associated with each calendar event.
- **Adding child care routines to the calendar.** As you create this shared schedule, review the Routines section of your Parenting Plan and add reminders of the routines to the schedule.
- **Get a bunch of car seats, or boosters.** When you and various other adults are regularly shuttling kids around, it can be a major hassle to constantly shuffle kid seats from car to car. If it's

financially feasible for you, skip this hassle by getting the needed seat for your child for each car they regularly ride in.

Selecting Your Ideal Types of Child Care

As you gather the adults who will help you raise your child, remember that these people don't have to be friends or family members. There are a variety of resources that can connect you with adults who will lovingly care for your child, such as day-care centers, co-ops, and babysitter services. Exploring these options can often reveal an exciting world of possibilities for getting some much needed help.

Common child care options include the following:

- **Daycare.** Many daycares accept children as young as a few months old up to about three and provide various programs that can suit a variety of schedules.
- **Preschool.** Preschools typically care for children who are between three and five years old and, like daycares, include a variety of programs and cost schedules.
- **Child care co-ops.** A child care co-op is owned and operated by the parents who are members. This type of co-op involves the members creating a consistent schedule for child care and taking turns providing that child care.
- **Parent's helper.** This is someone you hire to care for your children while you're also at home. Because you'll be home in case of emergency, parent helpers are often teens or tweens and don't charge as much as professional babysitters.
- **Babysitter.** A babysitter, or nanny, is typically someone who can legally drive your child, if needed, and is responsible enough to care for them without you. Services like Care.com can connect you with babysitters who have been carefully vetted.

Creating Child Care Criteria

As you explore child care options, bring elements of your Parenting Plan into the mix. Here are questions that can help you clarify the types of child care you want to explore, and the criteria you'd like your final picks to meet.

- What is their policy on screen time?
- How do they handle food allergies?
- Will they be making food for my child? If so, what type of food will they be making?
- Do they have communication philosophies they follow?
- How do they navigate disciplining?
- How do they handle conflict resolution?
- What do they do when a child has a big emotion?
- What activities will they facilitate?
- Do they have training in child development?
- Are they trained in child first aid and CPR?
- Do I trust this person or people?
- Does my child seem to feel comfortable with this person and/or in this care environment?
- Are there other adults my child will be around when being cared for by this person? If so, do I trust those adults?
- Do their services cost money? If so, is the cost feasible for my budget?
- Are they able to accommodate a consistent child care schedule?
- How do I feel about the safety, cleanliness, and overall ambiance of the area or areas where they'll be caring for my child?
- Will my child be with other children? If so, how many? What is the age range of the other children?
- Will they be transporting my child? If so, do they have a clean driving record and safe vehicle?

NOTE: Go to the following site to review additional resources for finding quality child care: https://www.childcareaware.org/start-your-child-care-search/.

After exploring these questions, list your resulting criteria in order of importance. This ranked list makes it easier to pinpoint the child care options that best suit your family.

Regularly Reevaluating Child Care

As your child's care needs will shift over time, you'll want to assess how a certain child care option is working out every six months or so. This review helps you determine if there are adjustments you'd like to request, or if you'd like to try something new.

Veins of Gold in the Challenges

In the fifteenth century, the Japanese art of *kintsugi* was born. *Kintsugi* consists of repairing broken ceramics with gold. *Kintsugi* is referred to in the realms of creativity and relationships, as often the breaking and then thoughtful repair of something like an idea or relationship results in it becoming stronger and more vibrant.

I find the idea of *kintsugi* to be especially relevant when navigating the relationships involved in parenting, as they can start out incredibly fragile, or be made fragile by the trials of caring for young children. This fragility can lead to breaks, and breaks result in two choices: leaving the pieces on the floor or repairing with gold. When we choose the latter, we not only make the relationship stronger but also are better able to view its beauty and value. The breakage and repair also offers juicy learning opportunities and hones our ability to mold adversity into possibility.

When we adopt this attitude toward hardship of any kind, we chip away at the fear of failure and can forge a life filled with courage and curiosity for all the glorious creations that can result from our stumbles. Holding this belief in the back of your mind when arguing with your partner about potty training or trying to coordinate confusing schedules with your village, for example, will help you maintain a flicker of hope that this challenge can lead to something spectacular.

This attitude saved me during the last trimester of my pregnancy with my daughter and the first few months of her life. A combination of stress, depression, and what was likely a hormonal imbalance caused my husband to experience a prolonged emotional breakdown. This broke us. But despite the pain I kept telling myself that something beautiful would grow from the struggle. I felt like a liar but held on to the belief.

More than a year later I'm noticing the veins of gold in our newly repaired relationship. My husband and I have learned how to argue with compassion, at least most of the time, and have gotten to know one another on a deeper level. We have a newfound commitment to doing life together. Our son got to witness this repair and learn that while his parents are deeply flawed, we will always protect and love him. Our family shines brighter.

Guided Meditation

In this meditation you'll visualize the ideal adults you'd like to support you in raising your child. You'll explore how they might be best able to help and then tune in to how that help makes you feel. Visit https://www.baileygaddis.com/parenting-village.

Writing Prompts

- What adults can enhance my family's life?
- If I don't know many adults in my area, where can I meet some?
- What do I most need help with?
- What are my expectations for each member of my parenting village?
- What communication techniques would I like to utilize with my parenting village?
- In addition to friends and family members, are there other types of child care I'm drawn to?
- What are my criteria for child care?
- What scheduling methods might work best for my village?

Parenting Plan

Members of my parenting village:

Specific support each helper provides:

Expectations for each helper:

Criteria and budget for additional child care:

Conflict resolution plan:

Parenting village schedule:

Conclusion

PUTTING IT ALL TOGETHER

Holy guacamole my friend, you made it! You've uncovered your beliefs about the essential aspects of parenting and crafted a plan for transforming those beliefs into action. You artfully dissected what parenting means to you and how you want to show up for your child and self. You've empowered yourself with inspired plans for how to interact with your child and are ready for those times when everyone seems to be melting down. You've got this. The positive impact you're going to (and already) have on your child will transform their lives.

To ensure you're clear on the material in your Parenting Plan, here are some final thoughts to tie up our journey.

Utilizing the Plan

Review your plan often, especially when faced with a tricky parenting situation. The more you review and enact the plan, the more it will embed in your mind, and living its contents will become second nature.

I also encourage you to give yourself kudos every time you view and enact the plan. You put so much love and thought into this. It's not just something a stranger made, but something you tailored for your life.

Prepare for Discomfort and Frustration

As growth and change are uncomfortable and often frustrating, you will probably experience challenges as you shift how you parent. While it's natural to resist this change in favor of comfort, committing daily to the parenting style you've developed can infuse your life with joy, inspiration, and deeply satisfying connection. Often, when we experience discomfort when trying something new, it's a sign we're heading in the right direction—that we're pushing through old ways that are comfortable only because they're familiar. Feel pride when that discomfort hits, because it means you're changing the trajectory of your life.

Building the Habits, One at a Time

It takes twenty-one days of doing something new to make it a habit. This stick-with-it-ness allows this "something new" to take root in your life. But because it would likely be overwhelming to cram all the new habits your Parenting Plan includes into a twenty-one-day period, you might just want to plant a few pieces of the plan at a time.

For example, for twenty-one days you can commit to utilizing the first few practices you outlined in the Communication section of your Parenting Plan, and so on.

In addition to helping you avoid overwhelm, this gentle pace provides time and space for you to notice how certain practices are working, and if they need to be adjusted or even scrapped.

There Is No End Point, Only Evolution

Many of us believe that once *x*, *y*, and *z* occur, and those proverbial ducks get their stuff together, all will be good. But that belief isn't in harmony with the reality of life, a reality often consisting of *c* and *f* happening instead of *y* and some of our ducks getting stuck in mud. Life is a beautiful mess no matter how neurotic and organized we are. This is especially true with parenting. Once we get little Lily pooing in the toilet, she develops the skill of scaling kitchen cabinets. Little Lucas has moved past his fear of the dark but is now wetting the bed. Everything and everyone are constantly changing, and that's what makes life so dynamic and engaging.

Remember, there's no finish line, just an ever-unfolding series of wonderful, complex, sometimes heart-wrenching moments and decisions that all serve to mold us and our children into the people we are destined to become. Embrace the ever-changing nature of your children and how you parent them. Be curious and open, as the changes come fast and sometimes hard. Honor yourself each time you parent in a way that feels good and true to you. Let parenting moments that make you cringe roll off you, because they contain golden drops of learning that open the bloom of wisdom.

The Parenting Plan Template

If you haven't already, download the printable Parenting Plan template at the following link and insert all the wisdom you've recorded: https://www.baileygaddis.com/parenting-plan.

My friend, I have no doubt you are an amazing, curious, strong, and resilient parent and person who has thoughtfully equipped yourself for your parenting adventures. These adventures will not always be enjoyable, but they will always be situations that you have the mind and heart to navigate. Always.

It has been one of the greatest honors of my life going on this ride with you.

With love,

Bailey

ACKNOWLEDGMENTS

I WAS ONLY ABLE TO WRITE THIS BOOK because of the love and support of many people. My children, Hudson and Grace, inducted me into the hallowed halls (or fun house) of parenthood and, through many twists, turns, and tantrums, taught me the power of curiosity, compromise, and of course cuddles. You two are the light at my core.

Thank you to my mom, Anna Lee Hicks, and husband, Eric Cowen, who provided the endless support that allowed me to sneak away to research and write. Mom, you are the life force of our family and selflessly provide the support and wisdom that allow me to stay sane. Having you and Dad as a daily presence in our lives is the greatest blessing. You both filled my childhood with compassion, exploration, and admirable values that have molded me into a parent I can be proud of.

Eric, being your partner in life has been an adventure filled with patience, understanding, and unconditional love. We've had high highs and low lows, but throughout it all we've stayed united and committed to providing our children with a stable, loving home. (And thank you for always taking out the trash!)

Thank you to Oak Grove School. Being part of your community, and learning from your treasure trove of teachers, has transformed how I parent, and do life.

To Michelle Williams, I am forever grateful that you saw the potential in *Customized Parenting* and provided the kindness, encouragement, and guidance that made the birth of this book possible. Also, a special thanks to Rachel McCumber, Melanie Roth, Devon Freeny, and the rest of the team at Chicago Review Press for helping me thoughtfully refine the book and get it out into the world.

NOTES

Introduction: The Seed of Your Plan

those who write down their goals: Gail Matthews, "The Impact of Accountability and Written Goals on Goal Progress," *PsycEXTRA Dataset*, 2007, https://doi.org/10.1037/e656862007-001.

2. Inviting Your Intuition on This Journey

"The first of the three elements": Bailey Gaddis, *Feng Shui Mommy: Creating Balance and Harmony Amidst the Chaos for Blissful Pregnancy, Childbirth, and Motherhood* (New World Library, 2017).

found that intuition does exist: Galang Lufityanto, Chris Donkin, and Joel Pearson, "Measuring Intuition," *Psychological Science* 27, no. 5 (2016): 622–634.

three types of intuition: Jean E. Pretz and Kathryn Sentman Totz, "Measuring Individual Differences in Affective, Heuristic, and Holistic Intuition," *Personality and Individual Differences* 43, no. 5 (2007): 1247–1257, https://doi.org/10.1016/j.paid.2007.03.015.

the dentists in the study: R. P. Nalliah, "Clinical Decision Making—Choosing Between Intuition, Experience and Scientific Evidence," *British Dental Journal* 221, no. 12 (2016): 752–754.

Your intuition is birthed: Lutz Kaufmann, Claudia M. Wagner, and Craig R. Carter, "Individual Modes and Patterns of Rational and Intuitive Decision-Making by Purchasing Managers," *Journal of Purchasing and Supply Management* 23, no. 2 (2017): 82–93.

found that taking the time now: Marco Sahm and Robert K. von Weizsäcker, "Reason, Intuition, and Time," *Managerial and Decision Economics* 37, no. 3 (January 15, 2015): 195–207, https://doi.org/10.1002/mde.2711.

intuitive awareness, composed of a mix: Viktor Dörfler and Fran Ackermann, "Understanding Intuition: The Case for Two Forms of Intuition," *Management Learning* 43, no. 5 (November 2012): 545–564.

top CEOs also rely on patterns: Modesto A. Maidique, "Decoding Intuition for More Effective Decision-Making," *Harvard Business Review*, July 23, 2014.

research participants were more likely: Ap Dijksterhuis and Loran F. Nordgren, "A Theory of Unconscious Thought," *Perspectives on Psychological Science* 1, no. 2 (2006): 95–109, https://doi.org/10.1111/j.1745-6916.2006.00007.x.

your body often responds: Joseph LeDoux, "Rethinking the Emotional Brain," *Neuron* 73, no. 5 (2012): 1052.

helpful resources to guide us: Jennifer L. Eberhardt, *Biased: Uncovering the Hidden Prejudice That Shapes What We See, Think, and Do* (Penguin Books, 2019); Louise Derman-Sparks, Julie Olsen Edwards, and Catherine M. Goins, *Anti-bias Education for Young Children & Ourselves* (National Association for the Education of Young Children, 2020).

a connection between the use: Howard Weiss and Russell Cropanzano, "Affective Events Theory: A Theoretical Discussion of the Structure, Causes and Consequences of Affective Experiences at Work," in *Research in Organizational Behavior*, vol. 18, eds. B. M. Staw and L. L. Cummings (Elsevier Science/JAI Press, 1996), 1–74.

A study of chefs: Marc Stierand and Viktor Dörfler, "The Role of Intuition in the Creative Process of Expert Chefs," *Journal of Creative Behavior* 50, no. 3 (September 14, 2015): 178–185, https://doi.org/10.1002/jocb.100.

intuition improves over time: Galang Lufityanto, Chris Donkin, and Joel Pearson, "Measuring Intuition," *Psychological Science* 27, no. 5 (2016): 622–634.

association between intuition and creativity: Judit Pétervári, Magda Osman, and Joydeep Bhattacharya, "The Role of Intuition in the Generation and Evaluation Stages of Creativity," *Frontiers in Psychology* 7 (2016).

3. Element 1: Crafting a Family Communication Philosophy

"an internal aura that encompasses": Eugene T. Gendlin, *Focusing* (Bantam Books, 1981).

an "autonomy-supportive" tone: Netta Weinstein, Maarten Vansteenkiste, and Silke Paulmann, "Listen to Your Mother: Motivating Tones of Voice Predict Adolescents' Reactions to Mothers," *Developmental Psychology* 55, no. 12 (December 2019): 2534–2546, https://doi.org/10.1037/dev0000827.

communicating through music can cause neurogenesis: Hajime Fukui and Kumiko Toyoshima, "Music Facilitate the Neurogenesis, Regeneration and Repair of Neurons," *Medical Hypotheses* 71, no. 5 (2008): 765–769, https://doi.org/10.1016/j.mehy.2008.06.019.

You can amp up all these benefits: Graham Welch, *The Benefits of Singing for Children* (Institute of Education, University of London, February 2012), https://efdm.org/wp-content/uploads/2017/10/ThebenefitsofsingingforchildrenGFW.pdf.

encouraging this skill can enhance: Sylvia Holmes and Susan Hallam, "The Impact of Participation in Music on Learning Mathematics," *London Review of Education*, 2017, https://doi.org/10.18546/lre.15.3.07.

whose parents regularly tell them stories: K. Salmon and E. Reese, "The Benefits of Reminiscing with Young Children," *Current Directions in Psychological Science* 25, no. 4 (2016): 233–238, https://doi.org/10.1177/0963721416655100.

"It is spoken at the right time": "Vaca Sutta: A Statement," translated from the Pali by Thanissaro Bhikkhu, *Access to Insight (BCBS Edition)*, AN 5.198 (2010), http://www.accesstoinsight.org/tipitaka/an/an05/an05.198.than.html.

4. Element 2: Navigating All the Emotions

prefrontal cortex plays an important role: Kevin N. Ochsner, Rebecca D. Ray, Jeffrey C. Cooper, Elaine R. Robertson, Sita Chopra, John D. E. Gabrieli, and James J. Gross, "For Better or for Worse: Neural Systems Supporting the Cognitive Down- and Up-Regulation of Negative Emotion," *NeuroImage* 23, no. 2 (2004): 483–499, https://doi.org/10.1016/j.neuroimage.2004.06.030.

ability to suppress an impulsive response: Shintaro Funahashi, "Prefrontal Cortex and Working Memory," *Brain Science* (2022): 515–543, https://doi.org/10.1007/978-981-19-7268-3_10.

emotion-related parenting practices: Alysia Y. Blandon and Meghan B. Scrimgeour, "Child, Parenting, and Situational Characteristics Associated with Toddlers' Prosocial Behaviour," *Infant and Child Development* 24, no. 6 (2015): 643–660, https://doi.org/10.1002/icd.1910.

how the child will navigate emotions: Veronica Ornaghi, Elisabetta Conte, and Ilaria Grazzani, "Empathy in Toddlers: The Role of Emotion Regulation, Language Ability, and Maternal Emotion Socialization Style," *Frontiers in Psychology* 11 (2020), https://doi.org/10.3389/fpsyg.2020.586862.

"literally become embedded in the architecture": Jack Shonkoff, "Children's Emotional Development Is Built into the Architecture of Their Brains," *Center on the Developing Child at Harvard University*, October 29, 2020, https://developingchild.harvard.edu/resources/childrens-emotional-development-is-built-into-the-architecture-of-their-brains/.

utilizing emotion regulation strategies: K. Kurki, H. Järvenoja, S. Järvelä, and A. Mykkänen, "Young Children's Use of Emotion and Behavior Regulation Strategies in Socio-emotionally Challenging Day-Care Situations," *Early Childhood Research Quarterly* 41 (2017): 50–62, https://doi.org/10.1016/j.ecresq.2017.06.002.

a contributing citizen of the world: Shonkoff, "Children's Emotional Development."

developing empathy is a crucial step: Ornaghi, Conte, and Grazzani, "Empathy in Toddlers."

three levels of empathy development: M. Hoffman, "Empathy and Prosocial Behavior," in *Handbook of Emotion*, ed. M. Lewis, J. M. Haviland-Jones, and L. Feldman Barrett (Guilford Press, 2008), 440–455.

empathy is connected to their verbal ability: Ornaghi, Conte, and Grazzani, "Empathy in Toddlers."

The COMT gene: S. J. Bishop, J. D. Cohen, J. Fossella, et al., "COMT Genotype Influences Prefrontal Response to Emotional Distraction," *Cognitive, Affective, & Behavioral Neuroscience* 6 (2006): 62–70, https://doi.org/10.3758/CABN.6.1.62.

health of the parasympathetic nervous system: Manjie Wang and Kimberly J. Saudino, "Genetic and Environmental Influences on Individual Differences in Emotion Regulation and Its Relation to Working Memory in Toddlerhood," *Emotion* 13, no. 6 (2013): 1055–1067, https://doi.org/10.1037/a0033784.

neural, cardiac, and neuroendocrine systems: Pamela M. Cole, Nilam Ram, and Mary Samantha English, "Toward a Unifying Model of Self-Regulation: A

Developmental Approach," *Child Development Perspectives* 13, no. 2 (2018): 91–96, https://doi.org/10.1111/cdep.12316.

neuropeptides, or chemical messengers: Brian J. Mickey, Zhifeng Zhou, Mary M. Heitzeg, Elizabeth Heinz, Colin A. Hodgkinson, David T. Hsu, Scott A. Langenecker, et al., "Emotion Processing, Major Depression, and Functional Genetic Variation of Neuropeptide Y," *Archives of General Psychiatry* 68, no. 2 (2011): 158, https://doi.org/10.1001/archgenpsychiatry.2010.197.

feel-good messages: D. Dfarhud, M. Malmir, and M. Khanahmadi, "Happiness & Health: The Biological Factors—Systematic Review Article," *Iranian Journal of Public Health* 43, no. 11 (November 2014): 1468–1477, PMID: 26060713; PMCID: PMC4449495.

the "pleasure chemical": Don E. Davis, Nathan Ballantyne, Joshua N. Hook, and Daryl R. Van Tongeren, "Conclusion to the Special Issue on the Interdisciplinary Study of Intellectual Humility: Unifying Themes from Divergent Theories and Research Programs," *Journal of Positive Psychology* 18, no. 2 (2023): 316–326.

specifically in the ventral striatum: Richard J. Davidson, Daren C. Jackson, and Ned H. Kalin, "Emotion, Plasticity, Context, and Regulation: Perspectives from Affective Neuroscience," *Psychological Bulletin* 126, no. 6 (2000): 890–909, https://doi.org/10.1037/0033-2909.126.6.890.

tells the brain it's safe to interact: Barbara L. Fredrickson, "The Role of Positive Emotions in Positive Psychology: The Broaden-and-Build Theory of Positive Emotions," *American Psychologist* 56, no. 3 (2001): 218–226, https://doi.org/10.1037/0003-066x.56.3.218.

physical, intellectual, and social resources: Fredrickson, "The Role of Positive Emotions."

positive emotions pump up: Sheldon Cohen, William J. Doyle, Ronald B. Turner, Carol M. Alper, and David P. Skoner, "Emotional Style and Susceptibility to the Common Cold," *Psychosomatic Medicine* 65, no. 4 (July–August 2003): 652–657, https://doi.org/10.1097/01.psy.0000077508.57784.da.

even prolong someone's life: N. Park, C. Peterson, D. Szvarca, R. J. Vander Molen, E. S. Kim, and K. Collon, "Positive Psychology and Physical Health: Research and Applications," *American Journal of Lifestyle Medicine* 10, no. 3 (2016): 200–206, https://doi.org/10.1177/1559827614550277; R. J. Davidson, M. Lewis, L. B. Alloy, D. G. Amaral, G. Bush, J. Cohen, et al., "Neural and

Behavioral Substrates of Mood and Mood Regulation," *Biological Psychiatry* 52, no. 6 (2002): 478–502.

positive emotions help the body: Fredrickson, "The Role of Positive Emotions"; J. A. Stern, M. Botdorf, J. Cassidy, and T. Riggins, "Empathic Responding and Hippocampal Volume in Young Children," *Developmental Psychology* 55, no. 9 (2019): 1908–1920, https://doi.org/10.1037/dev0000684.

"wear and tear" on the body: Carol D. Ryff, Burton H. Singer, Edgar Wing, Gayle Dienberg Love, and Meg Wise, "Elective Affinities and Uninvited Agonies: Mapping Emotion with Significant Others onto Health," in *Emotion, Social Relationships, and Health*, ed. Carol D. Ryff and Burton Singer, Series in Affective Science (2001; online edition, Oxford Academic, 2012), https://doi.org/10.1093/acprof:oso/9780195145410.003.0005, accessed October 2, 2023.

negative emotions can impair thinking: R. J. Davidson, M. Lewis, L. B Alloy, D. G. Amaral, G. Bush, J. Cohen, et al., "Neural and Behavioral Substrates of Mood and Mood Regulation," *Biological Psychiatry* 52, no. 6 (2002): 478–502.

problem-solving skills improve: Rebecca L. Gómez and Jamie O. Edgin, "The Extended Trajectory of Hippocampal Development: Implications for Early Memory Development and Disorder," *Developmental Cognitive Neuroscience* 18 (2016): 57–69, https://doi.org/10.1016/j.dcn.2015.08.009.

size of a person's hippocampus: Stern, Botdorf, Cassidy, and Riggins, "Empathic Responding."

nine to eleven years old: Akiko Uematsu, Mie Matsui, Chiaki Tanaka, Tsutomu Takahashi, Kyo Noguchi, Michio Suzuki, and Hisao Nishijo, "Developmental Trajectories of Amygdala and Hippocampus from Infancy to Early Adulthood in Healthy Individuals," *PLoS ONE* 7, no. 10 (2012), https://doi.org/10.1371/journal.pone.0046970.

become pros at communicating: Gómez and Edgin, "The Extended Trajectory."

long-term potentiation: J. Kim, and D. Diamond, "The Stressed Hippocampus, Synaptic Plasticity and Lost Memories," *Nature Reviews Neuroscience* 3 (2002): 453–462, https://doi.org/10.1038/nrn849.

affecting the limbic system: S. W. Cole, L. C. Hawkley, J. M. Arevalo, et al., "Social Regulation of Gene Expression in Human Leukocytes," *Genome Biology* 8 (2007): R189, https://doi.org/10.1186/gb-2007-8-9-r189; Catharina S. Hamann, Julian Bankmann, Hanna Mora Maza, Johannes Kornhuber, Iulia Zoicas, and Angelika Schmitt-Böhrer, "Social Fear Affects Limbic System

Neuronal Activity and Gene Expression," *International Journal of Molecular Sciences* 23, no. 15 (2022): 8228, https://doi.org/10.3390/ijms23158228.

intervention from a compassionate caregiver: Hillary Franke, "Toxic Stress: Effects, Prevention and Treatment," *Children* 1, no. 3 (2014): 390–402, https://doi.org/10.3390/children1030390.

an upstairs and downstairs: Daniel J. Siegel and Tina Payne Bryson, "Building the Staircase of the Mind," in *The Whole-Brain Child* (Robinson, 2012).

a certain negative emotion: Fredrickson, "The Role of Positive Emotions."

joy has been found to create: Judy Dunn, Jane Brown, and Lynn Beardsall, "Family Talk about Feeling States and Children's Later Understanding of Others' Emotions," *Developmental Psychology* 27, no. 3 (1991): 448–455, https://doi.org/10.1037/0012-1649.27.3.448.

reasoning skills improve: Cole, Ram, and English, "Toward a Unifying Model of Self-Regulation."

Caregivers can nurture: Ornaghi, Conte, and Grazzani, "Empathy in Toddlers."

handle difficult social situations: Judy Dunn, Jane Brown, and Lynn Beardsall, "Family Talk About Feeling States and Children's Later Understanding of Others' Emotions," *Developmental Psychology* 27, no. 3 (1991): 448–455, https://doi.org/10.1037/0012-1649.27.3.448.

their desires and emotions: Ilaria Grazzani, Veronica Ornaghi, Elisabetta Conte, Alessandro Pepe, and Claudia Caprin, "The Relation Between Emotion Understanding and Theory of Mind in Children Aged 3 to 8: The Key Role of Language," *Frontiers in Psychology* 9 (2018), https://doi.org/10.3389/fpsyg.2018.00724.

actually feeling sad: Fredrickson, "The Role of Positive Emotions."

especially outside the home: Jennifer A. Silvers, "Adolescence as a Pivotal Period for Emotion Regulation Development," *Current Opinion in Psychology* 44 (April 2022): 258–263, https://doi.org/10.1016/j.copsyc.2021.09.023.

emotion regulation strategies: Gustavo A. Rangel-Rodríguez, Montserrat Badia, and Silvia Blanch, "Encouraging Emotional Conversations in Children with Complex Communication Needs: An Observational Case Study," *Frontiers in Psychology* 12 (2021): 674755, https://doi.org/10.3389/fpsyg.2021.674755, PMID: 34295286; PMCID: PMC8290146.

understand what they're experiencing: Ashley L. Ruba and Seth D. Pollak, "The Development of Emotion Reasoning in Infancy and Early Childhood,"

Annual Review of Developmental Psychology 2, no. 1 (2020): 503–531, https://doi.org/10.1146/annurev-devpsych-060320-102556.

emotions don't last forever: P. M. Cole and T. Hollenstein, *Emotion Regulation: A Matter of Time* (Routledge, 2018), https://doi.org/10.4324/9781351001328.

the upper limit problem: Gay Hendricks, "Chapter One: Preparing for Your Big Leap," in *The Big Leap* (HarperCollins, 2009).

calm, happy headspace: Rangel-Rodríguez, Badia, and Blanch, "Encouraging Emotional Conversations in Children."

ability to regulate emotions: Tia M. Panfile and Deborah J. Liable, "Attachment Security and Child's Empathy: The Mediating Role of Emotion Regulation," *Merrill-Palmer Quarterly* 58, no. 1 (2012): 1–21, https://doi.org/10.1353/mpq.2012.0003.

deep breathing can reduce pain: X. Ma, Z. Q. Yue, Z. Q. Gong, H. Zhang, N. Y. Duan, Y. T. Shi, G. X. Wei, and Y. F. Li, "The Effect of Diaphragmatic Breathing on Attention, Negative Affect, and Stress in Healthy Adults," *Frontiers in Psychology* 8 (2017): 874, https://doi.org/10.3389/fpsyg.2017.00874, PMID: 28626434; PMCID: PMC5455070.

repetitive nature of counting: Aviva Berkovich-Ohana, Meytal Wilf, Roni Kahana, Amos Arieli, and Rafael Malach, "Repetitive Speech Elicits Widespread Deactivation in the Human Cortex: The 'Mantra' Effect?" *Brain and Behavior* 5, no. 7 (2015): e00346, https://doi.org/10.1002/brb3.346, PMID: 26221571; PMCID: PMC4511287.

production of oxytocin and endorphins: Asmir Gračanin, Lisa M. Bylsma, and Ad J. J. M. Vingerhoets, "Is Crying a Self-Soothing Behavior?" *Frontiers in Psychology* 5 (2014): 502, https://doi.org/10.3389/fpsyg.2014.00502, PMID: 24904511; PMCID: PMC4035568.

drawing can also elevate: Jennifer E. Drake, "How Drawing to Distract Improves Mood in Children," *Frontiers in Psychology* 12 (2021): 622927, https://doi.org/10.3389/fpsyg.2021.622927, PMID: 33603704; PMCID: PMC7884745.

genetic damage of stress: S. Venditti, L. Verdone, A. Reale, V. Vetriani, M. Caserta, and M. Zampieri, "Molecules of Silence: Effects of Meditation on Gene Expression and Epigenetics," *Frontiers in Psychology* 11 (2020): 1767, https://doi.org/10.3389/fpsyg.2020.01767, PMID: 32849047; PMCID: PMC7431950.

their own emotion regulation: Kristin W. Samuelson, Casey E. Krueger, and Crystal Wilson, "Relationships Between Maternal Emotion Regulation, Parenting, and Children's Executive Functioning in Families Exposed to Intimate Partner

Violence," *Journal of Interpersonal Violence* 27, no. 17 (2012): 3532–3550, https://doi.org/10.1177/0886260512445385, PMID: 22610834.

how a child regulates emotions: Ornaghi, Conte, and Grazzani, "Empathy in Toddlers."

especially true of anger: Esther M. Leerkes and Lindsay G. Bailes, "Emotional Development Within the Family Context," in *Handbook of Emotional Development*, eds. Vanessa LoBue, Koraly Pérez-Edgar, and Kristin A. Buss (Springer Nature Switzerland AG, 2019): 627–661, https://doi.org/10.1007/978-3-030-17332-6_24.

nonverbal cues of others: Elisabeth Norman and Mark Price, "Social Intuition as a Form of Implicit Learning: Sequences of Body Movements Are Learned Less Explicitly than Letter Sequences," *Advances in Cognitive Psychology* 8, no. 2 (2012): 121–131, https://doi.org/10.5709/acp-0109-x.

same kind of brain changes: John M. Weir, Arthurine Zakama, and Uma Rao, "Developmental Risk I: Depression and the Developing Brain," *Child and Adolescent Psychiatric Clinics of North America* 21, no. 2 (April 2012): 237–259, https://doi.org/10.1016/j.chc.2012.01.004.

5. Element 3: Building Healthy Boundaries

"Part of being human": Glennon Doyle, "Boundaries: Are Too Few (or Too Many) Why We Stay Stuck?," season 1, episode 2, of *We Can Do Hard Things*, Apple Podcasts, May 18, 2021, https://podcasts.apple.com/us/podcast/2-boundaries-are-too-few-or-too-many-why-we-stay-stuck/id1564530722?i=1000522110392.

sensory processing sensitivity: Beatrice P. Acevedo, Elaine N. Aron, Arthur Aron, Matthew D. Sangster, Nancy Collins, and Lucy L. Brown, "The Highly Sensitive Brain: An fMRI Study of Sensory Processing Sensitivity and Response to Others' Emotions," *Brain and Behavior* 4, no. 4 (2014): 580–594, https://doi.org/10.1002/brb3.242, PMID: 25161824; PMCID: PMC4086365.

understand boundary advocacy: M. Scott Peck, "P. 189," in *The Road Less Traveled and Beyond: Spiritual Growth in an Age of Anxiety* (Touchstone, 1998).

6. Element 4: Exploring the Messy Art of Discipline

"non-abusive spanking": Elizabeth T. Gershoff and Andrew Grogan-Kaylor, "Spanking and Child Outcomes: Old Controversies and New Meta-Analyses," *Journal of Family Psychology* 30, no. 4 (2016): 453–469, https://doi.org/10.1037/fam0000191.

an intergenerational cycle: Dominique Simons and Sandy Wurtele, "Relationships Between Parents' Use of Corporal Punishment and Their Children's Endorsement of Spanking and Hitting Other Children," *Child Abuse & Neglect* 34 (2010): 639–646, https://doi.org/10.1016/j.chiabu.2010.01.012.

each spanking episode reinforced: Mary Jane MacKenzie, Elise Nicklas, Jane Waldfogel, and Jeanne Brooks-Gunn, "Corporal Punishment and Child Behavioral and Cognitive Outcomes Through 5 Years-of-Age: Evidence from a Contemporary Urban Birth Cohort Study," *Infant and Child Development* 21, no. 1 (2012): 3–33, https://doi.org/10.1002/icd.758, PMID: 24839402; PMCID: PMC4024048.

performance IQ: Akemi Tomoda, Hiroshi Suzuki, Keisuke Rabi, Yu-Shin Sheu, Alaptagin Polcari, and Martin H. Teicher, "Reduced Prefrontal Cortical Gray Matter Volume in Young Adults Exposed to Harsh Corporal Punishment," *Neuroimage* 47, Suppl 2 (2009): T66–T71, https://doi.org/10.1016/j.neuroimage.2009.03.005, PMID: 19285558; PMCID: PMC2896871.

stress hormone production: Elizabeth T. Gershoff, "Should Parents' Physical Punishment of Children Be Considered a Source of Toxic Stress That Affects Brain Development?" *Family Relations* 65, no. 1 (2016): 151–162, https://doi.org/10.1111/fare.12177, PMID: 34334857; PMCID: PMC8323998.

emotion regulation and threat detection: Jorge Cuartas, David G. Weissman, Margaret A. Sheridan, Liliana Lengua, and Katie A. McLaughlin, "Corporal Punishment and Elevated Neural Response to Threat in Children," *Child Development* 92, no. 3 (2021): 821–832, https://doi.org/10.1111/cdev.13565.

no longer support: Cindy Miller-Perrin and Robin Perrin, "Physical Punishment of Children by US Parents: Moving Beyond Debate to Promote Children's Health and Well-being," *Psicologia: Reflexão e Crítica* 31, no. 1 (2018): 16, https://doi.org/10.1186/s41155-018-0096-x.

banned in over fifty countries: "What Is Corporal Punishment?" End Corporal Punishment, 2018, https://endcorporalpunishment.org/introduction/.

promotes a child's identity formation: Ben M. Law, Andrew M. Siu, and Daniel T. Shek, "Recognition for Positive Behavior as a Critical Youth Development Construct: Conceptual Bases and Implications on Youth Service Development," *Scientific World Journal* 2012: 809578, https://doi.org/10.1100/2012/809578, PMID: 22666155; PMCID: PMC3361320.

experiment with disruptive behavior: Susanne Schulz, Patricia Leijten, Daniel S. Shaw, et al., "Parental Reactivity to Disruptive Behavior in Toddlerhood: An

Experimental Study," *Journal of Abnormal Child Psychology* 47 (2019): 779–790, https://doi.org/10.1007/s10802-018-0489-4.

"A hurtful child is": Pam Leo, *Connection Parenting: Parenting Through Connection Instead of Coercion, Through Love Instead of Fear* (Wyatt-MacKenzie, 2022).

four elements of negativity bias: Paul Rozin and Edward B. Royzman, "Negativity Bias, Negativity Dominance, and Contagion," *Personality and Social Psychology Review* 5, no. 4 (2001): 296–320, https://doi.org/10.1207/S15327957PSPR0504_2.

Negative differentiation has also: Ryan M. Knuppenburg and Christina M. Fredericks, "Linguistic Affect: Positive and Negative Emotion Words Are Contagious, Predict Likability, and Moderate Positive and Negative Affect," *Inquiries Journal* 13 (03), http://www.inquiriesjournal.com/a?id=1884.

focusing on deep breathing: Laura G. Kiken and Natalie J. Shook, "Looking Up: Mindfulness Increases Positive Judgments and Reduces Negativity Bias," *Social Psychological and Personality Science* 2, no. 4 (2011): 425–431, https://doi.org/10.1177/1948550610396585.

toxic and destructive: Nhất Hạnh, *The Art of Communicating* (HarperCollins, 2014).

nonviolent communication (NVC): Marshall B. Rosenberg, *Nonviolent Communication: A Language of Life* (KNVC, 2011).

no cutting the other off: Harville Hendrix and Helen Hunt, *Doing Imago Relationship Therapy in the Space-Between: A Clinician's Guide* (W.W. Norton, 2021).

have a pretend tantrum: Alan E. Kazdin, "Clinical Dysfunction and Psychosocial Interventions: The Interplay of Research, Methods, and Conceptualization of Challenges," *Annual Review of Clinical Psychology* 11 (2015): 25–52.

7. Element 5: Discovering Your Family Values

Project P.A.T.H.S.: Daniel T. Shek, "Adolescent Developmental Issues in Hong Kong: Relevance to Positive Youth Development Programs in Hong Kong," *International Journal of Adolescent Medicine and Health* 18, no. 3 (2006): 341–354, https://doi.org/10.1515/ijamh.2006.18.3.341.

writing about your values: Kelly McGonigal, *The Upside of Stress: Why Stress Is Good for You, and How to Get Good at It* (Avery, 2015).

exploring creativity and dreaming big: Emily Winfield Martin, *The Wonderful Things You Will Be* (Random House, 2015).

8. Element 6: Traversing the Jungle of the Parent-Child Social Scene

who exhibit social competencies: Damon E. Jones, Mark Greenberg, and Max Crowley, "Early Social-Emotional Functioning and Public Health: The Relationship Between Kindergarten Social Competence and Future Wellness," *American Journal of Public Health* 105, no. 11 (November 2015): 2283–2290, https://doi.org/10.2105/ajph.2015.302630.

spark positive emotions: Fredrickson, "The Role of Positive Emotions."

"Empathy is really important": "Being with Jane Goodall," *NOVA's Secret Life of Scientists and Engineers*, PBS, September 2, 2014, https://youtu.be/0Qu7Wn1mRYA?si=2lI5du6pD2FobZiF.

children predisposed to anxiety: C. M. Middeldorp, D. C. Cath, R. Van, and D. I. Boomsma, "The Co-Morbidity of Anxiety and Depression in the Perspective of Genetic Epidemiology. A Review of Twin and Family Studies," *Psychological Medicine* 35, no. 5 (2005): 611–624, https://doi.org/10.1017/S003329170400412X.

enough emotional support: Geoffrey D. Borman, Christopher S. Rozek, Jaymes Pyne, and Paul Hanselman, "Reappraising Academic and Social Adversity Improves Middle School Students' Academic Achievement, Behavior, and Well-Being," *Proceedings of the National Academy of Sciences* 116, no. 33 (July 29, 2019): 16286–16291, https://doi.org/10.1073/pnas.1820317116.

bullying is "intentional and repeated": Xiaoou Man, Jiatong Liu, and Zengxin Xue, "Effects of Bullying Forms on Adolescent Mental Health and Protective Factors: A Global Cross-Regional Research Based on 65 Countries," *International Journal of Environmental Research and Public Health* 19, no. 4 (February 18, 2022): 2374, https://doi.org/10.3390/ijerph19042374.

Bullying goes beyond the standard: Man, Liu, and Xue, "Effects of Bullying Forms."

most effective ways parents can help: Man, Liu, and Xue, "Effects of Bullying," https://doi.org/10.3390/ijerph19042374.

from friend to good friend: J. A. Hall, "How Many Hours Does It Take to Make a Friend?" *Journal of Social and Personal Relationships* 36, no. 4 (2019): 1278–1296, https://doi.org/10.1177/0265407518761225.

challenges with interpersonal relationships: Joseph P. Allen, Megan M. Schad, Barbara Oudekerk, and Joanna Chango, "What Ever Happened to the 'Cool'

Kids? Long-Term Sequelae of Early Adolescent Pseudomature Behavior," *Child Development* 85, no. 5 (June 11, 2014): 1866–1880, https://doi.org/10.1111/cdev.12250.

This fixation on status: Allen, Schad, Oudekerk, and Chango, "What Ever Happened to the 'Cool' Kids?"

the science of popularity: Mitchell J. Prinstein, *Popular: The Power of Likability in a Status-Obsessed World* (Viking, 2017).

9. Element 7: Creating a Family Schedule and Routines

as high-endurance athletes: Anthony Birat, Pierre Bourdier, Enzo Piponnier, Anthony J. Blazevich, Hugo Maciejewski, Pascale Duché, and Sébastien Ratel, "Metabolic and Fatigue Profiles Are Comparable Between Prepubertal Children and Well-Trained Adult Endurance Athletes," *Frontiers in Physiology* 9 (April 24, 2018), https://doi.org/10.3389/fphys.2018.00387.

In Finland, elementary-aged kids: Agata Glapa, Joanna Grzesiak, Ida Laudanska-Krzeminska, Ming-Kai Chin, Christopher R. Edginton, Magdalena Mo Ching Mok, and Michal Bronikowski, "The Impact of Brain Breaks Classroom-Based Physical Activities on Attitudes Toward Physical Activity in Polish School Children in Third to Fifth Grade," *International Journal of Environmental Research and Public Health* 15, no. 2 (2018): 368, https://doi.org/10.3390/ijerph15020368.

neurons that produce serotonin: Stefan O. Reber, Philip H. Siebler, Nina C. Donner, James T. Morton, David G. Smith, Jared M. Kopelman, Kenneth R. Lowe, et al., "Immunization with a Heat-Killed Preparation of the Environmental Bacterium *Mycobacterium vaccae* Promotes Stress Resilience in Mice," *Proceedings of the National Academy of Sciences* 113, no. 22 (May 16, 2016), https://doi.org/10.1073/pnas.1600324113.

lower a child's anxiety: D. M. Matthews, and S. M. Jenks, "Ingestion of *Mycobacterium vaccae* Decreases Anxiety-Related Behavior and Improves Learning in Mice," *Behavioral Processes* (2013): 27–35, https://doi.org/10.1016/j.beproc.2013.02.007.

having enough exposure: J. F. Bach and L. Chatenoud, "The Hygiene Hypothesis: An Explanation for the Increased Frequency of Insulin-Dependent Diabetes," *Cold Spring Harbor Perspectives in Medicine* 2, no. 2 (2012): a007799, https://doi.org/10.1101/cshperspect.a007799.

Playing in dirt: Thomas W. McDade, Julienne Rutherford, Linda Adair, and Christopher W. Kuzawa, "Early Origins of Inflammation: Microbial Exposures in Infancy Predict Lower Levels of C-Reactive Protein in Adulthood," *Proceedings of the Royal Society B: Biological Sciences* 277, no. 1684 (December 9, 2009): 1129–1137, https://doi.org/10.1098/rspb.2009.1795.

The Tooth Book: Marc Bacera, *The Tooth Book: For Children to Enjoy and Learn About Teeth, Cavities, and Other Dental Health Facts* (Rounded Specs Publishing, 2020).

Brush! Brush! Brush!: Alicia Padron, *Brush, Brush, Brush!* (Scholastic Singapore, 2019).

to keep germs to themselves: Katie Daynes, Marta Álvarez Miguéns, and Suzie Harrison, *What Are Germs?* (Usborne Publishing Limited, 2023).

Germs Are Not for Sharing: Elizabeth Verdick, *Germs Are Not for Sharing* (Free Spirit Publishing, 2017).

Starting the potty-learning process: Nathan J. Blum, Bruce Taubman, and Nicole Nemeth, "Relationship Between Age at Initiation of Toilet Training and Duration of Training: A Prospective Study," *Pediatrics* 111, no. 4 (April 1, 2003): 810–814, https://doi.org/10.1542/peds.111.4.810.

both bowel and urinary control: T. Berry Brazelton, "A Child-Oriented Approach to Toilet Training," *Pediatrics* 29, no. 1 (January 1, 1962): 121–128, https://doi.org/10.1542/peds.29.1.121.

the time a child needs: B. Taubman, N. J. Blum, and N. Nemeth, "Stool Toileting Refusal: A Prospective Intervention Targeting Parental Behavior," *Archives of Pediatrics & Adolescent Medicine* 157, no. 12 (2003): 1193–1196, https://doi.org/10.1001/archpedi.157.12.1193.

stool toileting refusal: Nathan J. Blum, Bruce Taubman, and Nicole Nemeth, "During Toilet Training, Constipation Occurs Before Stool Toileting Refusal," *Pediatrics* 113, no. 6 (June 1, 2004), https://doi.org/10.1542/peds.113.6.e520.

children aren't developmentally able: R. J. Butler and J. Heron, "The Prevalence of Infrequent Bedwetting and Nocturnal Enuresis in Childhood," *Scandinavian Journal of Urology and Nephrology* 42, no. 3 (2008): 257–264, https://doi.org/10.1080/00365590701748054.

still wet the bed: Butler and Heron, "The Prevalence of Infrequent Bedwetting."

bedwetting tapers off: U.-B. Jansson, M. Hanson, U. Sillen, and A.-L. Hellstrom, "Voiding Pattern and Acquisition of Bladder Control from Birth to Age 6

Years—a Longitudinal Study," *Journal of Urology* 174, no. 1 (July 2005): 289–293, https://doi.org/10.1097/01.ju.0000161216.45653.e3.

10. Element 8: Promoting Healthy Food, Sleep, and Safety Choices

early childhood nutrition: E. J. Reverri, M. B. Arensberg, R. D. Murray, K. W. Kerr, and K. L. Wulf, "Young Child Nutrition: Knowledge and Surveillance Gaps Across the Spectrum of Feeding," *Nutrients* 14, no. 15 (2022): 3093, https://doi.org/10.3390/nu14153093.

over five million children: Jodi Shroba, and Susan McElroy, "Including Young Children in Their Food Allergy Care: A Pilot Study," *Journal of Food Allergy* 2, no. 2 (December 1, 2020): 161–163, https://doi.org/10.2500/jfa.2020.2.200034.

coping with stress and regulating emotions: A. F. Santos, C. Fernandes, M. Fernandes, A. J. Santos, and M. Veríssimo, "Associations Between Emotion Regulation, Feeding Practices, and Preschoolers' Food Consumption," *Nutrients* 14, no. 19 (2022): 4184, https://doi.org/10.3390/nu14194184.

good nutrition improves: E. L. Prado and K. G. Dewey, "Nutrition and Brain Development in Early Life," *Nutrition Reviews* 72, no. 4 (April 1, 2014): 267–284, https://doi.org/10.1111/nure.12102.

lessen symptoms of ADHD: S. A. Ryu, Y. J. Choi, H. An, H. J. Kwon, M. Ha, Y. C. Hong, S. J. Hong, and H. J. Hwang, "Associations Between Dietary Intake and Attention Deficit Hyperactivity Disorder (ADHD) Scores by Repeated Measurements in School-Age Children," *Nutrients* 14, no. 14 (July 16, 2022): 2919, https://doi.org/10.3390/nu14142919.

teach, act, model, and shape: David C. Schwebel, *Raising Kids Who Choose Safety: The T.A.M.S. Method for Child Accident Prevention* (Parenting Press, 2022).

11. Element 9: Parenting with Your People

people who typically take conflict personally: Eun Joo Kim, Ayano Yamaguchi, Min-Sun Kim, and Akira Miyahara, "Effects of Taking Conflict Personally on Conflict Management Styles Across Cultures," *Personality and Individual Differences* 72 (January 2015): 143–149, https://doi.org/10.1016/j.paid.2014.08.004.

ABOUT THE AUTHOR

Robin Emtage Photography

Bailey Gaddis is the author of *Asking for a Pregnant Friend: 101 Answers to Questions Women Are Too Embarrassed to Ask about Pregnancy, Childbirth, and Motherhood* and *Feng Shui Mommy: Creating Balance and Harmony for Blissful Pregnancy, Childbirth, and Motherhood*. She is also a certified HypnoMothering parenting coach, certified hypnotherapist specializing in children and parents, certified birthing doula, and HypnoBirthing practitioner. She has written on parenting topics for *Cosmopolitan*, *Redbook*, *Woman's Day*, *Good Housekeeping*, *Scary Mommy*, *HuffPost*, and more. Gaddis also supports families navigating cancer and parenthood at the cancer resource center OjaiCARES. In addition, Gaddis volunteers for the Parent Care Program at the Nan Tolbert Nurturing Center, where she offers in-home support to parents of newborn babies. She often stays involved with these families, who have limited supplemental support, offering her transition into toddlerhood guidance pro bono. She lives in Ojai, California, with her husband, son, and daughter.